PORTUGUESE DISCOVERIES DEPENDENCIES AND MISSIONS IN ASIA AND AFRICA

PORTUGUESE DISCOVERIES DEPENDENCIES

AND

MISSIONS IN ASIA AND AFRICA

REV: ALEX J D D'ORSEY

ISBN : 978-93-5324-597-9 (HB)

First Published, London, 1893

Published, 2020

Published by

Facsimile Publisher
12 Pragati Market
Ashok Vihar, Ph-2
Delhi-110052
E-mail: books@facsimilepublisher.com

Printed at: G. Print Process, Delhi.

**Portuguese
Discoveries Dependencies
and
Missions in Asia and Africa**

Rev: Alex J D D'Orsey

PORTUGUESE
DISCOVERIES DEPENDENCIES
AND
MISSIONS IN ASIA AND AFRICA

COMPILED BY THE

REV ALEX J D D'ORSEY BD

CAMBRIDGE

Knight Commander of the Portuguese Order of Christ late Professor in King's College London

LONDON

W H ALLEN & CO LIMITED

13, WATERLOO PLACE, S.W.

1893.

PREFACE.

THERE are some subjects which, at first sight, seem to present little difficulty, and to demand but a very moderate amount of research. When, however, the student has commenced his investigations, he sees new fields opening up on every side; and the difficulty is not to find materials for his work, but to select from the vast mass before him such elements as are solely, or chiefly, suitable for his enterprise. This has been our principal embarrassment in the preparation of the following Essay; for it was soon discovered that the volumes bearing upon our subject would have furnished matter for a history, instead of contributing to the pages of a monograph.

In writing an account of "The Portuguese Missions in Southern India in the XVIth Century, with Special Reference to the Syrian Christians, and to Modern Missionary Efforts in that Quarter," the

Author must obviously depend more upon ***industry in research, accuracy in quotation***, and ***judgment in selection***, than on the more brilliant qualities of intellect and imagination. He must make up his mind not to trust to second-hand authorities, ordinary compilations and translations, often indifferently rendered, but to go at once to the fountain head, examine carefully for himself, compare conflicting statements, verify citations, reconcile discrepancies, and out of chaos, as far as possible, produce order. He will, of course, have to study many a ponderous folio in mediæval Latin, in singularly quaint and difficult Portuguese, in Spanish, Italian, French, and English, all more or less differing from those of the present day. He must be prepared to encounter various, and sometimes contradictory, versions of the same transaction, according to the national or political bias of the writers whom he consults. And above all, he will find himself perplexed by the strong party colouring given by antagonistic religious factions to events which are made to tell for or against a theory, in proportion to the light in which they are represented. To all which must be added the subjective difficulty, for, unless perpetually on his guard, he will be prone to follow the example of those Procrustean writers who allow their own predilections to influence their manner of recording facts, and who sometimes so far forget what is due to truth as to diminish, magnify, or suppress, as may best suit the party they wish to serve.[1]

In the particular case before us the first duty was to divide the general theme into such portions as would enable the reader to form a clear idea of the whole question. The next object was to obtain from public libraries, from official reports, political and religious, and from private information, such authentic details as would fill in this outline, selecting such portions as are calculated by their shape, size, and colour, to combine for the production of a faithful and harmonious picture. The third part of our task, subordinate, but still important, was to indicate, by constant reference, the sources from which we derived our information, not only to steer clear of any suspicion of plagiarism, but to afford anyone interested in our subject the means of verifying our quotations, or of following up the stream to its fountain-head.

1 For a striking illustration of dishonesty in quotation, see Marshall's "History of the Christian Missions."

The First Book treats of the Portuguese themselves, and gives a very brief sketch of the circumstances which led to their maritime discoveries in the XVth Century, as preliminary to their brilliant conquests in the East in the XVIth Century. It affords also an outline of Portuguese India when their Eastern Empire was at its height, and concludes with a description of Southern India as the scene of the transactions recorded in this paper. This book is, of course, merely introductory, and may be omitted by such of our readers as are familiar with the subject.

The Second Book discusses the Portuguese Missions, their origin, progress, prosperous and adverse circumstances, first in reference to the heathen, and then with regard to the Church of Malabar. It includes a condensed narrative of the rise of the Jesuits, their settlement in Portugal, and their subjugation of the heathen in Southern India by Francis Xavier and his successors in the XVIth and early portion of the XVIIth Century.

The Third Book is devoted to the influence of the Portuguese Missions on the Syrian Christians, and records the various attempts made by Franciscans, Jesuits, and others, during the last forty years of the

XVIth Century, concluding with the triumph of Rome at the Synod of Diamper.

In the Fourth Book an attempt is made to bridge over the interval between the subjugation of the Syrian Church under Menezes, and the modern missionary efforts in South India. Though this is not included in the title of the paper, the link seems absolutely necessary to render the concluding book intelligible. This Fourth Book, therefore, comprehends the missionary movements from the College of St. Paul at Goa, the famous Madura Mission, the conversion by Jesuits and Capuchins, from Pondicherry to Cape Comorin, and the struggles of the Syrian Church during the XVIIth and XVIIIth Centuries.

The Fifth Book relates to modern missionary efforts in South India, and exhibits, in an extremely condensed form, the history of the first Protestant Missions in the Deccan, the temporary union between the English and Syrian Churches, the disruption and its results, the present state of the Syrian Christians as a proof of the still existing operation of Portuguese influence, and the revival of the Romish Missions in Madura, and surrounding districts.

If anyone will carefully peruse this summary, he will have no difficulty, without our encroaching on his patience, or tacitly censuring his understanding, in drawing his own inferences, and making his own reflections. If "one fact is worth a thousand arguments," this historical sketch, full of facts, will afford the most ample proof of the extent to which Portuguese Romanism has damaged Syrian Christianity, and will probably suggest that it is the duty of the Church of England to do her utmost to remedy the evil.

Coatham, Redcar,
March, 1893.

CONTENTS.

BOOK I.

INTRODUCTORY.

THE PORTUGUESE IN EUROPE AND ASIA.

BOOK II.

THE PORTUGUESE MISSIONS IN SOUTHERN INDIA.

BOOK III.

THE SUBJUGATION OF THE SYRIAN CHURCH.

CHAPTER VII.

BOOK IV.

SUBSEQUENT MISSIONS IN SOUTHERN INDIA, WITH SPECIAL REFERENCE TO THE SYRIANS.

BOOK V.

THE PORTUGUESE MISSIONS, WITH SPECIAL REFERENCE TO MODERN MISSIONARY EFFORTS IN SOUTH INDIA.

BOOK I.

THE PORTUGUESE IN EUROPE AND ASIA.

THE PORTUGUESE IN EUROPE AND ASIA.

CHAPTER I.

PORTUGAL AND THE PORTUGUESE.

"Il n'y avait pas quarante mille Portugais sous les armes, et ils faisaient trembler l'Empire de Marve, tous les barbares d' Afrique, les Mammelus, les Arabes, et tout l'Orient, depuis l'isle d' Ormuz jusqu 'à la Chine. Ils n'etaient pas un contre cent; et ils attaquaient des troupes, qui souvent avec des armes égales, disputaient leurs biens et leur vie jusqu 'à l'extrémité. Quels hommes devaient donc être alors les Portugais, et quels ressorts extraordinaires en avaient fait un peuple de hèros?"—"Hist. des Indes." Abbé Raynal. Tom. I., p. 119.

THE kingdom of Portugal, occupying the south-western extremity of Europe, seemed but little entitled to play a leading part in the world's drama. Yet no European nation can exhibit more brilliant pages than those to which the Portuguese proudly points in his country's annals from the early part of the XIIIth to the end of the XVIth Century. A rapid survey of the chief features will form a fitting introduction to the main subject of this Essay.

For many centuries the Lusitanians were an obscure people of the Roman Empire, remarkable for their utter want of civilisation. During the Middle Ages they were held in subjection by the Moslem invaders, till, in 1107, Count Henry, after severe conflicts, laid the foundation of the Portuguese power. His heroic son Alfonso by the victory of Ourique in 1139,[1] secured his title of King on the battle-field; but the country was not completely freed from the Moors till the conquest of Algarve in 1252, by Alphonso III.[2] Under the fostering care of Sancho I.; and especially of Diniz the Just, peace and prosperity were restored. Manufactures, commerce, and agriculture revived, and by his construction of the first Portuguese fleet at Lisbon in 1293, the King prepared the way for the glorious work of a later age. He founded the University of Lisbon, granted Municipal rights to newly-made towns, protected the merchants and trading classes against the tyranny of the nobles; and, while building cathedrals and monasteries, checked with a strong hand the arrogant pretensions of the clergy. Alphonso IV. reigned from 1325 till 1357, formed an alliance with Castile and Aragon against the Moors, caused the assassination of Inés de Castro, and was succeeded by his son Pedro I. During

[1] La bataille de campo d' Ourique fut livrèe le 25 Juin, 1139, et c'est de cette grande époque qu'il faut faire dater la monarchie Portugaise.—"Hist. de Port.," p. 7.

[2] Ribeiro-Dissertaçoes Chronologicas Criticas.

these reigns perpetual conflicts raged between the crown and the nobility, often in combination with the military orders and the clergy. Yet all the efforts of the Kings, though occasionally successful, failed to curb the turbulence of the feudatories till the battle of Aljubarrota in 1385, gained by John I. over the rebels, effectually crushed insubordination, and restored the dignity of the crown.[1]

Thus for many centuries the Portuguese had been trained to war. In the stern school of adversity the latent energies of the race had been gradually developed. Religion, or rather religious fanaticism was the inspiring principle, the very mainspring of every movement, of every heroic exploit. Their wars were rather crusades than patriotic struggles. They fought the Moor rather as an enemy to the faith, than as the invader of their country. As one of their own historians (De Barros) has said, "The kingdom was founded in the blood of martyrs and by martyrs was spread over the globe"; for, of course, he considered all who fell in battle against the infidel as perfectly entitled to the crimson crown.

Portugal, thus formed into a kingdom, was about 1450 divided into five provinces:—(1) Entre-Douro-e-Minho, with the ancient capital Guimarães, Oporto and Braga. (2) Tras-os-Montes, with Bragança, the

[1] "Dialogos de Varia Historia," 1648, p. 127. Faria e Souza "Europa Portugueza." "L'Univers Pittoresque Portugal," pp. 51-53.

cradle of the Royal House, Castello Rodrigo and Almeida. (3) Beira, containing Visen and Laniego, the latter famous for the Cortes in 1143 and 1181, Coimbra for its University founded in 1318. (4) Estremadura, the most important and populous province of the Portuguese realm. Lisboa had a Moslem population long after the time of Alphonso in 1147. Beautifully situated at the mouth of the Tagus, it afterwards became the centre of Portuguese manufactures and commerce, as well as the permanent residence of the King. Santarem, Torres Vedras, Almada, Restello (now Belem), Cintra Mafra, Leiria, Aljubarrote, Batalha, Alcobaça, are all famous in the history of the Spanish and Moorish wars. (5) Entre-Tejo-e-Guadiana or Alem-Tejo, possessing Evora, Beja, Ourique and Albuquerque.

Besides these provinces, there was the kingdom of Algarve divided into D'Alem Mar, "on this side of the sea," and Aquem Mar, or "beyond the sea"; the former containing Lagos, Faro, and Loulé, the last strongholds of the Arabs in Portugal. On Cape St. Vincent stood Sagres, where Henry the Navigator erected the world-renowned "Villa do Infante."[1]

[1] In days long past there had stood upon the sister headland of St. Vincent, at about a league's distance, a circular Druidical temple, where, as Strabo tells us, the old Iberians believed that the gods assembled at night, and from the ancient name of Sacrum Promontorium, hence given to the entire promontory by the Romans, Cape Sagres received its modern appelation. As may be imagined, the motive for the Prince's choice could not have been an ordinary one.—Major's "Prince Henry the Navigator," p. 2.

Here the scientific and enterprising Prince, in full view of the broad Atlantic, planned the various expeditions for the exploration of the African coast, and the discovery of Madeira and the Western Islands.[1] Algarve (now a province) was one of the most beautiful and fertile portions of the realm, its ports crowded with ships, and its towns full of warlike adventurers thirsting for foreign conquests. The inhabitants, Christians, Jews, and Moors, lived happily together till the Inquisition, in the XVIth Century, kindled the fires of persecution, and converted that happy region into a desert. The other Algarve ("beyond the sea") stretched from Ceuta (Abyla) to Cape Espartel, and contained Almina, Alcazar, Tanjier, and Arzilla. The African conquests began in 1415 (the year of Agincourt) with the capture of Ceuta, and ended, after years of heroism and glory, with the terrible defeat at Alcazar-el-Kebir, in 1578, and the death of King Sebastian.

This brief summary of the early history and geographical position of Portugal will enable the reader to understand the circumstances in which that country stood at the commencement of its discoveries. The warlike character of the population, the long range of coast bordered by the unknown Atlantic, and the desire to avenge the thraldom under which their native land had groaned, inspired the Portuguese

[1] Chronica de Guiné, por Gomez, Eamez, de Azurora, p. 385.

with a desire to carry the war into the enemy's country and to subdue the territory of the infidel to the Faith of the Cross.

In confirmation of these views we may partly extract, and partly condense, the opinion of a great writer on India a hundred years ago.[1] Speaking of the conquests of Albuquerque and his followers in Malabar he says, "If we are astonished at the number of his victories and the rapidity of his conquests, how much more should the brave men whom he commanded excite our admiration? Have we ever seen a nation, apparently so powerless, do such great deeds? There were never more than 40,000 Portuguese under arms, and they struck terror into the empire of Morocco, the barbarians of Africa, the Mamelukes, the Arabs, and all the East, from Ormuz to China. They were not one against a hundred, and they attacked troops, which, as well armed as they were, fought for their lives and property to the last extremity." What wonderful men must the Portuguese of that period have been, and what remarkable training must have converted them into a nation of heroes. They had been for a century warring against the Moors, when Count Henry of Burgundy landed in Portugal with some French Knights,

[1] Histoire Philosophique et Politique des Etablissemens et du Commerce des Européens dans les Deux Indes.—A. Paris 1778. Par M. Abbé Raynal.

with the intention of fighting in Castile under the Banner of the Cid, whose fame had attracted them to the theatre of war. The Portuguese invited these chivalrous adventurers to assist them against the infidels; the knights assented, and most of them settled in Portugal. The institution of chivalry, one which has so much elevated human nature, that love of glory instead of mere country, that spirit purified from the contamination of surrounding barbarism appeared upon the banks of the Tagus, with all the splendour which had characterised its origin in France and England. The Portuguese Monarchs strove to preserve it, and to extend its power by the establishment of various orders formed upon the old models, and whose spirit was the same, that is to say, a union of heroism, gallantry, and devotion.

The Kings of Portugal still further elevated the spirit of the nation by the equality with which they treated the nobility, and by the restrictions which they placed on their own authority. They often assembled the States-General, without which there is not properly a nation. It was from these States that Alphonso received the sceptre after the capture of Lisbon. It was in combination with these States that his successors, for centuries enacted laws, several of which seemed peculiarly calculated to inspire the love of glory. The Peerage was granted as a reward for distinguished services. For instance, to one who had killed or taken a General of the enemy, or to one who, when prisoner amongst the Moors, had refused to purchase his liberty by the sacrifice of his faith. On the other hand, whoever insulted a woman, bore false witness, broke his word, or concealed the truth from the King, forfeited his nobility.

The wars which the Portuguese had carried on in defence of their country and their liberty, were, at the same time, religious wars. They were full of that fierce but brilliant fanaticism which the Popes had excited during the Crusades. The Portuguese then were Chevaliers, armed in defence of their fortunes, their wives, their children, and their kings, Chevaliers like themselves. They were, in fact, Crusaders, who, in defending Christianity, fought for their country too. Add to this, that they were a little nation, an extremely feeble power, and we have another illustration of a well-known fact that small States often in danger, display a patriotic enthusiasm, rarely felt by great nations, enjoying uninterrupted security.

The principles of activity, force, elevation, and grandeur, which characterised the nation at that period, continued after the expulsion of the Moors. The victorious Portuguese, not satisfied with driving out these enemies of their country and their creed, pursued them into Africa itself. Then followed certain conflicts, more or less important, with the Kings of Castile and Leon, serving to maintain the spirit and the training required in war, if securing no other end. At last, during the period which immediately preceded the expeditions to India, the nobility, retiring from the court and the great towns, had but little to occupy them in their castles but the pictures and the virtues of their ancestors;[1] and they naturally longed for some enterprise worthy of their powers.

As soon as the question arose of attempting conquests in Africa and in Asia, a new passion was added to the motives of which we have just spoken, to give additional force to the genius of the Portuguese. This passion, which at first had the effect of stimulating all the others, but which soon annihilated their generous principles, was cupidity. They set off in crowds to make their fortunes to serve the State, and to convert the heathen. They appeared in India as superhuman beings down to the death of Albuquerque. After that event, the very riches which were the object and fruit of their conquests, corrupted them to the core. Noble passions gave way to luxury and self-indulgence, which never failed to destroy the strength of the body, and the virtues of the soul. The weakness of the successors of the great Immanuel, the men

[1] Enfin, pendant les tems qui précéderent les expeditions de l'Inde, la noblesse, eloignée des Villes et de la Cour, conservait dans ses châteaux les portraits et les vertus de ses pères.—Abbè Raynal. Vol. I., p. 122.

of mediocre talent, selected by him as Viceroys of India, gradually effected the utter ruin of the Portuguese Empire in the East.

These remarks will probably suffice to introduce the people who are to play so conspicuous a part in our narrative. The reader, who desires more information, is referred to the voluminous works of João de Barros, to the elegantly written "Historia de Portugal," by Ercolano (the Macaulay of his country), or to an exceedingly interesting compendium in the second and third chapters of Prince Henry the Navigator, by Mr. R. H. Major, of the British Museum.

CHAPTER II.

PORTUGUESE DISCOVERIES IN THE XVth CENTURY.

"The mystery, which since Creation had hung over the Atlantic, and hidden from man's knowledge one half of the surface of the globe, had reserved a field of noble enterprise for Prince Henry the Navigator."—R. H. MAJOR.

JOHN I., who reigned from 1383 till 1433, made the first attempt at discovery on a very limited scale, and in connection with an expedition to the Coast of Barbary. In 1415, Portugal, assured of peace with Castile, had reached a high degree of prosperity, and the King availed himself of domestic tranquility to attack the northern coast of Africa, and thus lay the foundation of an empire beyond the seas. A fleet was soon after dispatched to survey the western shore of Morocco, and, if possible, to trace the whole outline of the African Continent. Unable to advance further than Cape Bojador, they returned without accomplishing their object; though this attempt excited them to further researches in the same direction. These efforts were now systematically guided by one of the most remarkable men of his age, Prince Henry, a younger son of John I., by Philippa of Lancaster, sister of Henry IV. of England. In early life he had devoted himself to mathematics, and he continued to acquire all the information which geographical and nautical science at that time afforded. He fixed his residence, as we have already said, at Sagres; and his house became a sort of Naval College, wherein knowledge was communicated, and encouragement given, for the prosecution of maritime discovery. Immediately after his return from the victorious expedition to Ceuta he determined to realise his project, and at once dispatched two young officers of his household, Gonçalvez Zarco and Tristam Vaz, to cruise along the coast, and to penetrate those undiscovered regions, of which but vague reports had occasionally reached Europe. Driven out to sea by a storm, they lost the coast line, but discovered first Porto Santo and then Madeira. The chronicles of the period are filled with glowing descriptions of the beauty of "The Pearl of the Seas," which space forbids us to transcribe. We must not however omit one important fact, as showing the religious tendencies of the Portuguese, that no sooner had this interesting island been partially peopled, than Prince Henry, as Grand Master of the Order of Christ, placed the whole under his powerful institution. Soon after the

Franciscans arrived, and founded at Funchal the extensive Convent of San Bernardino.

About fourteen years after the discovery of Madeira, the Azores were explored for the first time, by Gonzalo Cabral, who had sailed from Sagres, under the Prince's auspices. But these successes, interesting as they are, form but the prelude to the explorations of the Portuguese along the Coast of Africa. There is in the narrative of the early triumphs, under the influence of the Prince, one fact which outshines all the rest—it is that which shows us the Portuguese *on the way to India*—it is the exact history of those exploring expeditions, creeping along the African Coast, which, preparing the downfall of Venetian commerce, were thereby destined to raise Portugal to the pitch of power which she enjoyed in the XVIth Century. Tempting, however, as this theme is, we are compelled to treat it superficially, as merely introductory to the main subject. A contemporary historian, Gomez Eannez de Azurara, gives five reasons for the Prince's desire to continue his researches, (1) his wish to know what land existed beyond the Canaries; (2) that he might find out whether there was any Christian Port with which he might maintain a profitable trade; (3) that he might ascertain precisely the extent of the Moorish dominions; (4) that he might discover any Christian Potentate who would aid him in his wars against the infidels; (5) *that he might extend the Holy religion* of Our Lord Jesus Christ, and bring to Him all the souls that wished to be saved. Animated then, by this desire, and guided by the reasons aforesaid, the Prince began to select his ships and his officers suitable to the nature of the case.[1] In 1433, Gil Eannez passed the famous Bojador, and thereby proved that the terror which this Cape inspired was simply imaginary. Baldaya, in 1436, commanded a second expedition, and about a hundred and twenty leagues south of the Cape saw, for the first time, the inhabitants of the land, the encounter being prophetically marked by bloodshed. These expeditions were renewed in 1441, under Gonçalvez and Nuno Tristam, who returned in triumph after having discovered Cape Blanco. "The Holy Prince," as he is called by Azurara, wished to possess the treasures of the Church, to distribute them amongst these bold Captains whom he intended to send into these desert countries. He therefore dispatched an embassy to Pope Martin V. to inform him of the marvellous discoveries just made; and his successor, Eugene IV., *conceded to the Prince and his successors* (1436) *not only the countries which he had already explored, but all that he might discover beyond Cape Bojador, however extensive they might be.* Nicholas V., in 1450, granted a second bull

[1] Chronica de Guinée.

confirming the first. Between 1445 and 1450, explorations were continued along the coast, the river Senegal and Cape Verde being then discovered. At this time one object was unquestionably the capture of slaves—this infamous traffic having been begun about this time, the first victims being sold at Lagos, in Portugal. So strangely were right and wrong confounded by *these pioneers of so-called Christianity* that the fifth part of the *proceeds of the sale of human beings* was granted to the Grand Master of the Order of *Christ*; and the historian, though indignant, calms himself with the consideration that the end justified the means, inasmuch as the *Negroes would thereby be converted.*

In 1448, King Edward left the throne to his Son, Alphonso V., who, furnishing Prince Henry with all the means required for pursuing his glorious career, received as his reward, in 1460, the discovery of the Cape Verde and adjacent islands. The progress of discovery was somewhat checked by the death of Prince Henry in 1463, but it soon continued to advance, for we find that the King granted to Gomez a monopoly for five years, on condition that he discovered, during that time, five hundred leagues more of the shores of Africa. In 1471, this Navigator succeeded in exploring the Gold Coast; the Castle of Elmina was erected, and the King of Portugal assumed the title of Lord of Guinea.

John II. ascended the throne in 1481, and immediately sent ambassadors to Innocent VIII. to request from the new Pontiff the bull of the "*Holy Crusade*," by means of which he hoped to realise the projects of his Father against the Mussulman States of the Coast of Barbary. About 1484 Diego Cam, setting sail from the new Castle of Elmina, advanced towards the south, and found himself, though out at sea, in a current of fresh water. Inferring that this indicated the near neighbourhood of a large river, he steered towards land, and discovered the mouth of the Congo. We next hear of settlements made by Evora and Anez in 1485-8 at Turcaral, Tombul, Congo, and in the country of the Zaloffes. "*Christianity was preached with success*," according to one of the historians, but we learn from the same source that the Portuguese were distinguished by a "burning thirst" for gold, by corrupt morals, by constant wars with the natives, and by the establishment of the Slave Trade.[1]

Success prompted John II. to further efforts for completing his exploration of the African Coast and, in 1486, he appointed B. Diaz, Commander of an Expedition, under orders to commence his investigations at the mouth of the Congo, and if

[1] "L'histoire des colonies ne nous offrent que trop souvent un spectacle de cruautés, que inspire l'horreur, et qui fait la honte de l'espèce humaine."—"Lettres Edifiantes." Tom. IV., p. XVII.

possible, to pass the southern extremity of the continent. We cannot accompany Diaz in his long voyage, the details of which are given with extreme minuteness by João de Barros[1]; but we may mention that he gave names to numerous capes, bays, and islands, and erected in every conspicuous place a "Padãro," that is a column of stone bearing the Cross and the Royal Arms, as a symbol of the subjugation of the country to *Christianity and Portugal.* A storm drove him beyond his destination, and when, after fourteen days' despair, they steered eastward, they found that they had overshot the mark, and unconsciously doubled the Cape. Forced by his mutinous crews to return home, he steered westward and discovered that mighty promontory which had lain concealed for so many centuries, and which formed, as it were, the boundary between two worlds. Diaz reached Portugal in December, 1487; and his "Cape of Storms" was changed by King John into the "Cape of Good Hope," a name ever since retained.

Desirous of affecting the discovery of the mysterious East, and of forming an alliance with "Prester John," the King sent Covilham and Payra overland in May, 1487. These bold travellers determined to go by way of the Red Sea. Payra died in Egypt, but his friend succeeded in reaching Sofala, Ormuz, and finally, Calicut and Goa; and Covilham was

[1] Primeira Decada. L. III., p. 42.

thus the first Portuguese that ever landed in India. About this time a Yolof prince from the banks of the Senegal arrived at the Court of John II. to ask for aid against a usurper of his throne. He availed himself of this favourable circumstance to receive instructions; and, surrounded by every element of regal magnificence and ecclesiastical pomp, *he was baptised by the name of John.* Soon afterwards, he did homage for his kingdom, returned to Africa, and, aided by by the Portuguese, regained possession of his throne. But poor Bemohi little knew the price to be paid for the blessings of civilisation; for though he had proved himself a zealous proselyte, and had persuaded or *forced twenty-five thousand of his subjects to embrace Christianity*, he fell beneath the dagger of General Bisagudo, to whose care he had been entrusted by the Portuguese King.[1]

The year 1492 is famous for the discovery of America by Columbus, whose service, offered, in the first instance, to John II. as the great promoter of naval enterprise, had been unfortunately declined. On the 6th of March, 1493, Columbus, returning from his first voyage, put into the Port of Lisbon, laden with the trophies of the New World, and was received by the dying King at his palace near

[1] Lorsque Joam II. examina sérieusement cette affaire, il trouva tan de hauts personnages compromis dans ce meurtre abominable, qu'il crut devoir garder le silence, et ne put décider a sévir. Voy. Vasconcellos. "Histoire de Jean II."

Santarem. John II., deeply mortified, held several Councils with the object of advancing a claim to the glories of the illustrious Genoese; and such was the intense chagrin of the courtiers, that they offered to assassinate Columbus on the spot.[1]

Emmanuel, or Manoel the Great, reigned from 1495 to 1521, and displayed a zeal in the cause of maritime exploration far surpassing that of his predecessors. A year after his accession, he determined to realise the immense projects which his father had planned. Diaz was charged with the task of building three vessels, strong enough to resist the stormy seas of the south. The command was conferred upon Vasco da Gama who sailed from Rastello (now Belem) on 7th July, 1497, amidst religious processions and the prayers of the whole population of Lisbon who crowded to the beach. After four months navigation, the expedition entered St. Helena Bay, and three days afterwards came in sight of the Cape of Good Hope. On the 20th of November, with a calm sea and gentle breeze Gama *doubled the Cape* amid the sound of trumpets and the ringing cheers of the crews. Before him lay the expanse of the Indian Ocean, and the road was now open to that unknown land, the object of all their hopes and expeditions. After numerous adventures on the eastern coast of Africa, during which he discovered Mozambique and

1 Barros, Dec. I., p. 56.

many other places, Gama sailed from the African Coast on the 26th of April, to steer three thousand miles through an unknown ocean. On the twenty-third day, they descried the peaks of the Ghauts, which their African pilot declared to be the coast of India, and, on the 20th of May he made the land at Capocate, two leagues from the town of Calicut; and thus was this great adventure crowned with triumphant success. This city was at that time one of the most powerful of the East; commerce flourished there to such an extent that the merchants of Arabia, Persia, and all India, resorted thither in crowds: and the King of Calicut was revered as the sovereign of all Malabar.

Da Gama waited upon the King (Rajah or Zamorin) to inform him officially of his arrival, of the object of his voyage, of the kingdom to which he belonged, of his position as ambassador, of his sovereign, and of the powers with which he was invested. Everything seemed to presage the greatest success; the Zamorin formed the highest opinion of those Europeans who had been bold enough to traverse a thousand leagues, and to brave all the perils of the deep, and gave the leader of the enterprise the most gracious reception, ordering that he should be entertained in his palace, and conceding to him and his people liberty to trade with all the ports of the empire.

This moment of good fortune was of short duration. The Mohammedans, monopolists of Indian commerce for many ages, foresaw their ruin if Gama remained in favour. They therefore bribed the ministers of the King to denounce the Portuguese Admiral as a piratical adventurer. After much negotiation and vacillation, mutual distrust broke into open war; and, at last, Vasco found himself compelled, though unprepared, to re-cross that formidable sea which lay between Malabar and Africa. After a passage of four months amidst storms and calms, the scurvy decimating his crew, he reached Magadoxo; but finding it in possession of the Moors, he anchored in the friendly harbour of Melinda. Supplied with provisions, he passed the Cape, and on the 29th of August, 1499, entered the Tagus with but one half of his hundred and eight men. Transports of admiration welcomed him home; Emmanuel ordered a universal thanksgiving, and honoured the discoverer with the new title of Grand Admiral of the East.

Taking advantage of this general enthusiasm Emmanuel hastened to equip thirteen ships, carrying twelve hundred men—a force sufficient to keep the sea against all the navies of India; and on the 8th of March, the King, having heard Mass, in the Convent of Belem, placed a consecrated banner in the hands of Cabral, who, *accompanied by eight Franciscan Mission-*

aries, was instructed to destroy all infidels, refusing to listen to the Christianity which the Friars preached.

A most remarkable event distinguished this second expedition to the East Indies. On the 25th of March, when the fleet had doubled Cape Verde, a tempest completely changed the course; and on the 24th of April, the Portuguese Admiral suddenly found himself in sight of a finely-wooded shore, which he rightly conjectured to be part of the Continent recently discovered by Columbus. The *Portuguese Missionaries then celebrated Mass* on the flowery turf of this unknown land, amid savage tribes who bent before the Cross; and thus the immense Empire of Brazil, the brightest jewel in the Portuguese Crown, "was won in a single day, Providence requiring merely to invoke the winds."[1] Cabral then steered straight for the Cape of Good Hope; and, after losing four of his ships (in one of which Diaz perished) rounded the promontory, touched at Mozambique, Melinda, and Quiloa, and arrived off Calicut on the 13th of September. His arrival was announced by several salvos of artillery, causing the greatest consternation amongst the inhabitants. Recovering from their fears, the natives went on board the Portuguese vessels, and Cabral was received at Court. Dissimulation, however, prevailed on both sides, and open war broke out. Cabral, everywhere

[1] "Chroniques Chevaleresques de l'Espagne et du Portugal" T. II.

victorious, forced the Zamorin to enter into alliance with Portugal. The Arab merchants, alarmed at the approaching ruin of their commerce, prevailed on the inhabitants to league with them against the intruders. The Admiral avenged himself by capturing the richly-laden vessels of the Moslems, who appealed to the King, declaring that the Portuguese had now shown themselves in their true colours as pirates. The King told the merchants they might seek redress as they pleased. They accordingly took the law into their own hands; and heading a tumult, stormed the Portuguese factory, and killed Correa and forty of his men. Cabral, witnessing this terrible scene, took summary vengeance. He attacked ten Moorish ships, seized their crews and cargoes, and burnt the vessels in full view of the citizens. He next drew up his fleet close to the shore, and bombarded the city, burying hundreds of the inhabitants under the ruins of their homes. After this rupture, Cabral abandoned Calicut, and went ninety miles south to Cochin, whose King was a reluctant vassal of the Zamorin. He therefore gave the strangers a hearty welcome, offered them full liberty of trading, entered into an alliance with Portugal, and appointed an ambassador to ratify the treaty at Lisbon. While Cabral was at Cochin, he heard that the enraged King of Calicut had fitted out a fleet of sixty sail, and the Admiral, judging "discretion the better part of valour," and avoiding the conflict, sailed for Lisbon, and left the Rajah of Cochin to his fate. He touched at Cananore, and *there met, for the first time, with two Christians of St. Thomas* who asked him to grant them a passage to Rome. The Portuguese fleet, reduced to half its original number, reached Lisbon on the 31st of July, 1501.

The voyage of Cabral completely changed European ideas of the East. The Christian monarch, known by the name of Prester John, invested with imaginary power and holiness, disappeared from the scene. People began to form a more *sober estimate of the Christians of St. Thomas*, by whom these rich countries were supposed to be peopled, reducing the number to about 20,000, being tolerated, rather than enjoying independence, behind the mountains of Cochin. Men began to admit the inflexibility of the Brahminical institutions; and the severe fasts endured by the hostages on board the Christian fleet, revealed a religious antagonism which the warlike Propagandists were, at first, far from suspecting. Caste, with its unalterable laws, its rigorous principles, and its numerous restraints, presented itself, for the first time, in its real essence to European eyes. Statesmen too, understood better than before the influence exercised by the Moslems over the timid people of the East; and, when the Rajah, forced by the demands of the Portuguese to state positively the line he intended to take with regard to his old allies, declared that he could not banish five thousand Arab families from his empire, he gave the Europeans to understand the nature of the contest in which they would have to engage, in order to crush the Mohammedan power, and to establish their own ascendancy. The almost harmless arrows of the Hindoos, and the rude fire-arms of the Moors, were no match for the well-served artillery of the western invaders, and this superiority ultimately decided the question.

The expedition of Cabral closes the maritime discoveries of the Portuguese in the fifteenth century, so far as India is concerned, several minor explorations in other regions not affecting the subject of this paper.

CHAPTER III.

PORTUGUESE CONQUESTS OF INDIA IN THE XVIth CENTURY.

"Vasco da Gama, o forte capitão
Que a tammanhas empresas se offerce
De suberboede altivo coracão,
A quem fortuna sempre favorece.

CAMOENS.

THE XVIth Century opens with the dispatch in March, 1501, of a squadron of four vessels under Nueva to reinforce the fleet in India. He was steering for Calicut, but found at St. Blas (an African port) a letter warning him of what had taken place, and advising him to go to Cochin. On his arrival, the Zamorin attacked him, but was utterly defeated.

Meantime, the greatest excitement prevailed in Lisbon. The first enthusiastic feeling was now chilled by the critical aspect which the affairs of India had assumed. While these voyages afforded adventures, extended knowledge, formed alliances, augmented the national wealth, exalted the honour of Portugal, and, above all, *enlarged the dominion of the Romish Faith*, the popular voice warmly seconded the sovereign will in fitting out one expedition after another. But, now when hostilities had broken out, and when it was evident that a mighty war had to be carried on against a Monarch almost at the other side of the world, it was feared that the resources of a small state would certainly be exhausted in the unequal conflict. King Manoel, however, was inflexible. Animated by political ambition and *religious zeal*, he relied on the *Papal grant, which had placed all the Eastern nations beneath his sceptre;* and he believed it both his right and his duty to follow up the conquests which his admirals had begun. Even on ordinary policy he calculated that the coalition of Cochin and Cananore would, in union with his own forces, be more than a match for the Rajah of Calicut. In a word, his great aim was to found an Empire in the East; and we, therefore, find him taking the proud title of "Lord of the Navigation, Conquest, and Commerce of Ethiopia, Arabia, Persia, and India." To justify these titles, and to accomplish his designs, an Armada was equipped, much more powerful than any hitherto dispatched to the East. A fleet of fifteen sail was destined to defend the Portuguese factories on the Malabar coast; while another squadron of five vessels was to intercept the Moorish traders at the mouth of the Red Sea. Vasco da Gama, with the title of Admiral of India, was invested with the chief command, and started from Lisbon on the 10th of February, 1502.

Independently of other motives, to which we have already referred, da Gama appears to have been prompted by a desire to punish the Moslems for the death of his friend Correa, as well as for the insults offered to religion. Chance soon furnished him with an opportunity of gratifying his revenge; and this instance (unfortunately but a specimen of many such) serves to account for so much of the hatred which Portuguese cruelty excited in the East, that we may, for a moment digress, to give an outline of the details. Da Gama encountered, on the 3rd of October, a large vessel belonging to the Sultan of Egypt, and crowded with pilgrims returning from Mecca. The Arabs, seeing resistance hopeless, offered an enormous ransom, which the admiral accepted, and yet ordered the vessel to be fired. The poor wretches succeeded in extinguishing the flames, but the merciless da Gama ordered his men to rekindle them. An eye-witness[1] relates that the women held up their children towards da Gama, and that in this scene of horror "l'intérieur du batiment offrait une représentation visible de l'enfer," and that "ce cruel souvenir lui était resté toute sa vie." This terrible episode in the second voyage of Vasco da Gama shows the spirit with which he was animated in his voyage to Malabar. And yet *the*

[1] Navegacãs as Indias Orientaes por Thomé Lopes. Chap. XVIII.

Jesuits treat this atrocity but lightly—"un vaisseau d'Egypte refuse de se rendre, il le crible de coups de canon, saute à borde, n'épargne que les enfans, et livre aux flammes le vaisseau et tous les hommes qui composaient l'équipage ; ce ne fut la qu 'un prelude de ses brillans succès.[1]

Da Gama then steered for India, and touched at Cananore, where he had an interview with the old Rajah, marked on both sides by great magnificence. As he sailed towards the hostile Calicut, he met a galley conveying noblemen from the Zamorin, as messengers of peace. They pleaded that his vengeance on the unfortunate ship ought to be accepted as full atonement of the murder of Correa. Gama haughtily replied that he would only treat with them on condition of the complete expulsion of the Moors. On anchoring before Calicut, the admiral received the Rajah's ultimatum, that, while he would give every advantage to the Christians, he positively refused to banish the Moorish residents. This answer was considered a declaration of war, and the Portuguese commander prepared to bombard the ill-fated city. Before making the attack, he wrote to the Zamorin by one of his prisoners, declaring that if he did not receive by mid-day a satisfactory response, he would burn the city. The time being past, he ordered all his captains to hang their Moorish prisoners at the

[1] "Lettres Edifiantes." Tom. IV., p., 25.

yard-arm ; and then commenced a bombardment which lasted all day. Towards evening he sent the heads, feet, and hands of the thirty-two victims on shore with a letter declaring that though these men were not the murderers of Correa, they were sufficiently related to justify the reprisal. He next threw the mutilated trunks into the sea, that they might float ashore, and strike terror into the people. For two days more he continued to cannonade the town, and then sailed for Cochin, which he reached on the 7th of November.[1]

It is unnecessary to multiply these frightful recitals; but it was requisite to give some idea of the arrogance and cruelty of the Portuguese conquerors. Of course, every attempt is made by their fellow countrymen to justify or palliate such atrocities as we have described. But though the bad faith of the Hindoo Monarchs, and the perfidious insinuations of the Moors, may explain the conduct of the admiral, the spirit of his age can alone excuse it. The summary of this expedition, *given by the Jesuits*, is characteristic :— " Vasco da Gama se trouve de nouveau aux côtes de Malabar ; il parle en maître, il veut venger la mort de Correa et de ses quarante compatriotes ; on lui offre des satisfactions, il les rejette avec dédain, s'empare d'un grand nombre de vaisseaux arabes, fait pendre

[1] This narrative is condensed from the History of João de Barros, Dec. I., B. VI., p. 130.

trente infidèles, détruit à coups de canon la plupart des maisons de Calicut, brûle les vaisseaux qui étaient à l'ancre, laisse Sodré dans les Indes, et retourne en Portugal avec ses vaisseaux richement chargés.[1]

The eyes of the Malabar princes were at length opened. Up to this time they had seen in their visitors only men urged by the desire of wealth, and anxious to gratify it in trading with India. Experience tore away the veil, and exposed the secret machinery of Portuguese policy. The alternative was evident; the Rajahs must either conquer the invader, or must lay their crowns at the feet of King Manoel. The Zamorin made every effort to rouse the apathetic sovereigns to take part in the common cause. It was too late; the first operations made the allies only the more sensible of their political weakness. And, when the King of Cochin, withdrawing from the coalition from policy, or in disgust, appeared as the ally of the Europeans, he naturally drew on himself the vengeance of his brother Rajahs. Too weak to offer effectual resistance, he was compelled to abandon his capital, and retire to the fortified island of Vipeen, where he would have been crushed, but for the opportune arrival of succour from Europe.

The Portuguese monarch fully resolved to maintain the footing which he had thus secured at Cochin, dispatched, in 1503, three squadrons of three ships each,

[1] Lettres Edifiantes. Tom. IV., p. 25.

under the two Albuquerques, Antonio de Saldanha, and Duarte Pacheco, called by Camoens, "the Portuguese Achilles." The fleet arrived at Malabar just in time, as already stated, to save the Zamorin and restore him to his throne. The Albuquerques immediately invaded the dominions of the enemy, and after a series of sharp conflicts forced him to conclude a hollow peace. They then set sail for Lisbon, leaving the defence of Cochin to Pacheco, with a handful of nine hundred Portuguese. The Zamorin, seeing his enemy thus almost defenceless, raised an army of 50,000 men, supported by a fleet of 160 vessels. Pacheco, nevertheless, resolved to protect the city to the last, and, after prodigies of valour, he succeeded, at the end of six months, in driving back the enemy with a loss of 15,000 men. This event took place in 1505, and may be regarded, as having *laid the foundation of the Portuguese Empire, in India.* Henceforward the natives were convinced, that their undisciplined armies, however numerous, could not resist a handful of well-armed soldiers, thoroughly trained to war. Pacheco thus pointed out the road to victory to his successor Albuquerque, by the brilliancy of whose exploits the fame of all other Portuguese leaders has been eclipsed.

From the year 1504, King Emmanuel had seen the necessity of regulating the administration of the East, and of establishing a permanent governor in these distant regions. He accordingly appointed Francisco d' Almeida, as first Viceroy of India, who set sail in 1505, and after certain petty conquests in Eastern Africa, sailed for Cochin, and soon found himself engaged in a desperate conflict with a Mohammedan fleet, dispatched by the Sultan of Cairo, to exterminate the European corsairs.

In the year 1506, fourteen vessels left Lisbon, under Tristam Dacunha, and Alphonso d' Albuquerque. Sailing first to Arabia, they reduced Muscat and other cities; making their king swear allegiance to Emmanuel. On Alburquerque's arrival at Cochin, Almeida was much disgusted at finding himself superseded by the new Governor-General of India; and persisted in retaining his authority till he had vanquished the Egyptian fleet, and avenged his son. After a dear bought victory, he disgraced his triumph by a general massacre of his prisoners. Almeida, having resigned, Albuquerque entered at once on those vast schemes of conquest which have made him one of the heroes of Portugal. His first object was the reduction of Calicut, the obnoxious centre of the Malabar alliance. In January, 1510, the town was taken and burnt; but the enemy, rallying at the palace, drove the Portuguese to their ships. Undeterred by this comparative failure, Albuquerque still resolved to secure some strong point which might become the Metropolis of

India, and the centre of conquest, colonisation and Christianity. An Indian pirate suggested Goa, a town on a small island separated by fordable salt marshes from the mainland; and the Viceroy, with his characteristic promptitude, cast anchor before this famous place in January, 1510. The outworks being taken, and a fleet close to the walls, the merchants, (Moslems, Hindoos, and Parsees), to whom commerce was more important than patriotism, offered to surrender on conditon of full protection. Albuquerque accepted these terms, fulfilled them strictly, took possession of the palace, and assumed the rank of sovereign. Meantime, Adelschah, the native Prince, hearing that his capital was in the possession of the detested Europeans, raised an army of 40,000 men, and, on the 17th of May, forced the enemy to evacuate the city. The Rajah, however, did not long enjoy the fruits of his *coup de main.* Albuquerque appeared before Goa on Christmas Day, 1510, at the head of a force of 1,800 men to attack a capital defended by 9,000. After a terrible bombardment, he stormed the city, and by a hand-to-hand fight of six hours in the streets, he won it a second time, and reunited it definitely to the Crown of Portugal. Goa, being thus secured as the Portuguese Metropolis, the Viceroy took effectual measures to render the conquest permanent by extensive fortifications, by just administration, by matrimonial alliances, and *by the propagation of the faith.* Then followed the expeditions to Malacca and Ormuz, and the discoveries, in 1511, of the Moluccas and other islands in the Indian seas, but as these do not bear upon our subject we may pass over the details.

Albuquerque died on 16th December, 1516, leaving the Portuguese empire at the height of its power "stretching twelve thousand miles from the Cape of Good Hope to the frontier of China."[1]

While these events were taking place in the East, King Emmanuel sent an embassy (1514) to Leo. X. presenting him with an elephant from Goa, bearing the richest gifts. The Pontiff received the Ambassadors with extraordinary honours. Pacheco made a Latin speech and had a reply in the same language: "Portugal offers to Christian Rome all these newly-explored countries;" and *the Pope granted what the Portuguese required, formal possession, in the face of the world, of these Oriental conquests.*

John III. ascended the throne in 1521, and found himself in a very different position from that which had marked the beginning of the last reign. A small fleet had grown to three hundred vessels, the trade of Lisbon at home and abroad had been prodigiously developed, and the influence of this little kingdom felt throughout the world. The new Monarch, was "appetite growing with what it fed on," determined to

[1] Faria e Souza.

pursue his conquests in India. Were we writing a history, instead of an introduction, we might give a long list of the Viceroys and Governors who succeeded Albuquerque, and enter into full details of their achievements. The history of the struggles of the Portuguese with the natives, who were goaded by the cruel bigotry of their oppressors into the most determined resistance, is too monotonous to render a circumstantial narrative of sufficient interest. One or two contests are, however, worthy of notice.

The Governor-General, Da Cunha, received the sanction of the Rajah to erect a factory and fort near the important city of Diu, close to Cambay and Guzerat. Bahador, Sultan of Cambay, at first friendly, soon became jealous; and during a visit to the port, lost his life in a sudden quarrel. This led to a combination against the strangers in which the Governor of Cairo was ordered by the Turkish Sultan to co-operate. Then began (1538) the first siege of Diu, when six hundred Portuguese successfully resisted twenty-thousand troops, sixty-five ships, and a splendid train of artillery. Seven years afterwards, Zofar, the chief of Guzerat, again attacked the fortress of Diu which was gallantly defended by two hundred men. In October, 1545, the new Viceroy, the famous João de Castro arrived, broke through the enemy's lines and defeated them with terrible slaughter. Taking the neighbouring city of Diu, he gave it up to plunder and massacre, and returned to Goa in triumph, crowned with laurel, the Royal Standard of Cambay trailing behind him. This able and distinguished Viceroy held office only three years, and was so disinterested that, though Governor of the richest provinces, he died in extreme poverty. The great stain on his character was the dreadful barbarity which he everywhere exercised over the conquered.

The Portuguese historians agree that at this period there was a revival of prosperity, similar to the almost fabulous success of the Albuquerques. This prosperity, the immediate consequence of a noble spirit and of severe integrity was but of short duration. Gradually, place-hunters and extortioners, gained the ascendency, so, that sixty years afterwards, an author writing on statistics could say, "such is the number of lawyers who besiege the Government offices at Goa, that one might call it a city of pleaders, and not a city of warriors." This political decline did not, however, arrive all at once, and the times which immediately followed the epoch of João de Castro were still glorious under Garcia de Sa, during whose government the Dominicans arrived, and under Cabral, during whose sway the Portuguese gained signal victories by sea and land.

In 1570, during the government of Luis de Ataide, the Mogul formed an alliance with the Zamorin, for the purpose of expelling the Portuguese. An army of

100,000 men laid siege to Goa, defended by only 700 troops in addition to 1,300 monks and slaves. After a long and unsuccessful siege, a desperate assault was made on the 13th of April. This too, failed, and the enemy withdrew with the loss of 12,000 men. Similar attacks were made on Chaul, near Bombay, and Chale near Calicut; but being defended with the usual vigour, the assailants were finally discouraged, and the coalition dissolved. By such achievements as these, the Portuguese maintained their supremacy, not only on the coasts, but on the seas of India, during nearly the whole of the sixteenth century. But the high degree of power and prosperity to which Portugal had attained, became the object of the envy, the ambition, and the cupidity of other nations. Dutch, French, Danes, and English poured into India, to conquer and to appropriate a share of its territory, its commerce, and its riches. In the autumn of 1596, Houtman arrived off Java. In 1599, a fleet of eight Dutch vessels returned from Sumatra and Java, laden with spices, and in 1600, several Dutch trading companies dispatched forty large vessels, and soon succeeded in depriving the Portuguese of nearly all their lucrative trade. During the next fifty years there was a long and bloody struggle between the Portuguese and Dutch, in which the latter were finally victorious; while in the western provinces, the Portuguese were supplanted by their new rivals the English. The successors of the Albuquerques and de Castros were stripped of their vast dominions almost as rapidly as they had gained them, and now Goa, Mozambique, Diu, Macao, and a few minor factories, all in a decayed condition, are the sole and sad remnants of that colossal power, which, in the XVIth Century, extended over so large a part of the Eastern Hemisphere.

This summary of the chief events which mark the Portuguese conquest of India will, we trust, *prepare the way for a clear understanding of the Portuguese Missions in the XVIth Century.* The difficulty has been not to obtain sufficient information, but to condense, with discrimination, the enormous mass of materials afforded by the historians of that age, whose discursive and pompous style fills page after page of ponderous folios and quartos, rarely taken from the shelves of our public libraries. Should any reader care to have a more detailed account of this interesting period, he may consult, with advantage, the original authorities named in the appendix.

CHAPTER IV.

THE PORTUGUESE EMPIRE IN THE XVIth CENTURY

"To understand a Mission thoroughly, we should know something of its locality; the people among whom it is carried on; their former condition and history; their habits of life, the history of Missionary effort among them; its discouragements and pleasing features; its present character and fruits."—"South India Missions," p. 91.

THOUGH some idea may be gained of the Portuguese acquisitions from the narrative already given, it may be useful to present a summary of the geographical questions relating to this volume. We may notice in the first place the conquests of the Portuguese in the XVIth Century with reference to their localities; next the political divisions of India at that period; and lastly, South India, especially Malabar, Cochin and Travancore, the abodes of the Syrian Christians.

I. Omitting the settlements on the West Coast of Africa, mentioned in our previous pages, we may adopt the condensed statement, appended to the Third Volume of "Asia Portuguesa," which describes the Portuguese Empire of the East as it existed at the close of the XVIth Century. The learned author, Faria y Sousa, writing with the advantage which a cotemporary possesses, informs us that the Lusitanian Settlements actually extended 1,200 miles from the Cape of Good Hope to China, and that these vast dominions were thus divided :—(1) From the Cape of Good Hope to Guardafui, and Socotra at the mouth of the Red Sea, in other words the whole range of the East Coast of Africa—the kingdoms of Sofala, Mozambique, Zanquebar, Magadoxo, Ajan, and Somauli, with the splendid island of Madagascar, and numerous ports (Quiloa, Melinda, &c.) enriched with the commerce of Arabia, and adjacent countries. (2) The coast line from Mocha to Muscat, *i.e.*, from the mouth of the Red Sea to the Persian Gulf, embracing Hadramant, Omaun and other regions of Arabia Felix. (3) The third division begins at Bosta or Bussora, where the Euphrates enters the gulf, passes Bussire, and other emporia, stretches along Beloochistan and Scinde, to the gulf of Cambay. This region was one of the first Portuguese possessions, and the names of Ormuz, Guadel, Scinde, Cambaya, Guzerat, with the fort of Bandel and Diu, so famous for its siege, occur perpetually in their early histories. (4) The fourth division ranges from Cambaya to Cape Comorin, and includes those districts to which our history specially refers, the coast of Bejapoor, Coukan, Canara, Malabar, Cochin and Travancore. The fortified factories of Damaun, Assarim, Danu, Bassaim, St. Gens, Agaçaim, Maini, Trapor, Cana, Savanja, Chaul and Moro. "The most noble city Goa," says Faria,[1] "large, strong and populous, is the Metropolis of our Eastern Dominions, and contains an Archbishopric, whose Prelate is the Primate of all the East. This is the residence of the Viceroys, and here are the courts of the Inquisition, Exchequer, Chancery, Custom House, Arsenals, and Magazines well provided. The city is seated on an island girt with strong walls, and defended by six mighty Castles" and much more to the same effect, which we need not quote, as we have elsewhere described the capital of India. (5) This lies between Cape Comorin and the mouth of the Ganges, including what was then called Madura (Tinnevelly, Dindigul, Tanjore, &c.) the Carnatic, Golconda, Narsinga, Orissa, and smaller states. Here the Portuguese possessed many factories, the chief being Negapatam, Meliapour, Masulipatam, and Vizagapatam, with smaller settlements, as far as the spot on which Calcutta now stands. (6) This division has little or no reference to our present subject; but, to complete the list we may state that it extends from Calcutta to Singapore, and includes part of Bengala, with Pegu, Tenasserim, and Malacca. (7) The last portion of this extraordinary maritime empire swept along from Singapore to

[1] "Asia Portuguesa," Vol. III.

Macao, thus completing one of the most singular phenomena in the history of the world; for, while other nations have aspired to the conquest of kingdoms or continents, it was the peculiar characteristic of Portuguese ambition to limit its colonial dominion to the mere sea-boards of the countries which it subdued.

II. The Political Divisions of India in the XVIth Century, are sufficiently intelligible for our purpose, without tracing their history to their source. Every classical student is perfectly aware, that at a very remote period, India was known to the Egyptians and Phœnicians, and possibly, to the Hebrews also.[1] As far back as 1491 B.C., Sesostris, King of Egypt, marched through Asia to the banks of the Ganges, and even, it is said to the Eastern Ocean. And though this rapid conquest is alleged to have left no permanent impression, it is plausibly conjectured that several customs now prevailing in India were introduced at the time of the Egyptian invasion.[2] Passing over the expedition of Darius, in 510 B.C., which seems not to have gone beyond the Indus, we may observe the famous invasion of Alexander the Great in 326 B.C. which may certainly be considered

[1] Robertson doubts this, saying "The Jews then, we may conclude, have no title to be reckoned among the nations which carried on intercourse with India by sea." Hist. of India, p. 12. Bruce's Travels Book II., C. IV.

[2] Diud. Sic. Lib. I., p. 64. La Croze Hist., p. 434. Rollin Vol. I., p 78. Robertson's India, p. 7.

the first disclosure of a knowledge of India to the people of Europe. His successor, Seleucus, fruitlessly endeavoured to prosecute Alexander's schemes of Oriental Conquest; but, Ptolemy Soter,[1] more fortunate in his choice of means, was able to make Egypt the peaceful centre of a prosperous trade with India. The Persians, hearing of this success, soon followed the example set by the Egyptians, transporting the commodities of India by land, while they left to their rivals the monopoly of the sea. Very early in the 1st Century, B.C. we find the Romans eagerly pursuing commercial intercourse with the East, and opening a third channel through Mesopotamia.

Nothing further is heard as to change of route, till the Egyptian Hippalus (50 A.D.) boldly sailing from the mouth of the Red Sea, crossed with the monsoon in forty days to Musiris, somewhere near Mangalore, on the coast of Canara. The student is referred to "Ptolemy's Geography of India" for a description of the whole region as then known. "Strabo's Geography," "Arian's History of the Indies" and D'Anville's well-known work, "Antiquités de l'Inde" will throw further light on this part of our subject.

In the year 200, Pantœnus is said to have visited India as its first Missionary;[2] and, in 325 Johannes,

[1] His son Ptolemy Philadelphus anticipated Lesseps in the idea of the Suez canal. Strabo. Lib. XVII., p. 1,156. Plin. Nat. Hist. Lib. VI., C. XXIX.

[2] Eusebius. Lib. III. Cap. X.

Bishop of Persia, and India, signed his name at the Council of Nice.[1] About the year 527, in the reign of Justinian, one Cosmas, an Alexandrian merchant, called Indo-Pleustes (Indian voyager) published some valuable information about India and the Indian Church, especially in Malabar:—"There is in the island of Taprobrane, in the farthermost India, in the Indian Sea, a Christian Church, with Clergymen and believers. In the Malabar country also, where pepper grows, there are Christians, and in Caliana, as they call it, there is a Bishop who comes from Persia where he was consecrated.[2] The VIIth Century is marked by the rise of Mohammedanism, which soon spread over the East and which, to this hour, affects the condition—political, moral, and intellectual—of Hindostan. In the IXth Century, an interesting episode connects England with India; for, in 883, Alfred the Great sent Sighelm, Bishop of Sherborne, on a mission to the shrine of St. Thomas, near Madras.[3] Omitting all accounts of visits to Malabar, by Persian Ecclesiastics in the Xth Century, and other irrelevant matters, we may advert to the Crusades as powerfully influencing European intercourse with

[1] Eusebius. Lib. III. Cap VI. Hough's Christ, Vol. I., p. 61.

[2] Asseman. Tom. XIII., p. 2. Robertson's India, p. 95. Lardner Vol. XI., C. 148. La Croge, pp. 37-8. Paulinus Ind. Orient. Christ, p. 14.

[3] Saxon Chron., p. 86. "William of Malmesbury De Gestis," Book II., Chap. IV., p. 44. Turner's, Hist. Ang. Sax., Vol. II., p. 145. Gibbon, Chap. XLVII.

India, and as preparing the way for the extensive trade which favoured the Venetians in the XIIIth Century, the Genoese in the XIVth and the Florentines in the XVth. The study of this question would be incomplete without examining the travels of the famous Venetian Marco Polo, who, for more than a quarter of a century (1255-80) explored the whole of Asia as far as Pekin, and who has left us the only trustworthy account of the East at the time of his travels.[1]

While Prince Henry and the captains, whom his genius and energy had called into action were exploring the coast of Africa, the Mongols and Hindoos were engaged in deadly conflict for the vast prize of Northern India. Timur, the Tartar, after desolating the country, destroyed Delhi and reduced the whole empire to the power of Mahomet. Baber, his lineal descendant, came to the throne in 1494; and, by the decisive battle of Panniput in 1526, succeeded in establishing the Mogul Dynasty in Delhi.

At this time, when the Portuguese first came in contact with Indian Princes, the whole of what we now call India contained five great Mohammedan empires, besides many Hindoo kingdoms. The old Patan sovereignty of Delhi had included Hindostan and the Punjaub, but was now divided into two main

[1] Herbelot Bib. Orient. arctic *Khathai.* Voyage of A. Jenkinson. Hakluyt, Vol. I., p. 333. Robertson's India, p. 154 and p. 395.

principalities. Guzerat, Malwa, and Bengal, had each its Sultan, possessed of formidable armies, and though brethren in the Moslem Faith, perpetually at war with each other. The Hindoo Princes were the Rajah of Beejanuggur in the Deccan, and the Rana Sanka of Mewar, with many others whose dominions were not affected by the Portuguese invasions. Of course the Zamorin and the Rajahs of Cochin, and other towns along the coast, have already been so frequently mentioned, that it is not necessary to refer to them again. An inspection of the map of the Deccan, about 1520, will give a better idea of the political divisions of India as they then were than any verbal description. Before leaving this part of our subject we may remark that the accession of Akbar, in 1554, produced an important effect on the political divisions of India. Internal dissensions had weakened the great Hindoo Monarchy of Beejanuggur, which was finally extinguished by a coalition of the surrounding states. Availing himself of this condition of the Deccan, Akbar invaded South India, and incorporated the greater part with the Mogul Empire in 1598. This monarch seemed disposed to cultivate friendly relations with the King of Portugal, encouraged Europeans to enter his service, and invited the Jesuits of Goa to resort to his Court.[1] At his death in 1605,

[1] Manonchi's "Life of Akbar," p. 136. Fraser's "History of the Mogul Emperors," p. 12. Hough's "Hist. of Christ," Vol. I., p. 261.

his extensive dominions were divided into fifteen Vice-royalties, each governed by a Subardar.[1] The reigns of Baber, Humayan, and Akbar covered the XVIth Century, and synchronise very nearly with the period of the Portuguese conquests and early missions.

III. South India demands a description more extensive than our space will afford as, it is not only the scene of the earliest missionary efforts of the Portuguese amongst the heathen and the Syrian Christians, but it is by far the most interesting field of modern operations for the conversion of the natives. This division includes the whole of the Peninsula of India, south of what we now call the Nizam's dominions, but was very little known to the Portuguese settlers, with the exception of a strip of land ten miles broad along the coast. In the XVIth Century, its boundaries differed from those which at present exist. It had Krishna on the north, and comprehended Bijnagur, Madura, the Empire of the Zamorin, subdivided into a number of petty states, such as Cannanore, Calicut, Canganor, Cochin, Coulon, Travancore, &c. South India extends from the sixteenth to the eighteenth parallel of latitude. The area is 200,000 square miles, and the population about 32,000,000. The physical aspect of the country is that of a large

[1] Tod's "Annals of Rajasthan." "South of India," Col. Wilkes, Vol. I., p. 169.

plateau, or table-land, bounded by the Eastern and Western Ghauts, and rising into Alpine ridges such as the Neilgherry Hills; while the Godavery, the Khistna, the Cauvery, and many other streams, supply abundant water for irrigation without which India would be a desert. The climate is influenced by the mountains and the monsoons; and though in temperature, the Madras coast is undoubtedly the hottest part of the peninsula, a climate, almost English, may be reached by railway in a few hours.

One of the common errors in England is the idea that India is one vast country, instead of being like Europe, a union of many states, races, languages, and religions. In South India the population is extremely diversified in origin, stature, and complexion. Most of these races profess the Hindoo Faith, and Brahmins are more numerous than in any other part of the peninsula. Caste still holds sway, but there are decided symptons of this formidable barrier being broken down, in spite of all the injudicious concessions made by the Romish missioners. Christian effort, the march of civilisation, continued intercourse with Europeans, and that remarkable movement among the Hindoos themselves, called the Brahmo-Somaj, of which Chunder Sen is the leader, seem all combining to remove this obstacle to the progress of India. The English language is now more than supplanting the Portuguese; though the natives, of course, still use

Tamil, Malayalim, Canarese, and Telegu, besides Urdu, employed in the camp.

Malabar is a long narrow strip between the Ghauts and the sea, containing 6,000 square miles and a million and a half of people. The mountains rise rapidly to the height of 5,000 feet, and are covered with magnificent forests of teak and cedar. The ravines and passes present scenes of romantic beauty, while the low grounds are laid out in paddy-fields, and the flat, sandy shores, are fringed with groves of cocoa-nut palms, the graceful arecas surrounding the small groups of mud cottages scarcely worthy the name of villages. The soil is extremely fertile, and produces rice, cardamums, coffee, and pepper, in great abundance; the latter, as far back as the days of Cosmas, was the characteristic of the country, and it is now often called the money of Malabar. The population of this coast is singularly varied: Brahmins, Nairs, Tiars, Moplays, Christians, and Jews, besides numerous foreigners, Asiatic and European, who have settled here for purposes of trade.

Cochin the chief seat of the Syrian Christians, though often included under the name of Malabar, is really an independent state of 1,100 square miles, and 400,000 people. This irregularly shaped mountain tract has British Malabar on the north, the Rajah of Travancore's dominions on the south, Coimbatore and Madura on the east. The physical features climate and productions, are almost the same as those of Malabar, but it is distinguished by a peculiarity in the distribution of its watercourses, of which we may quote from an eye-witness the following account:—"It is watered by numerous streams, which descend from the mountains towards the sea; but these little rivers, instead of pouring their waters separately into the ocean, spread out before they reach it into wide channels just within the coast line, and communicating with one another, form what is called "The Back-water"—a land locked lake of every varying depth and width, with an outlet here and there, through which the water finds its way into the ocean."[1] The population consists of Naimhoories, or Aboriginal Brahmins, Nairs, Pollayers (a wretched race), and Christians of various nations and churches. The inhabitants are generally very poor, there being no middle-class between landowner and labourer. On the coast many find employment in ship-building, rope-making, fishing, and gathering cocoa-nuts, and are, therefore, somewhat better off. With rare exceptions the clothing of the upper class natives consists of nothing more than a few yards of calico or muslin, wrapt round the middle; while the poorer people are scarcely clad at all. This, of course, does not apply to the Christian converts, many of whom have been persuaded to assume more ample garments. The

[1] Howard's "Christians of S. Thomas," p. 2.

country is at present ruled by a Rajah under the British Government; and many evidences of civilisation, such as churches, schools, and hospitals, are everywhere springing into existence.

Travancore is a very important government under its own sovereign, extending from Cochin to Cape Comorin, one hundred and fifty-five miles. The climate is extremely hot and moist, in the lowlands the thermometer rising to above 90°; and though the heat is much less in the mountains, the air is not so bracing as in the Neilgherries. Animal life is abundant, the forests teeming with tigers, leopards, snakes, and an immense variety of birds. The soil in the level districts is prolific in rice, sago, coffee, &c. Like Cochin and Malabar, Travancore possesses a remarkably diversified population in race and creed. Christianity is professed by about one-eighth of the population, and is spreading rapidly, not only under the English and other Protestant Societies, but also under the Romanists. The Rajah, one of the most enlightened Princes, has established police, schools and hospitals, formed excellent roads, granted perfect religious toleration, and removed all restrictions on commerce. His handsome palace, is at the modern capital, Trevandrum; the old one, Travancore, being now deserted. Allepi and Quilon are also important harbours.

Madura, Tinnerelly, and other districts of South

India are so well known from the reports of the Missionary Societies, "Les Annales de la Foie" and similar publications, that it seems quite unnecessary to notice them here. Occasional references in the following chapters will be sufficient to illustrate geographical names as they occur.[1]

[1] Further information will be found in Thornton's "Gazetteer of India," George Duncan's "Geography of India," 1868; Professor Ansted's "Geography of India," 1870; the Rev. G. Rowe's "Colonial Empire—The East Indian Group." S.P.C.K., and similar works.

BOOK II.

THE PORTUGUESE MISSIONS IN SOUTHERN INDIA.

CHAPTER I.

EARLY HISTORY OF THE CHURCH IN INDIA.

"That St. Thomas was the Apostle of the Indies is attested by all Ecclesiastical Records, Greek, Latin and Syriac"—Asseman, "Dissert de Syris Nestorianis," Tom. IV., p. 439.

> "Choraram te, Thorné, o Gange, e o Indo ;
> Choron-te-toda a terra, que pizaste ;
> Mais te choram as almas, que vestindo
> Se iam da sancta fè, que lhe ensinaste."
>
> CAMOENS.

WE have hitherto spoken of the conquests of the sword, the only ones which, generally speaking, attract the attention of mankind, and furnish themes for the historian. There are, however, other victories which, beginning with the early part of the XVIth Century, have exercised an immense influence over Southern India. We allude, of course, to the missions established there soon after these regions were discovered and subdued.

When the Portuguese had obtained a firm footing upon the coasts of Malabar, and partially penetrated into the interior of the country, they found those vast tracts peopled by three sorts of inhabitants. First, there were the Christians of St. Thomas, who, during at least eight centuries, had been cut off from the rest of Christendom, and had, according to some writers, corrupted the true faith by engrafting on it the errors of Nestorius and the superstitions of Paganism ; secondly, the Moors, or Arabs, fanatical followers of Mahomet, divided into many sects ; and thirdly, the Hindoo population, the learned men believing in various systems of philosophy, the middle and lower classes being plunged into the thick darkness of the grossest idolatry. Our business being briefly to sketch the early history of the Indian Church, as introductory to the Portuguese Missions, it seems unnecessary to describe, except incidentally, the errors of Mohammedanism, or the superstitions of the heathen.

The Church of India acknowledges St. Thomas as its first founder. This Holy Apostle had carried the gift of religion to the Parthians, the Hircanians, the Persians, and the Arabs. In the ardour of his zeal, he counted it as scarcely anything that he had announced his Divine Master in all the places which the Grecian hero had rendered illustrious by his conquests. Not satisfied with finishing his course where the ambition of Alexander the Great had ended his, he penetrated into the interior of India, preached the Gospel to nations whose very names were hardly known, and founded, amidst tribes where idolatry had been hitherto triumphant, a Church of earnest worshippers of the true God.

There is, of course, much discussion on this point. While, on the other hand, the Roman Catholics and some reformers maintain the truth of what we have just stated, others declare that the Syrian Church was founded by another St. Thomas of the IVth Century. According to one view, the Apostolic origin of this Church is not one of those obscure traditions which dread the severe investigations of criticism, as it unites in its favour all the proofs which can attest its truth: the accumulated evidence of the first ages of the Church of St. Jerome, St. Chrysostom, St. Augustine, St. Athanasius, and amongst the historians nearest to this epoch, Eusebius, Nicetas, Sophronius, Abdias, and Nicephorous. To the authority of these testimonies may be joined that of usages and monuments still in existence, and which ascend to the period when the name of Christian began to be known in Hindostan. St. Chrysostom writes that from the earliest times of Christianity, the tomb of St. Thomas was, in the East, as much venerated as that of St. Peter at Rome. To this very day, and from time immemorial, the city of Meliapour, to which the Christians of India have given the name of St. Thomas, sees, every year, the two neighbouring hills covered by a multitude of

Christians, old and new, who flock thither from the coasts of Malabar, from Ceylon, from the most distant parts of India, and even from Arabia, to deposit their offerings and to pray at the shrine of the Holy Apostle. The Communion office, the liturgy, and all the services of this Indian Church were celebrated in Syriac, a language which, as all students know, was much used in the Holy Land amongst the Jews in the time of Our Lord. This may be considered an additional proof that the faith was introduced into India by St. Thomas, and in the words of the Jesuit historian, "on ne voit pas qu'il soit possible de trouver, dans l'historie de cette Eglise, un autre fondateur que Saint Thomas lui-meme."[1]

The Portuguese, on their first expedition into India, found there 200,000 Christians; the wreck of a wretched people, plunged into gross ignorance and bending under the yoke of slavery. Interrogated as to their faith, these Indians could give no other account of their religion than that they bore the name of Christians of St. Thomas, and the practice which they had, following the example of their ancestors, of going every year to offer their homage to their protecting saint, on the very spot where, according to the constant tradition of their Church, he had consummated his martyrdom. These Christians of St. Thomas related marvellous things of his

[1] "Lettres Edifiantes," Tom. IV., p. 3.

Apostolate, taken from their annals. They had composed from these materials canticles, or sacred songs, translated into the language of the country, and chanted by the inhabitants of Ceylon, and of the coasts of Malabar.

The traditions of an ignorant and barbarous people are always confused and often mixed with fable. Amidst the clouds which cover the traditions of the Christians of St. Thomas, the following account seems to possess the greatest amount of probability, and the nearest approach to truth. After having established Christianity in Arabia Felix, and in the island of Dioscorides (now called Socotora), the Holy Apostle landed at Cranganor, at that time the residence of the most powerful King on the Malabar Coast. We know, from the historians of the Christian people, from Josephus and from the Sacred Books themselves, in the account of the Miracle of Pentecost that before the birth of Jesus Christ, there went forth from Judea a great number of its inhabitants, and that they were scattered throughout Egypt, Greece, and several countries of Asia. St. Thomas learnt that one of these little colonies had settled in a country adjacent to Cranganor. Love for his nation inflamed his zeal; and faithful to the command of Jesus Christ who had enjoined his Apostles to proclaim the faith to the Jews, before turning to the Gentiles, he repaired to the country which his compatriots had chosen for their asylum; he preached to them the Gospel, converted them, and changed their Synagogue into a Christian Church. *This was the cradle of Christianity in India.* Very soon this precious seed, cultivated by the Holy Apostle, bore fruit a hundredfold; the faith was carried to Cranganor, to Coulan, a celebrated city of the same coast, and to several kingdoms of Southern India. The converted Gentiles were united to the Jews; Churches were multiplied, and the Syriac language was adopted in Divine Service. St. Thomas, after having given a constitution to these infant Churches, proceeded to new conquests; and, directing his steps towards the coast of Coromandel, reached Meliapour. The fame of his miracles and of his wonderful success had preceded him; the Rajah's eyes were opened to the light of the faith, he received baptism; and by his example, a part of his subjects embraced the Gospel. These numerous conversions excited the jealousy and hatred of the Brahmins, two of whom urged the populace to stone the Holy Apostle. One of these Priests observing some trace of life in the Saint, pierced him with his lance, and St. Thomas thus received the reward of his love and devotion as a missionary, the crown of martyrdom. The Church of Meliapour, thus founded in the Apostle's blood, flourished for centuries; it had its Bishops, Priests, and faithful congregations; but a time came when the Gentile Kings took possession of the city and its dependent provinces, and the Christians suffered the most violent persecutions from the destroying Pagans. To escape from their cruelty, the greater part fled towards Cape Comorin; and passing thence they took refuge *in the mountains of Malabar, amongst the other Christians whom St. Thomas had taught.* They spread into Cranganor, Coulan and Travancore, *i.e.*, into the district called the empire of the Zamorin in the XVIth Century.

From the end of the second Century of the Christian era, an evil, much more to be feared than persecutions, afflicted the Church of India; the divisions which arose within her bosom weakened the purity of the faith and the vigour of primitive discipline. At this period the school of Alexandria (founded by St. Mark) so famous throughout the Roman empire, by a succession of such men as the Clements and the Origens, spread the brilliancy of its knowledge over the Christian world. The Christians of India, groaning under internal dissensions, sent deputies to Demetrius imploring him to commission some eminent man to arbitrate amongst them and to restore the authority of their Church. Pantænus, being chosen for this mission passed several years in India; but history is silent as to the success of his visitation. There is only one tradition which has been preserved to us by St. Jerome and Eusebius, that Pantænus found in India the Gospel of St. Matthew written in Hebrew. This important fact, the designation of "Christians of St. Thomas," transmitted from age to age to the faithful of this Church, the custom of celebrating public worship in Syriac, the name of a bishop amongst the signatures at the first general Council of Nice, with the title of Bishop of Persia and of great India—all these united proofs strongly confirmed the general opinion that St. Thomas was the first Apostle of India.

In the fourth Century, St. Athanasius also came to the aid of this Church. St. Fromentius had been, for many years, reduced to slavery; but, having found means of effecting his escape, he succeeded in reaching Alexandria and there fixed his abode. St. Athanasius, whom Providence had placed over this great See, thoroughly recognised the merits, the virtues, and the zeal, of the illustrious fugitive whom he therefore raised to the episcopate. St. Fromentius then returned to his old companions in misfortune, preached Jesus Christ to them, and to the people of India; and received the reward of his zealous labours in the Crown of Martyrdom.

The Gospel made rapid progress, and new conquests in India; Churches were multiplied in all directions and the virtues of the Christians of St. Thomas secured for them extensive popularity, and even the favour of the monarchs of the country. Ceram Peromal, founder of Calicut, became Emperor of all Malabar, divided the provinces of his realm amongst his relations and favourites, and thereby gave origin to that multitude of small states with which the coast of Malabar is filled. This Prince, though an infidel, granted the most important privileges to the Christians, and they were placed on a level with the superior Castes. They further enjoyed the prerogative of depending solely on the authority of their Bishop, even in things temporal. These privileges were renewed to them in the ninth century, and time has preserved to us the authentic title-deeds in a most durable form; for they were written upon plates of copper in characters of Malabar, Canarin, Bisnagare and Tamil, the languages most in use on these coasts.

This continued prosperity had the effect of rendering these Christians enterprising and ambitious. Powerful enough to shake off the yoke of the infidel princes, they elected a monarch of their own religion; and Baliartes was proclaimed King of the Christians of St. Thomas. This state of independence was but brief, for one of these Kings, having adopted the Prince of Diamper, was succeeded by this youth. A similar adoption placed them under the Rajah of Cochin, who, being a Pagan, persecuted his Christian subjects. The prosperity of the Church ended, and its subsequent history is but a chain of misfortunes. The heresies predicted by Our Lord and His Apostles were at that time rending the Catholic Church; the faith persecuted by Christian Emperors was exposed to greater dangers than all that it had endured under the Pagan Sovereigns; in fact the powers of darkness were making the greatest efforts to destroy, by their own hand, that body which the persecutions of the Cæsars had but strengthened. Nestorianism, originating in the Vth Century had extended its ranges throughout the East.[1] The Church of India had long groaned under the yoke of the infidel Princes, the successors of the Christian Kings. A calm indeed, had followed the storm, but it was the calm of spiritual death. Deprived of the Priesthood, the Indian branch was obliged to apply to the Churches of the North West. The Patriarch of Armenia, a Nestorian, was delighted to embrace the opportunity thus presented, and eagerly sent Priests fitted to extend his jurisdiction.[2] The Indians, who had suffered so long from the want of pastors welcomed these missionaries, paid them full obedience, and received, necessarily from such teachers all the evils of heresy and schism. "As a natural consequence, they cut themselves off from the centre of Catholic unity, abjured the *obedience which*

[1] Neander, Vol. IV., p. 123. Mosheim, Cent. V., Part II., Chap. V. Hough's "Hist. of Christ." Vol. I., p. 74. Bishop Browne, XXXIX. Art.

[2] "Nestorianism took deep root in many soils, and the Nestorians proved themselves zealous missionaries. Their opinions spread rapidly into Armenia, Chaldea, Syria, Arabia and India." — Bishop Browne, p. 63. Bishop Pearson, p. 178.

bound them to the Bishop of Rome (!) and acknowledged no other Superior than the Patriarch of Armenia.[1]

The misfortunes of the Church of India approached their crisis. Towards the VIIth Century, the Mahommedans over-ran all India to the East of the Ganges. The ferocious Mahmoud proclaimed Islamism, and, on both sides of his march, levelled with the dust, or committed to the flames, the Churches of the Christians, and the Pagodas of the idolaters. The victims had to choose between the acceptance of the Koran, or the loss of liberty, property, nay life itself. The Disciples of St. Thomas on the Malabar Coast, as well as those near Meliapour, were happily at a safe distance from the Moslem invaders. They were thus able to maintain, in most cases, the religion of their Fathers, and to read, in their Churches, their Syriac Bibles. The worship of images was ignored, but they continued, in a certain sense, to "venerate" the Cross. They asserted the dogma of the real presence of the Eucharist, and the viaticum was administered to the sick. The fasts of Lent and Advent, and the eves of solemn Festivals were religiously observed. The celibacy of the Priesthood was not strictly enforced, but second marriages were interdicted. With regard to the remaining rites and

[1] It is scarcely necessary to inform the reader that this extraordinary sentence is translated from a Jesuit's writings in the "Lettres Edifiantes." Tom. IV., p 9.

ceremonies, these Indian Christians were sufficiently in conformity with the Roman Catholic Church.

It is quite impossible, with due regard to the main purpose of our work, to say more on this part of the subject, however interesting it might be to the student of Ecclesiastical History. We must therefore remark, in conclusion, that the Syrian Church continued for Centuries, in what the Jesuit Fathers called, "the depths of schism and heresy." Renaudot, in his "History of Liturgies," speaks of Nestorian Patriarchs coming from Persia, whose See was first established at Modain—the *Seleucia* of the Parthians, and, he adds that after the destruction of that city by the Caliphs, they retired to Bagdad, and thence to Mosul. From this source the Christians of St. Thomas received their Bishops, and continued to yield obedience to this distant Patriarchate till 1599, when, under circumstances, to be narrated in a future book, the Syrian Church was forcibly united to that of Rome. Previously to this, many of the outlying Churches had fallen, step by step into a lifeless indifference, if not apostacy, in the hope of averting persecution from Moslem and Pagan. "Thus in consequence of the gross ignorance to which they became more and more enslaved, they had formed an extraordinary compound of various faiths, the religion of their ancestors, blending itself with the absurdities of idolatry, and the superstitions of Islamism, so that nothing remained but the faintest trace of true Christianity. It was in this deplorable condition that our Missionaries found them on arriving in Hindostan."[1]

In compiling this chapter we have done our best to let the Romanists state their views of the early history of the Syrian Church, as they came first in contact with its members. Even their own writers, however, (Tillemont, Renaudot, Trigant, and others) consider much of the account apocryphal, and express grave doubts of the legend of St. Thomas. Several members of our own Church, on the other hand, such as Bishop Heber, Archdeacon Robinson, and Dr. Claudius Buchanan, see no improbability in the tradition, and "favòur the claim of the Syro-Malabaric Church to this Apostolic origin."[2] La Croze, Hough, and others, treat the whole as a myth, and the latter certainly adduces most powerful arguments and quotations in proof of his opinion.

The chief Roman Catholic authorities are Emmanuel Anger, 1571; Martino Martinez, 1615; Gothard Artus, 1660; Gouzales d'Avila, 1649; Urbano Cerri, 1716; and, of course, the "Lettres Edifiantes."

[1] This sentence is of course the opinion of a Jesuit writer, and many such may be found in the "Lettres Edifiantes:"

[2] "Dean Pearson's Life of Schwartz," Vol. I., p. 2. "Heber's Journal," Vol. II., p. 278. "Dr. Claudius Buchanan's Christian Researches," "I am satisfied that we have as good authority for believing that the Apostle Thomas died in India as that the Apostle Peter died at Rome," p. 113. Hough, Vol. I., p. 32.

CHAPTER II.

FIRST MEETING OF THE PORTUGUESE WITH THE SYRIANS.

"The Portuguese entered India with the sword in one hand and the Crucifix in the other; finding much gold, they laid aside the Crucifix to fill their pockets."—João de Castro (Viceroy of India, 1548).

THE love of conquest, the thirst for gold, the flattering hope of personal or political aggrandizement, influenced the early Portuguese adventurers to such an extent that all restraint on their passions and conduct was abandoned. Their leaders were ordered to invade the dominions of all those Princes who refused to become vassals of the King of Portugal; and the pompous titles which Emmanuel, intoxicated by success, had added to his Crown, showed the area which he proposed to cover with his Empire. The Portuguese effectually disguised their schemes and objects. They represented themselves as a friendly nation, coming to offer a commerce reciprocally advantageous, and whose chief aim was to propagate the only religion acknowledged by Heaven as the means of man's salvation.

The Christians of St. Thomas were the first to be ensnared by these specious appearances. These people, ignorant and credulous, persuaded themselves that Christians who had travelled 1,200 leagues, braving the perils of a painful navigation, to extend the empire of their religion, could not but be just and benevolent men. These poor Syrians were, with few exceptions, miserable wretches, reduced to the lowest servitude by Pagan and by Moslem. Naturally enough, then, they saw in the Portuguese, envoys from Heaven, liberators who were come to break their chains, and restore them to the privileges which their ancestors had enjoyed. The first meeting took place at Cranganor in 1501, when Pedro Cabral succeeded in inducing two brothers, Matthias and Joseph, to accompany him to Lisbon ; and thus communicated to Europe the interesting fact of the existence of a native Christian Church amongst the heathens of South India.[1] After the first victories of da Gama, 30,000 of these Syrian Christians sent deputies to Cochin to render homage to the conqueror. According to Gouvea's account, they presented to Vasco da Gama a sceptre or bâton of vermilion wood, the ends of which were tipped with silver, and surmounted by three little bells. This

[1] "Joseph went first to Rome and from thence to Venice where, upon his information, a tract was published in Latin of the State of the Church of Malabar, and is printed at the end of 'Fasciculus Temporum.'" Gouvea, translated by Geddes, p. 2. La Croze, p. 49.

was the sceptre of their Kings, the last of whom had died shortly before the arrival of the Europeans. They told the admiral that they had received the gift of the faith, and that they were the spiritual subjects of the Assyrian Patriarch from whom their Bishops received consecration. They declared in the name of their constituents, that they believed King Emmanuel to be the most zealous of all Princes in the propagation of the Gospel; and, therefore, desiring to have him as their sovereign, they begged the admiral to effect their adoption, and to take them under his own special protection.[1] The number of the Christians of St. Thomas was supposed to reach 200,000; and Gama was astute enough to perceive the vast gain to Portuguese ascendency that would result from the devoted alliance of these brave, but oppressed Christians. He replied that he thanked Heaven for directing his steps to find, amongst the infidels, so many servants of Jesus Christ; and he assured them both by his flattering promises, and by his distinguished reception, that his Royal Master, who only made war to promote Christianity and destroy infidelity, would declare himself their zealous protector, and would defend them against all their enemies. This news, spreading through the mountain

[1] Gouvea's "Jornada," p. 72. João de Barros, Dec. I., Liv. III. Osorio, Vol. I., p. 134. La Croze, p. 52. Geddes, p. 3. Hough's History, Vol. I., p. 154.

Churches of Malabar, Cochin, and Travancore, everywhere excited the liveliest joy. Too soon, however, the bitterest disappointment succeeded, as the Portuguese Ecclesiastics gradually discovered the Nestorian tenets[1] of their new friend; and the native Christians began to experience those vexatious persecutions which culminated at the close of the century, in the Synod of Diamper.

In proportion as the affairs of Portugal prospered in India, King Emmanuel dispatched new fleets, and augmented the number of their crews. The European forces then became truly formidable, and everything on the coast of the Deccan was compelled to yield to their valour. But what was the composition of this army of adventurers. They were men too much resembling the fillibusters or buccaneers, who, at the same period, made the West Indies tremble, and whose chief merit was reckless courage.[2] All the historians of the period agree in painting these marauders in the blackest colours. At the time of embarkation in Lisbon, selection was impossible; everyone was enrolled who wished to go, vagrants, jail-birds, debtors, criminals of every description, wretches, incapable by immorality and loss of

[1] Bishop Osorio gives an interesting account of the Syrian Church as to its creed, ceremonies, &c., in Vol. I., p. 212 of his "History of the Reign of Emmanuel." He mentions the Christians also at p. 119.

[2] Towards the close of this century Drake, Raleigh, and many other of our own countrymen bore too close a resemblance to these adventurers.

character of obtaining employment at home, whom Portugal was glad to banish to save the honour of their families. It must not be supposed that the Portuguese were peculiar in this respect; for such seems to have been the characteristic of most of the emigrants of every nation. The English were not a whit better, if we may believe the description of one who has thoroughly examined the condition of the early settlers in British India. "From the moment of their landing on the shores of India the first settlers cast off all those bonds which had restrained them in their native villages; they regarded themselves as privileged beings—privileged to violate all the obligations of religion and morality, and to outrage all the decencies of life. They who went thither were often desperate adventurers who sought those golden sands of the East to repair their broken fortunes; to bury in oblivion a sullied name; or to wring, with lawless hand, from the weak and unsuspecting, that wealth which they had not the character or capacity to obtain by honest industry at home. They cheated, they gambled, they drank; they revelled in all kinds of debauchery."[1] Without doubt every Portuguese was not depraved; the annals of the country exhibit many noble specimens of the highest virtue; but still the description is, in the main, correct, and such was the miserable aspect under

[1] Kaye's "Christ in India," p. 46.

which European Christianity was first exhibited to the natives of India. In spite of vigorous laws, and of the wisest regulations published by the Court of Lisbon, the Portuguese were seen on all sides with the voracity of vultures, devouring the property of the unhappy natives, whose countries they had subdued. The Christians of St. Thomas fared no better than their compatriots, for the invaders, giving full swing to their rapacity were not likely to be discriminating in their choice of victims, or to recognise, as friends and brethren, those who professed a religion so nearly allied to their own. A natural re-action took place, for the Bishops and Clergy of the Syrians, aggrieved by attempts, even thus early made, to interfere with their Church, eagerly took advantage of the misconduct of the Portuguese settlers to hold up the Roman Church as an object of hatred, and thus to hinder the union which the European missionaries so ardently desired to accomplish. While this was the condition of things on the Malabar Coast, King Emmanuel was making every effort at Lisbon to give effect to his zeal in the propagation of the faith, for he felt that it was no less a policy than a duty, subjects being always better disposed to obey a Sovereign who cultivates and protects their religion. How the pioneers of the Portuguese missions in India carried into execution the benevolent schemes of their monarch will be seen in our next chapter.

CHAPTER III.

PIONEERS OF THE PORTUGUESE MISSIONS.

"Only when the Church is rich internally in the gifts of the spirit will the Divine fulness flow over outwardly, and the water of life, while it fructifies the heathen world, will flow back with a blessing to the districts from which it issued; but where the Spiritual life is wanting, no salutary influence can go forth on those who are without the pale of the Church."—NEANDER.

WHEN Cabral returned to Europe in 1501, he brought an account, as we have already stated, of the existence of numerous Christian congregations scattered amongst the mountains of Malabar. The natives, who accompanied him, confirmed his statement, and excited the liveliest interest amongst the Propagandists of Lisbon, who not only desired to cultivate friendly relations with their Indian fellow-Christians, thus romantically discovered, but to make use of the Syrian Church as a centre of missionary operations amongst the surrounding heathen.

The first pioneers of the Portuguese Missions to India belonged to the Order of the Capuchins. "His Majesty," says Bishop Osorio, "sent likewise, in the fleet, five Franciscan Friars, men of known piety and zeal for religion. These men were to remain at Calicut, if amicable terms could be agreed upon with the Zamorin, to perform divine service to the Portuguese who should settle there on account of trade, and to instruct in the mysteries of our Holy Religion any people of the country who might be willing to embrace the truth of Christianity. The chief of these religious persons was Henry, afterwards Bishop of Ceuta, a man of the most exemplary piety and sanctity of manners."[1] Another account by Cordozo in the Agwlogio Lusitano, speaks of seven monks having embarked in 1501, and states that three of them died at Calicut a month after their arrival, the other four sharing the same fate in the following spring. Pedro Covillam is said to have been the first to administer baptism in India.[2]

A long interval exists between these early efforts and subsequent attempts at Evangelisation. It is quite possible, however, that the work was going on, though no record has come down to us of the number and names of the missionaries, the fields of their operations, and their successes or reverses. Were our work designed to give a full account of these early Crusaders,

[1] Osorio's "History of the reign of Emmanuel," book ii., p. 85.

[2] He had travelled to India by land before the Cape of Good Hope had been doubled; and he has published his adventures under the title of "Relazao do Viage de Pedro Covillam de Lisboa a India, per Terra, evolta do Cairo."

or proselytisers in arms, we might find abundant materials in the ponderous volumes of the Romanist Historians to fill many pages of our book, even though the annals of the first thirty years are a blank. As our purpose, however, is to condense to the greatest extent consistent with an intelligible narrative, we must rest satisfied with stating one or two leading facts.

In 1530 Miguel Vaz was appointed Vicar-General of Goa, and seems to have produced an extraordinary effect on his victorious countrymen by the ardour of his zeal. He led into the fields of Paganism a numerous and devoted body of missioners, whose names Cardosa, that indefatigable Biographer of Saints, has not thought worthy of enrolment in his list. It is, however, recorded of this first Vicar-General that he not only overthrew the pagodas of the Brahmins, but laid the foundations of the famous Missionary College of Goa in 1546. In that year John III. sent to this Miguel Vaz a letter dated the 8th of March, addressed to the Viceroy of Goa, in which he commanded him to care for the interests of Christianity, and to protect the Paravas (fishermen) and other Christians, meeting the expense out of his revenue.[1] On the death of Bishop Vaz in 1548, we find Diego da Barba, Simao Vaz, Francisco Alvarez, and others, carrying on the

[1] In 1537 Pope Paul III. had made Goa the seat of a Bishop, of which Vaz was the first.

work of the mission, as yet chiefly limited to the Pagans. Besides these, Gaspar Coelho, ranking with the earliest Apostles of India, took up his abode at Meliapour (near the modern Madras), and it was there that he was found by St. Francis Xavier in 1548. Geddes, the translator, or rather paraphraser, of Gouvea's "Jornada," says, "We hear no more of these Christians till about the year 1545, the Portugueses being all that while too busie in making new conquests, and the Friars, who were sent thither, too much employed in building and providing commodious seats for their convents to attend to any foreign business, of what nature soever. This forty years' neglect of a Christianity which was just under their noses puts me in mind of what a Minister of State said of the Portuguese zeal in the Indies. 'It is a vain conceit, if it please your Majesty (speaking to Philip IV.) that the world has entertained of the zeal of the Portuguese upon account of the conversions that have been made by them in the Indies, for it was covetousness, and not zeal, that engaged them to make all those conquests. The conversions that have been made there were performed by the Divine Power, and the charity of a few particular Friars, the Government and Crown, having no other aim therein but the robbing of kingdoms and cities; and there were still the greatest Conversions where there was most to gratify their covetousness. But where there was nothing to be had, there the people were obdurate, and not to be wrought upon. And so we see their zeal expired quickly in all places, where it was not animated by covetousness, and how they who had nothing else to say but Lord open unto us, were not thought fit to enter into Heaven.'"[1]

This opinion of the neglect of Christianity, even by the early missionaries themselves, is confirmed by the testimony of Manoel de Faria, who says, "It is a shameful thing that this Church should continue an hundred years in the neighbourhood of the Portugueses without being reduced to the Roman Faith, and which makes it still the worse, under the eye of the Bishops of Goa; but the truth is, those merchants whom Christ whipped out of the Temple, were such as these."[2]

It will thus be seen that the Portuguese missionaries who first broke ground in Southern India had to encounter, as we have already said, three distinct classes of opponents, the Christians of St. Thomas, the Mohammedans, and the Pagans. We learn that King Emmanuel sent the most positive orders to the missionaries to declare to the Indian Christians, unless they abjured the heresy of Nestorianism, renounced all communication with the schismatic Patriarch, and

[1] Geddes, pp. 4-5.

[2] Manoel de Faria "Asia Portuguesa." Vol. III., *passim*. Geddes's "Translation of Gouvea," p. 6.

acknowledged the Holy See of Rome, as the centre of Catholic Unity, he would neither own them as his faithful subjects, nor interfere to protect them against their enemies. This menace was a part of that systematic course of persecution which the native Church has had to endure from her Roman Sister for more than three centuries. As, however, we shall give an account of this in its proper place, we may refer at present to pioneer work amongst the heathen, for it is especially in the conversion of the Indian idolaters that the triumph of Apostolic virtue shines most conspicuously in the really good members of the Portuguese missions. Every organisation has some obstacle to overcome, but the Indian missions seemed called upon at this period to encounter not single difficulties, but an assemblage of every special embarrassment, the Asiatic races clinging with greater pertinacity to their customs, to their social distinctions, and to the peculiarity of Caste,[1] than to fortune and liberty itself. The Portuguese saw at first in the Hindoos merely a nation of slaves, whom they could easily master by frightening them into subjection ; they sought out the Pariahs in

[1] The Hindoos are divided into four classes, the Brahmins, sacerdotal ; the Cshatrya, or military ; the Vaisya, or industrial ; and the Sudras, or servile. See "Translation of the Laws of Manu," by Sir William Jones. Elphinstone's "History of India." Trevor's "India," p. 38. Irving's "Theory and Practice of Caste," p. 7 ; and, in confirmation of our view, p. 122.

preference to the higher class associated with them, and took a great number of them into their service. Ignorant of the extraordinary strength of Hindoo prejudice with regard to Caste, the missionaries committed an error by this step, which affects, to this day, the opinion of the less educated natives, not only with regard to European religions, or the original Propagandists, but also with reference to all settlers, no matter of what race or creed. For when the high Caste Hindoo saw the Portuguese in familiar intercourse with Pariahs, his contempt was transferred from the outcast to the Portuguese themselves, and from the Portuguese to all Europeans, whom they confound to this day with them, under the general name of Prangius—the Hindoo mode of pronouncing Franks. To this well-meant but injudicious movement on the part of the missionaries must be added an obstacle for which there is no excuse. The confession is a sad one, but the security of historical truth forces from us the admission that the conduct of most Europeans, whether civil, military, or commercial, in India, the violence and vexations to which they were prompted by the desire of making rapid fortunes, their insulting pride, their scandalous immorality, have but too powerfully contributed to render natural to the Hindoos that burning hatred which three centuries of intercourse have not been able to extinguish, and which periodically bursts out in such terrible forms as at Vellore, Meerut, and Cawnpore. That this conduct was not limited to the Portuguese we have already shown, and but too much testimony to the same effect may be gleaned from works on India in the XVIth and XVIIth centuries.[1]

Thus it happened during the early days of the Portuguese missions in South India, that, with some remarkable exceptions, only four sorts of natives embraced Christianity, (1) the inhabitants of Salsette, and the neighbourhood of Goa, with those of the Pescaria, who were forced to take the European yoke as a protection from Moorish tyranny, (2) Pariahs or outcasts, objects of contempt to all the Indian population, (3) a certain number of the Malabars who were constrained to embrace the religion of their oppressors to renounce their Castes, and to adopt European customs, and lastly, the scum of the people—purchased slaves, and degraded Indians.

Everything, therefore, conspired against the spread of the Gospel, everything up to the moment of its first success. The missioners sent at this time into the heathen lands of Southern India felt this keenly.

1 "There had been two Christian nations in India before us. We found the name of Christian little better than a synonym for devil, and for some time we did nothing to disturb the popular belief in the Satanic origin of our saving faith, and so not only was nothing done for our Christianity during the first century of our connection with India, but very much against it. We made for ourselves impediments to the diffusion of Gospel light."—Kaye's "Christianity in India," p. 43.

Strong in their virtue, and in their ardour for the faith, they saw clearly that the only hope left for its extension was to adopt a policy in every respect opposed to that which had hitherto been employed by the Portuguese. To name the Great Apostle of India, St. Francis Xavier, is, to tell in one word, the whole history of the early missions. For his glorious example was the sacred model on which nearly all future action was based. In the vast field of missionary enterprise, the most successful labourers were but imitators of this great leader, as he himself was of the first founders of Christianity. "What marvellous men were the Barsees, the companions of Xavier, Lopez, Bishop of St. Thomé—Robert de Nobilibus, nephew of the celebrated Cardinal de Bellarmin[1]; Father Borgèse, whose illustrious birth was the least of the favours which this new Apostle had received from heaven! But we must not rise to the style of the panegyrist, but content ourselves with following a simple narrative of facts."

As the price of their conquests, the first Europeans had to endure the universal hatred of the races whom they had subdued. The missionaries, on the contrary, aimed only at winning the affections of the natives. Strict observers of the laws and customs of the countries into which they carried the light of the

[1] Robert is, of course, an admirable missionary, according to the *Jesuit* view.

Gospel, they became "all things to all men," in order to secure the great end which their constant preaching had in view. "They, therefore, respected the prejudices and the usages of the tribes amongst whom they laboured, however ridiculous or repulsive they might appear to European sense or taste."

The Indian idolaters naturally refused to believe a religion introduced by men who abused their power, to violate the sacred laws of hospitality, to press them under the sceptre of tyranny, to deprive them of their legitimate sovereigns, to plunder them of their precious metals, and to dishonour, by the scandalous immorality of their lives, the sanctity of the doctrine which they proclaimed. On the other hand, these bewildered natives, turning to the missionaries, beheld in them all those noble and estimable qualities which could attract their love and secure their confidence; they saw, in the heroes of the Cross, all the characteristics of a religion fresh from Heaven. "No," said they, astonished by the moral beauty of this spectacle, "it is only God, the supreme God, which could fill the hearts of these missionaries with zeal and charity, who could induce them to tear themselves from their native land, from the flattering hopes assured to them by their birth, their talents, their virtues, in order to come to us, crossing the boundless ocean, and braving every peril, that they might announce to us the oracles of God, and make us partakers of the happiness of

Heaven. What purity in their manners, what austerity in their lives! What ardour in teaching us, what sweetness in their pathetic exhortations, what patience in listening to our stories, what love speaking in the eloquence of the heart in bending our stubborn wills! What a life of disinterestedness, of privation, of devotion and self-sacrifice! All that they could command is dedicated to us; their talents, their labours, their life itself, they give us all. They share our miseries that they may be the better able to relieve them. They refuse all the gifts which gratitude would be tempted to offer them, and they desire nothing from us in return for such benefits, but the satisfaction of seeing us enjoy the truth which they preach at the peril of their lives." Profoundly modest, the missionary Priests, thinking nothing even of their best works, were only raised above their disciples by their greater fidelity to the sacred dictates of religion; and if the Bishops were at all distinguished from the ordinary Priests, it was by greater simplicity in dress, greater love of poverty, and greater desire for martyrdom.

Such are the outlines presented to us by the early history[1] of the Portuguese Missions to Southern India in the XVIth Century. Their first Apostles have

[1] The reader must bear in mind that these praises of the missionaries are put into the mouths of the converts by the missionaries themselves, for the greater part of this chapter is condensed (often literally translated) from the original letters of the Jesuit Fathers.

shared the fate of men superior to common souls, for they have suffered from the malice of foes and the falsehood of detractors. But not one of these slanderers has presented himself before the severe tribunal of criticism to substantiate his charge, and to invalidate the facts transmitted to Europe, as it appears in the letters of Xavier and in the valuable correspondence of the French and Portuguese missionaries.[1] Every lover of truth should read therein the wonderful history of the foundation of Churches, the progress of the Gospel, the change in the manners and habits of Indians newly Christianised—and he will admit that the virtues of these reformed tribes are not less worthy of exciting the curiosity, and attracting the attention of the true philosopher, than is the admirable life of their Apostles and Fathers in the Christian faith.

The ambition of the first conquerors of India had roused against them and their religion the feelings of all the princes who had not yet submitted to their yoke. Every Christian was to them an object of suspicion, and if we find them frequently wielding the sword of persecution, their action may be regarded as the result less of religious sentiment than of state

[1] This is utterly untrue, for at least a hundred volumes have been published against the Jesuits and their missions. We may refer the reader to the letters of Abbé Dubois, whose work on the state of Christianity in India tells many an unpleasant tale; also to the admirable account founded on the Jesuits' own statements by the Rev. W. S. Mackay, in the "Calcutta Review," Vol, II.

policy. Every Hindoo who embraced the new religion seemed to the Rajah an enemy of his throne, a traitor ready to yield on the first occasion to the European power, which would put a price on his rebellion against his lawful sovereign. They little knew the spirit of true Christianity. Experience, in due time, undeceived those princes, who, by an ambitious policy on the part of the invaders, had been forced into misconceptions which, in the early ages of missionary efforts, had given so many martyrs to the Church of India. This change of feeling was the fruit of the life and lessons of the missionaries. The princes not only ceased to be enemies, but actually became protectors of the Gospel Teachers against the jealousy of the Brahmins and the Bonzes, whose prejudices and self-interest made them naturally the persecutors of Christianity; several of them indeed became fervent neophytes. These Rajahs, certain of the fidelity of the Christians, offered them every inducement to serve in their armies, and many granted them the same prerogatives formerly enjoyed by the Christians of St. Thomas.[1] Another remarkable fact may be noticed as a proof of the influence thus acquired. The missionaries, authorised by the Sovereigns of the country, administered justice to the members of their flock. The princes thought that their Christian subjects would be better governed, even in temporal

[1] M. Perrin, Tom. II., p. 197.

matters, by their Pastors than by judges, strangers to their faith. The Jesuits, writing in 1760, say "This custom has existed for more than two centuries, and far from regretting the surrender which they have made of a part of their sovereign authority, the Nabobs offer daily increased proofs of their confidence in the missionaries of their states. It was doubtless under the same impression that the first Christian Emperors invested the bishops with a similar power of jurisdiction."[1]

[1] Choix des "Lettres Edifiantes," Tom. IV., p. 45. This is, of course, the Jesuit view of the case, but it is not borne out by their own sad experience in China, Japan, &c.

CHAPTER IV.

THE RISE OF THE JESUITS.

"While Alburquerque and his successors were prosecuting their conquests in the East, and the Portuguese power was extending itself from the Arabian Gulf to the very confines of China, a greater than Alburquerque was achieving that greater conquest of self, and a mightier power than that of the arms of Portugal in the East was rising among the peaceful Colleges of the West."—Kaye's "Christianity."

IT is impossible to obtain a clear insight into the progress of the Portuguese Missions in Southern India, without thoroughly understanding the nature of that singular organisation by whose agency they were mainly conducted. The Society of Jesus, the Order of Jesuits, or the "Company," as it is often called, was founded, or at least received the Papal sanction, in 1540, and, as no institution has, in modern times, exercised so powerful an influence as this throughout the world, we may here give a brief outline of its origin, constitution, history, and effects.

Ignatius Loyola,[1] a Spaniard, was descended from

[1] Helyot. "Histoire des Ordres Monastiques." Vol. VII. p. 452 "History of the Jesuits," by G. B. Nicolini. Edin. 1853, p. 10. Maffei Vita Ignatii.

an illustrious house long established at Loyola in Biscay. Born about 1491, he received an imperfect education and entered life as page to Ferdinand V., a career common at that age to scions of noble houses. Entering the army when still young, he distinguished himself by the most dauntless courage, and, after several years of a soldier's life, he was severely wounded at the seige of Pampeluna, in 1521.[1] His French captors, instead of sending him prisoner to France, carried him to his father's neighbouring castle of Loyola, where he was, of course, watched and nursed by the members of his own family. While slowly recovering from the effects of the shot which had wounded both legs, Ignatius beguiled his weary hours with the "Life of the Saints," and his ardent mind was stirred to its very depths with admiration of their deeds and with an enthusiastic resolution to follow their example.[2] Abandoning all hope of ever serving again under the standard of Spain, he resolved, with God's help, to become, not only a soldier, but a leader in the

[1] "It was in defending the ancient citadel on the Plaza del Castillo, (1521) that Ignacio Loyola was wounded; and just before you reach the Puerta de San Nicolas, is a chapel, founded in 1691, on the very site which some paintings illustrate."—Ford's "Spain," p. 954.

[2] The tradition runs that he was cured by St. Peter, who came down from heaven on purpose; and having done penance for a year in a cave within view of the "jagged Moulserrat," he dedicated himself to the Virgin, collected a few disciples and proceeded to Rome.—See "Ribad," II., 407.

army of Christ. His first act under this impression was one of religious chivalry. He prayed to the Virgin Mary[1] for her intercession on behalf of himself and his nascent scheme, and he dedicated himself to her and her service as her true knight. The practice of good works immediately followed this self dedication, for, as soon as he was sufficiently recovered, we find him, so recently a sufferer himself, becoming the kind and faithful nurse of the poor and sick in the Hospital at Marenza, this early reduction of theory to practice giving an indication of what was afterwards to be one of the salient features of the Order. Then the Spanish soldier, whose experience of men and things had been limited to his native land, determined to visit other countries, and selected, as the first object of his travels, the early scenes of that Christianity which his successors were to spread so widely over those regions of east and west then just made known to Europe. Returning from the Holy Land, he resolved to repair the defects of his early education by studying at the Universities of Spain, and subsequently at Paris, where, it is believed, he laid the first stones of the great edifice of which he was the chief founder. We say chief founder, because there is no doubt that Loyola himself was almost a tool in the hands of Laynez, Salmeron, and Acqua Viva especially.

[1] Nicolini's Hist., p. 14.

This committee were the real authors of the Secreta Monita, the Disciplina Arcana, containing some rules for the conduct of the members which have been justly stigmatised as diabolical.[1] Ignatius prepared two sets of rules for his followers, one for their personal government called "Spiritual Exercises," the other consisted of the "Constitutions of the Order," containing principles opposed not only to other societies, but hostile to the liberty and welfare of the human race. Loyola, having presented his institutes to Paul .III., the Pontiff consulted the Cardinals, and was advised by them to withhold his sanction. But Loyola proposing that, in addition to the three ordinary vows, the members of his new order should take a fourth, pledging themselves to implicit obedience to His Holiness, and devoting themselves to him absolutely without remuneration, offered a bait which the Pontiff could not resist. Paul III., feeling that Luther's movements were shaking the Church to its foundation, accepted with joy the services of enthusiasts, who came to the rescue, animated by burning zeal and organised with consummate skill. The shrewd old man confirmed the institutions of the Order by the Bull of September 27th, 1540;[2] conferred the most exten-

[1] Nicolini's Hist., p. 15.

[2] This was the famous bull "Regimini militantis Ecclesiœ."—Nicolini, p. 28.

sive privileges on the new society, and appointed the Biscayan soldier to be the first general of the new religious army.[1] The event justified the Pope's decision, for, from that moment, the tide of battle turned. The Reformation, which for twenty years had been carrying all before it, was checked in its career. Within half a century the Jesuits had planted the Cross in every part of the world, besides securing permanent establishments in all European countries that acknowledged the Roman obedience. Within a hundred years the Order had filled the earth from India to America, with memorials of great things done and suffered for the faith. "No religious community could produce a list of men so variously distinguished: none had extended its operations over so vast a space: yet in none had there ever been such perfect unity of feeling and action. There was no region of the globe, no walk of speculative or of active life in which Jesuits were not to be found."[2]

The condition, constitution, and genius of this energetic and self-devoted society merit particular attention, not only from the student of general history, but from every one interested in Christian Missions. The Laws of the Order, if not originally

[1] On Easter Day, 1541, he became General of the Jesuits, and on the following Friday renewed his vows in the magnificent Basilica of St. Paul's at Rome.—Maffei "Vita Ignatii," p. 90. Nicolini. p. 58.

[2] Macaulay's "Hist. of Eng." Vol. I., p. 208.

formed by Laynez and Acqua Viva, were certainly brought to perfection by them, and reduced to that system of marvellous policy which is the essential characteristic of this powerful organisation.[1] Based on the old Castilian military and monastic obedience, "they enlisted soldiers into the camp of Mary," for the purpose of fighting against civil and religious liberty, upholding Popery, not Christianity, governing the human race by means of superstition, reviving the spirit and in many respects the action of the old Crusades, and compensating the Papal tiara for losses in the old world by enormous acquisitions in the new.

There is a marked contrast between the Order of the Jesuits and other monastic institutions, which has a distinct bearing on the influence which this Society at once exerted, and still continues to exert in the propagation of Christianity. The monk in the silence of his cloister, devoted to self-mortification, is shut out from the world, and possesses no influence, except possibly by the example of his piety and prayers.

[1] "These famous Constitutions were composed by Loyola in the Spanish language. They were not at first the perfect system we now find them, and it was not till about the year 1552, that, after many alterations and improvements, adapting them to the necessities of the times, they assumed their ultimate form. They were translated into Latin by the Jesuit Father, John Polarcus, and printed in the College of the Society at Rome in 1558. They were jealously kept secret, the greater part of the Jesuits themselves knowing only extracts from them. They were never produced to the light until 1701, when they were published by order of the French Parliament, in the famous process of Messieurs Leonci and Father Laralette."—Nicolini, p. 30.

The Jesuit, on the other hand, is from his earliest years trained as the Soldier of the Cross, sworn to contend zealously for the service of God and of the Pope, God's Vicar upon earth. "Whatever might be their residence, whatever might be their employment, their spirit was the same, entire devotion to the common cause, unreasoning obedience to the central authority."[1] The instruction of the ignorant, the reclaiming of the wanderer, the *conversion of the heathen*, the persecution of the heretic, formed their chief objects. For these purposes, they claimed exemption from all the ordinary duties of monasticism. They wasted no time in pompous processions, or in tedious repetitions of religious offices.[2] But they made it their leading duty to enter thoroughly into the business of life, to study every transaction that might *influence the propagation of the faith.* They were ordered to insinuate themselves into the society of men of rank and influence, and to penetrate the secrets of every Government and every family. Deeply impressed with the importance of education, they almost entirely monopolised the training of the young, and displayed in the manage-

[1] Macaulay's "History of England," Vol. II., p. 309. Robertson's "History of Charles V.," Vol. II., p. 430. Macaulay is indebted to Robertson for many of the ideas, and even the language in his description of the Jesuits.

[2] "Compte rendu par M. de Monibar," Part XIII., p. 290. "Sur la Destruction des Jesuites, Par Mons. d'Alembert," p. 42.

ment of their schools and colleges an amount of tact and ability worthy of a better cause. Their bitterest enemies were forced to admit that as teachers they had no rivals; but "they appear to have discovered the precise point to which intellectual culture can be carried without intellectual emancipation."[1] In the sixteenth Century the pulpit held its own against the rising power of the press; and the Jesuits, without neglecting the latter, estimated at its full value the influence of the former, and prepared their young members by a long course of practical instruction for the successful exertion of sacred eloquence. Every other instrumentality which could reduce mankind to mental and moral slavery was pressed into the service of this despotic order. The ministry of the Confessional was wielded with the greatest craft, assiduity, and success. There they became "all things to all men." Casuistry itself was exhausted to supply the means of dealing pleasantly with men's consciences. Sins of the most trivial character were magnified, if it suited the Confessor's purpose to terrify the penitent, while crimes of the deepest dye were explained away if the interests of "the Society" required the transgressor to be secured as a victim or a tool. In short, the religion which they inculcated was so far from being the basis of morals, that it might justly be regarded as a system

[1] Macaulay's History, Vol. II., p. 310.

of iniquity, having, for its chief end, the promotion of the Order, utterly regardless of the destruction of truth, honour, virtue, law, or whatever else the Jesuits might consider an obstruction.

Such being the objects of this famous "Company," the form of its Government[1] was no less remarkable. Voluntaryism is, in a certain sense, the guiding principle of the other monastic orders, that is, the members enter of their own free will, and, though yielding obedience to an executive head, retain a share of power in the general congregation of the community. But the stern spirit of Loyola, trained in the military school of implicit obedience, resolved that the government of his new order should be a despotism, pure and simple. The very name "General," by which this religious monarch was designated, represented the idea of absolutism. The chief, elected by representatives from different provinces, wielded supreme and independent power over every individual, and in every cause. His undisputed authority appointed and removed every officer in the society. No Eastern Potentate ever ruled his slaves more absolutely than the General governed his

[1] The Government is purely Monarchical, and the General is its absolute and uncontrollable King. The members of the Society are divided into four Classes, the Professed, Coadjutors, Scholars, and Novices.

For a well-written account of the Hierarchy, consult Nicolini's History, chap. III.; also, Examen IV., p. 10-15, and Const., part V., cap. IV.

passive instruments. The members of the Order were to be so completely at his disposal, that they were to give up their own wills, and even their understandings into his keeping, and to hold themselves in readiness to listen to his commands and to execute his orders as if uttered by Christ himself. "If he was wanted at Lima, he was on the Atlantic in the next fleet. If he was wanted at Bagdad, he was toiling through the desert with the next Caravan."[1] "In short, they were to be like clay in the hands of the potter, or like dead carcases, incapable of resistance."[2] Such centralisation necessarily impressed a unity of purpose and a decision in action on all the members of this singular organisation, and contributed to crown its operations with success. History furnishes no other example of so absolute a despotism not ruling slaves in a court, soldiers in a regiment, or monks in their cells, but stretching its mysterious sway over its subjects apparently free in the most distant parts of the world, and binding them all with invisible chains to the central throne.

Thus invested with absolute and irresponsible power, the General of the Jesuits possessed, by the laws of the Order, the most ample means of studying

[1] Macaulay's History, Vol. II., p. 309. Nicolini's "History of the Jesuits," Int. II.

[2] Compte rendu au Parlem de Bretagne par M. de Chalotais, p. 41. Robertson's "Charles V.," Book VI., p. 430.

the characters of his subjects. Every novice had to "manifest his conscience," that is, to confess his sins, defects, inclinations and passions—a declaration to be renewed every six months.[1] During the novitiate, a universal system of espionage is established; and when, at the age of thirty-three, they take the full vows and become "professed," the superiors are thoroughly acquainted with the disposition and talent of every pupil. The results of these long-continued scrutinies are digested in the form of regular reports, transmitted by the Provincials, and entered in registers, so that the General may, at a glance, see the whole state of the society in every region of the globe, observe the abilities, temper, attainments and experience of every member, and thus select the most suitable instruments for employment in any duty which the interests of the Order may require. A calculation has been made of this wonderful system of reports which the General annually receives; from which it appears that there are thirty-seven provinces in the Order, that the average number of reports from each is a hundred-and-seventy-seven, thus making the total amount six thousand five hundred and eighty-four. The reader must not suppose that these reports were mere dry tables of figures such as modern statistics frequently exhibit; they were rather general accounts, first, of the Society itself in all its departments, and

[1] Compte rendu, par Mons. de Monclar, p. 121.

secondly, of the affairs of the country, so far as a knowledge of these could contribute to the interests of what was called religion. The writers entered into the most minute particulars, and, when secresy was important, ciphers were employed, each Provincial, or Rector being furnished with a cipher for his own special use.[1]

The progress of the new Order was distinguished as much by its rapidity, as by its universality and absolute power. When Loyola, early in 1540, humbly petitioned the Pope to recognise his new Order, he could only boast of ten disciples. But, during the period to which our Essay refers, that feeble band had increased to 10,581. In the year 1710, there were twenty-four professed houses, fifty-nine houses of probationers, three hundred and forty residences, six hundred and twelve colleges, two hundred missions, one hundred and fifty seminaries and boarding-schools, and the total number of the Jesuits was twenty thousand.[2] The ostensible profession of this great order was to *secure the salvation of mankind*, not by prayer and contemplation solely, but by the most decided and vigorous action. We have already seen their employment of education, the pulpit, the press, the confessional, *missions to the*

[1] "Hist. des Jesuites," Amsterdam, 1761, Tom. IV., p. 56. Compte par Mons. de Mond, p. 431. Compte de M. Chalstais, p. 52. "Lettres Edifiantes," *passim*.

[2] "Hist. des Jesuites," Tom. I., p. 20.

heathen, and other instrumentalities; and to these they added matchless skill and tact in originating and conducting every variety of intrigue, which rendered them masters of the situation in all Courts of Europe and Asia. And not only did the power of the Order increase, but its wealth grew in proportion. One calculation shows that the property of the Jesuits in Spain alone, under Charles III. exceeded three millions sterling.[1] Plausible subterfuges were invented to reconcile these enormous possessions with the monastic vow of poverty. Their vast estates, accumulated treasures of coin, plate, and jewels, and the architectural grandeur of their public buildings, while belying their professions, added immensely to their influence. One source of wealth was peculiar to this Order—a monopoly obtained from Rome of trading with the *nations which they desired to convert*—their plea being that they could thereby *render their mission self-supporting.* These priestly merchants planted the warehouse beside the Church; and, so far from considering this as a temporary expedient, they almost invariably aimed at the permanent establishment of "factories," or commercial settlements, like those of trading companies.[2]

[1] Ford's "Spain," p 425.

[2] Ces vastes et fertiles contrées sortiraient bientôt de l' obscurité où elles sont plongées, si l'Espagne savait profiter de l'ambition active des Jesuites. On sait que ces hommes admirables comme société, dangereux comme citoyens, détestables comme religieux, etaient parvenus à tire du fond des forêts un nombre considérable de sauvages; à les fixer sur

We find this the characteristic of many of their operations in India and China, while in South America, they secured a firm footing in the fertile province of Paraguay, and reigned as sovereigns over a hundred thousand converts.[1]

While rendering justice to the distinguished energy, disinterestedness, and self-sacrifice, which characterised the "Society of Jesus," we must admit, unhappily for mankind, that great vices were mingled with great virtues. The enormous influence which the Order had acquired before the close of the XVIth Century was quite as often employed for the worst purposes, as for the best. Every Jesuit was trained to consider the interests of the "Company" to be the sole object of his existence to which all considerations—ease, liberty, health, life itself, must be unhesitatingly sacrificed. Though the beautiful expression "ad majorem Dei gloriam" was his motto, "the end justifies the means" was practically his watchword. Attachment to his Order was the key to his public policy, as well as to individual peculiarities in character and conduct. To promote the honour and interests of the fraternity, it was, of course, important

les bords de l'Orenoque, et des rivières la plupart navigables, qui s'y jettent, à leur donner quelques principes de sociabilité un peu de goût pour les arts les plus nécessaires, et surtout pour l'agriculture.—Abbé Raynal "Hist. des deux Indes," Vol. IV., p. 278.

[1] Abbé Raynal, Vol. III., p. 326. Robertson's "Charles V.," Vol. II., p. 434. Macaulay, Vol. II., p. 309, and "Hist. des Jesuites," Vol. IV., p. 168.

that every brother should secure an ascendency over the Civil Power, Christian or Pagan ; and, to this end, the most unscrupulous use of means was made to play upon the passions of men, to apologise for vice, to tolerate imperfections, and to authorise violations of every law, human and Divine.[1] In point of fact, the Jesuits' code seems to have been composed, less with the view of elevating human nature to the level of Divine morality, than with the object of lowering the standard till it was beneath the average of ordinary humanity. Another point must not be omitted. The Jesuits were the stoutest champions of the Papacy, we might almost call them the Pontiff's body-guards, or the Papal Zouaves of the XVIth century. The tendency of all their teaching was to assert and to strengthen the doctrine of unlimited obedience to the Pope. Their aim was to erect an enduring edifice of ecclesiastical power on the ruins of civil government and religious freedom. They therefore claimed for Rome absolute jurisdiction, asserted the independence of the clergy, and maintained, that Sovereigns who opposed the Catholic faith, might lawfully be dethroned.[2] As a natural

[1] "Compte par M. de Moncc.," p. 285. Robertson's "Hist. Charles V.," p. 415. Macaulay's "Hist. of Eng.," Vol. II., p. 310.

[2] Robertson's "Hist. Charles V.," p. 435. Macaulay's "Hist. of Eng.," Vol. II., p. 13. Cretineau, Vol. II., p. 269. Bartoli dell' Ing., F. 101, 102, 104. Ranke's "History of the Popes," Vol. I., p. 512. Nicolini's "History of the Jesuits," p. 154.

consequence of these opinions, the Jesuits considered themselves the especial champions of the Church of Rome, against the Protestants. Every act of intrigue, every weapon of violence, every measure that the most bitter hatred could dictate, was employed without scruple to check the progress of the Reformation. The historian of the centuries which have elapsed since Paul III., armed Loyola and his ten disciples with his fatal sanction, cannot hesitate to acknowledge that this remarkable Brotherhood is answerable for many a dark deed, the result of that union of ingenious casuistry, extravagant despotism, and intolerant persecution which characterised their system.

But, while every impartial student admits the truth of our description, he must also own that the picture has its bright side, and that in this case as in many others "none are all evil." We have already said that the Jesuits had wisely secured the almost exclusive management of education, not so much in its elementary as in its superior aspect. The Universities were naturally alarmed at the threatened loss of their ancient supremacy; and the Jesuits were therefore bound to prove their claim by the exhibition of a higher grade of learning. Hence they devoted themselves with the most wonderful ardour, to the cultivation of literature, science, and art; to the revival of ancient learning, as well as to the acquisition of foreign languages, to the preparation of valuable text-books, and to the invention of improved methods of communicating knowledge. Nor were their attainments limited to those branches which are generally considered to constitute a liberal education They were equally at home in the pursuit of the ordinary and humbler duties of life. As one historian has said "the Jesuits set themselves to instruct and to civilise these savages. They taught them to cultivate the ground, to rear tame animals, and to build houses, they brought them to live together in villages. They trained them to arts and manufactures. They made them taste the sweets of society; and accustomed them to the blessings of security and order."[1]

[1] Robertson's "History of Charles V." Book VI., p. 438. "Hist. du Paraguay." par Pere de Charleovix. Tom II., p. 42.

CHAPTER V.

THE JESUITS IN PORTUGAL.

"So strangely were good and evil intermixed in the character of these celebrated brethren; and the intermixture was the secret of their gigantic power."—MACAULAY.

JOHN III. came to the Portuguese throne at the age of nineteen, and reigned from 1521 till 1557. His contemporaries were chiefly Charles V. of Germany, Francis I. of France, and Henry VIII. of England, and the great events of European History which synchronise with his reign, were the civil and religious wars which sprang from the Reformation. The little kingdom which John governed was, however, so far removed from the centre of Europe, as to be but slightly disturbed by these movements, and the annals of his reign are chiefly filled by internal reforms in the Cortès, by wars with the Moors, negociations with Spain, and, above all, with the extension of his power in the East.

The cares of diplomacy, the pursuit of commerce,

the glories of war, did not, however, prevent this pious King from thinking of the honour of God, or, from taking what he believed to be the most effectual measures for promoting the Kingdom of Christ. He had heard a rumour that a new institution, entitled the "Company of Jesus," had been founded at Rome, or, at least sanctioned there, by Paul III., and that its author was the great St. Ignacio de Loyola, the Soldier Saint of Gui puscoa. The King, therefore, wrote to Mascarenhas, his Ambassador at Rome, for further information, and was assured, in reply, of the great good that the Saint and his companions were doing to the souls of men, and of the high opinion which the Pontiff entertained of their labours. He saw, at a glance, that such an institution was the very thing which he most ardently desired as the foundation of a mission to those parts of the East which Portuguese Navigators had discovered, and Portuguese warriors had subdued. He believed that he should now be able to have his vast dominions illuminated by the light of the true faith, and subject to the sweet yoke of Christ our Redeemer, and of His Holy Church.[1] It appeared to him that to create, as it were, a new religion, at a time when all the heathen nations of India were eagerly seeking for Baptism, would be

[1] "Allumiadas com a luz da verdadeyra fè, e svgeitas av jugo suavissimo de Christo nosso Redentor e de su Igreja sagrada."—Annaes de Elrei Dei João Terceiro, p. 321.

an acceptable offering to the Supreme. He reflected that as the wine was new, it should therefore have new cultivators. He considered this fresh field of enterprise so vast that it would exhaust the energies of the religious Orders already established in Portugal —an additional reason for his seeking the co-operation of the recently organised missionary power. Impressed with these sentiments he wrote again to Mascarenhas, requesting him to communicate with Ignatius, and to submit an account of the extensive field which God offered to him in India for the exercise of the great mission begun by himself and his companions, adding that, though he was aware that the new Order numbered as yet but few adherents in proportion to the vast work that had to be accomplished, he trusted that Ignatius would send him at least six of the brethren, the most zealous that he could select, and, with the utmost possible dispatch. The Ambassador entered warmly into the views of his master; a lively correspondence ensued, and, at last, the business was submitted to His Holiness. Finally, of the six which King John demanded, St. Ignatius could only spare four, who arrived at Lisbon, accompanied by the Ambassador, at the very moment when the new Governor-General of India was on the point of embarking. This was on the 30th of May, 1540, in point of fact, nearly four months before the granting of the Bull which confirmed the foundatio of the Order. In the words of the old Chronicler "the King received the new guests with the same love which had sought them and brought them."[1] He rejoiced greatly when he became more intimately acquainted with the missionaries, for he found much more in them than he had been led to expect. On their arrival they were lodged at All Saints' Hospital, close to the Palace at that time known by the name of Estaos; and it was from this lowly residence, significantly near the throne however, that the Jesuits issued forth to subjugate the Oriental world and to civilise, a century later, the solitudes of America. Although all the brethren that came from Rome had devoted themselves to the Missions in the East, the King accepted only three for that object, and retained one in Portugal. The three that embarked were S. Francis Xavier, Padre Paulo, and the Brother Francisco de Mausilhas, liberally provided by the King's munificence with every necessary for the voyage. The Jesuit that remained was a Portuguese named Rodriguez de Azevedo, who became the head and founder of all those Houses and Colleges which the Company possessed in Portugal, and in all the lands subject to the Portuguese Crown throughout the world. To carry into effect the scheme which the King had formed, he determined to transfer the College

[1] Recebeo El Rey os novos hospedes com o mesmo amor e voutade que os buscara e pedira,—" Luiz de Sousa, Annaes de João," III., p. 322.

which his Father Emmanuel had founded in Lisbon to Coimbra, with the same statues and laws, and with the King as its President. He appropriated to this University the revenues of the commandery of Carquere. These endowments entitled Portugal to be considered the first country in Europe in which the Jesuits possessed their own property — substantial riches, destined to increase to a fabulous amount. The Father P. S. Rodriguez, whose name is but little known in history, had been resident in Lisbon for two years subsequent to his arrival from Rome, and there filled the post of Rector of the College of St. Anthony. His intimate friend was Father Medeiros, and it is to these two Ecclesiastics that one must attribute the influence which the Order soon began to exercise over the mind of John III. The Portuguese historian, Alvaro de Liamo, who seems to have been ignorant of these facts, but who follows, step by step, the progress of the Order in Portugal, expresses himself with his accustomed energy as to the results of this skilful seduction which changed the whole political aspect, and which, addressing itself at first to the King, in a short time subdued the country. After referring to the arrival of these two Founders at Lisbon, he says "The first was always a stranger to the Court and avoided the honours with which he was loaded; he had no rest till he quitted Lisbon to embark for India. Simon Rodriguez devoted himself to establish in Portugal the empire of the ambitious Society of Loyola. This fanatic, aided by ten companions as indefatigable as himself succeeded in usurping the rights of the Episcopate, seized all the sources of public opinion, of the Government in Church and State, and of the education of the young. Even the King himself (John III.) took the vows, and the Portuguese nobility saw themselves thenceforward surrounded, if not oppressed, by the corrupters of Christian morality."[1]

It does not enter into our plan to follow, in minute detail, the encroachments of the Jesuits in the various Courts and countries of Europe. We have noticed their settlement in Portugal, because that event forms an important link in the chain which we are attempting to construct. Further information will be found in Herculano's "History of Portugal," Nicolini's "History of the Jesuits," Ranke's "History of the Popes," Maffei's "Vita Ignatii," the "Litteræ Annuæ Societatis Jesu," Pasquier's "Catéchisme des Jesuites," Michelsen's "Modern Jesuitism," and similar works.

We may conclude this chapter by reminding the reader that two centuries after the foundation of the Order, when Pombal undertook to crush the power of the successors of Rodriguez, they counted twenty-four great Colleges, being then considered the richest corporation in the kingdom, and that then was verified

[1] Quoted in "Portugal," par M. F. Denis, p. 412.

the celebrated prophecy of St. Borja, who saw in their apparent prosperity, the very causes of their destruction—"Veniet tempus cum se societas multis quidem hominibus abundantem, sed spiritu et virtute destitutam, mœrens intuebitur."

CHAPTER VI.

ST. FRANCIS XAVIER'S MISSION IN INDIA.

"In the History of the Jesuits Missions in India, Francis Xavier stands out in solitary grandeur, as the one Apostolic man."—KAYE.

ABOUT twenty miles from Pampeluna[1] at the foot of the Pyrennees, and in the midst of the most romantic scenery of Navarre, stands the baronial castle of the noble family of Xavier. Here lived Don Juan de Jasso, and his wife Mary Xavier, and here their youngest son, Francis, was born, 7th April, 1506. Thus by a singular coincidence the great Apostle of the Indies, and the first great missionary of the new Order was, like Loyola, not only a Spaniard, but a Navarese. The early years of Xavier were spent in solitary wanderings at every spare moment amidst the romantic scenery of his mountain home. For him the rough sports of the field had no charms. Under several private tutors, whom the wealth of his parents

[1] "Pampeluna, or Pamplona, the ancient Pompeiopolis ("Strabo," III., 245) was founded by the sons of Pompey, 68. B.C. and the Latin name was corrupted by the Moors into Bambilonah."—Ford's "Spain," p. 952.

secured, he became eminent as a classic and metaphysician. In 1524, he was enrolled as a student of the College of St. Barba, at Paris, and while still a mere youth he was selected to fill the Chair of Lecturer on the philosophy of Aristotle.[1] Here he might have passed his life in academic obscurity, or with merely local fame, but for the arrival of his enthusiastic countryman Loyola. The Founder of a new Order was then preparing himself for his great work. The schemes first dawning on his mind when suffering from his wounds at Pampeluna were now gradually gaining strength. Feeling his own deficiencies, he too became a student at Paris, and there heard of Xavier's reputation. The old soldier at once sought the acquaintance of the young noble, read with a wonderful penetration the mind of his future disciple, and employed every argument to convert this splendid intellect and powerful will into instruments for the promotion of his great plan. Philosophy, casuistry, metaphysics, were to give way to action, and that action was to be the Propagation of the Faith. For a long time Ignatius importuned in vain. The quiet student clung to his books and resisted all entreaties. But one day, when every appeal had failed, Ignatius,

[1] "He was about the middle size, had a lofty forehead, large, blue, soft eyes, with an exquisitely fine complexion, and with the manners and demeanour of a prince." Nicolini, p. 88. See Lucena's "Life of Xavier," "Life of S. Francis Xavier" by Bartoli and Maffei, translated by Faber, "Venu's Life of Xavier," and Nicolini's "Jesuits," pp. 106.

fixing his eyes on the still hesitating scholar, said, "What shall it profit a man if he shall gain the whole world and lose his own soul?" Then, with a few rapid strokes, he drew a picture of worldliness as contrasted with spiritual blessings. He pointed out the hollowness of all earthly happiness, the privations and self-sacrifice which must fall to the lot of the disciples of the Cross, and, with burning eloquence, exhibited the glories of the Martyr's Crown. Xavier listened, wavered, and was won.

Montmartre, a short walk from the College of St. Barbe, was, soon after this interview, the scene of a remarkable act. There, in the Church of St. Denis, on Assumption Day, 15th August, 1534,[1] Ignatius Xavier, and five other proselytes,[2] met one morning, and, in circumstances of peculiar solemnity, after Mass, dedicated themselves to the Holy Father, and to the Church of which he was the head. How much of the world's history depended on this meeting!

Six years passed. Xavier, true to his vows, had renounced the world, and was spending his life in toilsome journeys, suffering every hardship, from poverty, exposure, and fatigue, when he was summoned by Ignatius to Rome. The scheme was now approaching its completion. Nearly nineteen years

[1] "This day was ever after regarded as the Birthday of the Society." —Bartoli translated by Faber, p. II.

[2] These were Lainez, Salmeron, Rodriguez, Bobadilla, and Lefevre.

had elapsed since the cannon shot of Pampeluna had prepared the way for the foundation of the Society of Jesus. The little Company numbered but seven when they mustered to be presented by Ignatius to Paul III. Two circumstances seemed to combine to train the future Apostle for his Eastern Mission—his appointment to the Pulpit of St. Lawrence, where he had ample training in extemporaneous preaching, and the occurrence of a terrible famine in which he displayed that unselfish devotion to the sufferers, which shone forth still more splendidly in the regions of the East.

While these things were passing at Rome, an old college companion of Loyola and Xavier happened to be sent by John III. as Ambassador to the Pope. Renewing his friendship with his fellow-students, he was deeply impressed by the extraordinary zeal and energy which they displayed. He saw in them the very *Missionaries whom the Portuguese monarch was engaged in seeking to plant the Church in Southern India.* In our last chapter we gave a brief account of this negotiation. Ignatius could not accept the invitation, as he was head of the Order. and was, of course, obliged to remain at Rome, the centre of operations. Rodriguez headed the mission that set out from Rome, though he was destined not to visit the East. The stern Loyola, delighted as he was with this first indication of the future greatness of his Order, could not part with his favourite disciple without emotion. Clasping his hands, he exclaimed in a voice, broken by sobs, "Go, my brother, rejoice that you have not here a narrow Palestine, or a single province of Asia in prospect, but a vast extent of ground—the *Indies, a whole world of people and nations.* This is reserved for your endeavours; and nothing but so large a field is worthy of your courage and your zeal. The voice of God calls you, kindle those unknown nations with the flame that burns within you." Xavier's words were, "It is impossible for me to forget you, Ignatius; or not to recall to my memory that sincere and holy friendship which you have shown me. Father of my soul, when I am afar, I will think that you are still present, and that I behold you with my eyes; write to me often. The smallness of my talent is known to you; share with me those abundant treasures which Heaven has heaped upon you."

They parted for ever, Ignatius remaining in the capital of the Christian world, Xavier setting forth to preach the Gospel to unknown nations in the East. On his way to Lisbon, the Apostle of India started from Rome, on 16th March, 1540, travelled by Loretto, Bologna, &c., crossed the Alps and the Pyrennees, and, it is said, passed within sight of his Castle Towers, but refused to stop, or even to make himself known, lest an interview with his mother (then dying) and family might shake his purpose.[1] On arriving at the Portuguese Court in June he found the next fleet for India was not to weigh anchor till the following spring, and he spent the intervening nine months in visiting the sick and dying in the hospitals, and the prisoners in the cells of the Inquisition.

In April, 1541, a Portuguese troop-ship lay ready for sea in the Tagus opposite Belem. Her destination was Goa, and she was to carry out a new Viceroy, and a reinforcement of a thousand men. But one was to sail in her who was to effect a revolution in the Eastern world, as well as to immortalise his name amongst the great-hearted workers in the cause of truth. Xavier, commissioned as Pope's Nuncio in the East, and bearing letters of recommendation to all the princes whom he might encounter, went silently on board the Flag Ship St. James, and bade adieu for ever to his home, his friends, and the first brethren of that Order in which he felt so deep an interest.[2] John III. had, with his characteristic kindness, ordered a cabin to be fitted up for this *leader of the Portuguese Missions;* but he, faithful to his vow, rejected everything in the shape of indulgence. He retained merely a few books, a warm rug

[1] Lucena, Liv. I., p. 62. Bartoli by Faber, p. 36. "The conduct attributed to Xavier is, however, scarcely consistent with his generous character."—Venn's Life, p. 13.

[2] "He sailed on 7th April with the Viceroy (Martin de Souza), on his 36th birthday."—Lucena.

to cover him during chilly nights, he made his pillow a coil of ropes, and shared the coarsest food of the common sailors. He conversed in the most friendly way with all around him, tended the sick, instructed the ignorant, and won all hearts. The rudest soldier was at no loss to recognise the gentleman and the scholar, even under the disguise of the poor raiment which Xavier felt it his duty to wear, and when, at the end of a tedious thirteen months' voyage (6th May, 1542) the battered vessel cast anchor, in the roadstead of Goa, he felt that he had had another course of probation for his great work in the golden land which now met his gaze. His parting words to Rodriguez, who escorted him on board at Belem, were (speaking of a vision of various forms of death which had appeared to him at Rome), "I then beheld all I was to suffer for the glory of Jesus Christ; I exclaimed in my dream 'Yet more oh my God! yet more!'—and I hope, that God will grant me that in India which he has foreshown to me in Italy." On landing he presented his letters to the Bishop of Goa by whom he was warmly welcomed, and assured of support in his mission. Declining the well-meant offers of Bishop Vaz, though at the same time acknowledging his authority, and delicately proposing to keep in abeyance his office of Nuncio, the Apostle resolved to seek in prayer encouragement from a Higher Power. It is recorded that he retired to a Church and spent the whole of his first night in India in earnest supplication—"an example worthy the imitation of missionaries of a purer creed."[1]

The social condition of his countrymen was the first thing that attracted his notice. Merchants, soldiers, sailors, emigrants, adventurers of all kinds, had crowded into Goa, as men rush, in our own day, to newly discovered diggings, petroleum-wells, or any other source of tempting wealth. The love of gold and the gratification of passion had rendered law and order almost unmeaning names, and though, it is true that the Portuguese Church had, at a very early period, sent out a Bishop with a full staff of Clergy,[2] yet the voice of religion received but little heed amidst the distractions of commerce, the clash of arms, and the temptations to self-indulgence. This state of things, Xavier saw, would entirely neutralise the success of his mission to the heathen; and he, therefore, devoted himself with a wonderful mixture of tact and courage to reform the Christians before attempting to convert the Pagans. His biographer[3] narrates the means employed (somewhat childish in our eyes) and recently to a certain extent, imitated in the East London Mission, but attended with remarkable success, inasmuch as a great reformation of manners took place,

[1] Hough's "Christianity," Vol. I., p. 173.

[2] "Fernando was first Bishop."—Lucena p. 99.

[3] Lucena, *passim*.

and the heathen could no longer point to the Christians as the very worst specimens of the religion which they professed.

This accomplished, he felt himself in a better position to devote all his energies to *the primary object of, his mission—the conversion of the heathen.* He, therefore, declined the Bishop's offer of the Rectorship of the new College at Goa, established for the purpose of educating heathen students. Yet he saw the importance of this academy as an instrument for the promotion of his great plan, and he introduced into its constitution several salutary reforms, made it a missionary college, and transferred it to the "Society of Jesus," under the title of "the College of St. Paul."[1] Another object attracted the attention of Xavier. He found that Christianity made very slow progress because the Hindoo converts, suffering loss and persecution on account of their change of faith, were neglected by the very Monks who had won them over. On his solicitation, the wealthy merchants of the Portuguese "factory" subscribed a large sum which enabled him to support destitute proselytes, and to found an orphanage for the children of deceased converts.

During all this time he missed no opportunity of still further preparation for his mission to the heathen.

[1] "The Jesuit Missionaries in India are therefore frequently called the Fathers of St. Paul."—Hough, Vol. I., p. 175.

India was then but little known, except those portions in the immediate vicinity of the European settlements, scattered, at wide intervals, along the coast. Xavier therefore, without guide-books, maps, dictionaries, or any knowledge of the native dialects[1] had to obtain as best he could (and one wonders how he did it), all the information as to manners and customs, laws, religion, and language, which the natives, visiting Goa, could supply. He then resolved to start on his mission, and we must try to picture to ourselves the Spanish Noble, the Parisian Professor, the Papal Nuncio, forsaking all dignities and honours going forth in lowly garb[2] his little silver bell in hand, summoning the apathetic Indians around him, and teaching them, in broken language, and with foreign accent, the elements of a strange creed. He first visited the Paravars, a low Caste, chiefly fishermen on the southern coast, who had been defended by the Portuguese against the Moslems. and who, *in gratitude, had adopted the religion* of their champions.

[1] "'I find it a most inconvenient position to be in the midst of a people of unknown tongue without the assistance of an interpreter,' says Xavier in his letter of 21st August, 1544; yet one of his panegyrists, John Vaz, determined to magnify his powers, declares that 'he spoke the language of the people fluently, though he had never learnt it.' Faber, of course, believes the miracle ("Life of Xavier," p. 98), and Marshall 'has no doubt that he could converse at the same moment with men of various nations and dialects, so that each thought he heard him speak his own tongue.'"—"Christian Missions," Vol. I., p. 211.

[2] "Father Xavier always went barefoot, wearing an old, faded, patched habit, with an old black cloth hat."—João Vaz.

Believing this to be a favourable opening he sailed from Goa for Cape Comorin in October, 1542. Two Priests, who fancied they knew the language (Tamil) accompanied him, but their attainments were not equal to the task. Still, he managed to make a translation, imperfect, no doubt, of the Apostles' Creed, the Lord's Prayer, and other portions of the Christian faith. One almost smiles, when reading the narrative of his biographer, at learning that he committed to memory this extraordinary compound of truth and error in religion, of right and wrong in language; and that, thus armed, he positively undertook to preach to the people in their native tongue.[1] Let us hear, in his own words, his extraordinary method of converting the heathen:—"I went about with my bell in my hand, and gathering together all I met, both men and children, I instructed them in the Christian doctrine. The children learnt it easily by heart, in the compass of a month; and when they understood it, I charged them to teach it to their fathers and mothers, then to all of their own family, and even to their neighbours. On Sundays, I assembled the men and women, little boys and girls, in the Chapel; all come to my appointment with an incredible joy, and most ardent desire to hear the Word of God. I began with the confessing God to be one in nature, and triune in person. I afterwards

[1] See Lucena. Dr. Faber's Translation. "Venn's Life."

repeated distinctly, and with an audible voice, the Lord's Prayer, the Angelical Salutation, and the Apostles' Creed. All of them together repeated after me; and it is hardly to be imagined what pleasure they took in it. This being done, I repeated the Creed distinctly, and, insisting on every particular Article, asked if they really believed it? They all protested to me, with loud cries, and their hands across their breasts, that they firmly believed it. My practice is, to make them repeat the Creed oftener than the other prayers; and I declare to them, at the same time, that they who believe the contents of it are true Christians.

"From the Creed, I pass to the Ten Commandments, and give them to understand, that the Christian Law is comprised in these precepts; that he who keeps them all according to his duty, is a good Christian; and that eternal life is decreed to him: that, on the contrary, whoever violates one of these Commandments is a bad Christian, and that he shall be damned eternally, in case he repent not of his sin. Both the new Christians, and the Pagans, admire our law, as holy and reasonable, and consistent with itself.

"Having done as I told you, my custom is to repeat with them, the Lord's Prayer, and the Angels' Salutation. Once again we recite the Creed, and, at every Article, besides the Pater Noster and the Ave Maria, we intermingle some short prayer: for having pronounced aloud the first Article, I begin thus, and they say after me: 'Jesus thou son of the living God, give me grace to believe firmly this first Article of thy Faith, and with this intention, we offer unto thee that prayer, of which thou thyself art the Author.' Then we add, Holy Mary, Mother of our Lord Jesus Christ, obtain for us, from thy Son, that we may have the grace to keep this first Commandment. After which we say the Ave Maria. We observe the same method through the other nine Commandments, with such little variations as the matter may require."[1]

It will thus be evident that Xavier's *hopes of success rested on bare rites and ceremonies, baptisms not understood or desired, but simply performed by the one party and endured by the other, dry formularies repeated as if the mere words would act as charms or spells in the work of conversion.* With all this, however, there was combined the influence which arose from untiring zeal, marvellous activity, and unwearied patience in enduring fasting, fatigue, poverty, sickness, and every kind of misery. To this we must add one characteristic feature of his mission, *his invariable kindness in ministering to the wants of the sick and the poor.*

The year 1543 was chiefly spent amongst the thirty villages of the fishery coast. His headquarters appear to have been the little town of Tuticorin, to the

[1] Hough's "India," Vol. I., pp. 178-9. This is an extract from Xavier's Letters to the Jesuit's Society at Rome.

East of Tinnevelly, but his biographers represent him as being constantly on the move, and devoting from one to three weeks to each village according to its population. During this time he sent a priest to Manaar, a little island near Ceylon, and succeeded in converting many of the natives, six hundred of whom were shortly afterwards massacred by the King of Jaffnapatam.[1] On leaving each village he appointed the cleverest proselyte to drill the converts regularly in the repetition of the formularies ; and that they might not trust to religious zeal alone, they were *handsomely paid* by certain "gold fanams" from the Portuguese treasury at Goa. When he left these simple people, he took with him a few of the most promising lads to be trained for missionary work in the College of St. Paul. We have no space to notice his unsuccessful attempts to convert the sharp-witted Brahmins, but the reader will find a full account in Lucena, Bartoli and Maffei, and in the Lives by Faber and Venn.

Early in 1544 he returned to Goa, secured the services of three missionaries, and went back to South India, dividing the coast into three districts, and assigning a priest to each. He advanced alone into the interior, pursuing the same course which we have already described. The Rajah of Travancore received him kindly, thousands of idolaters were baptised,

[1] Lucena, Liv. II., p. 238.

idols and their temples were destroyed by the proselytes, and forty-five churches erected for the new Christians. His own words are: "In the kingdom of Travancore, in the space of one month, I have made ten thousand Christians."[1] This work of conversion was promoted by a romantic episode, in which the chivalrous courage of the Spanish noble shone forth from the squalid garment of the Jesuit. A band of mountaineers had poured down upon the plains of Travancore, and were plundering the possessions. The Rajah's forces, inferior in number, went out to meet the invaders, but Xavier resolved, if possible, to save their lives by being himself their champion. Raising the crucifix aloft, he rushed forward to meet the advancing foe, and exclaimed in a voice of thunder, "I forbid you, in the name of the living God, to pass further. Return to your homes, and leave the land in peace." Astounded by this apparition, the superstitious multitude broke and fled. We give this story as it is recorded. Though improbable, it is not impossible; and there must be some foundation for it, as the Rajah, grateful for this heroic deed, did all in his power to further the interests of Xavier and his mission. Convinced that the way was now open, we

[1] Xavier's Letters, 45. This exaggeration is supposed to be the work of a copyist, for Xavier writes only "*plurimos* Christianos." Venn, p. 65. But the Roman Catholic writers do not doubt the ten thousand. See Faber, p. 74; and "Marshall's Missions," Vol. I., p. 215

find him writing the most urgent letters to Europe, imploring the Jesuits in Italy, France, and Portugal to come over and help him. "I take God to witness," he exclaims, "that, not being able to return into Europe, I have resolved to write to the University of Paris, that millions of idolaters might be easily converted, if there were more preachers who would sincerely mind the interests of Jesus Christ, and not their own concernments." His appeal was admired and applauded, but no action followed. Then, as now, approbation was easier than imitation.

The early part of 1545 was spent at Cochin and Nagapatam in missionary labours of the same kind, and with the same results. We find him writing to the Portuguese king (John III.) a very strong letter against the administration of the Viceroy, conveyed to Europe by the hands of Michael Vaz.[1] The effects of this appeal were the recall of the obnoxious Viceroy, and the appointment of the famous João de Castro. A letter from the King to the new Viceroy, dated Almelrem, 8th March, 1546, is printed *in extenso*, and shows how deeply interested the King was, not merely for the promotion of his dominions, but for the co-extensive propagation of the faith.[2] He commands that the idols should be broken to pieces, the

[1] Lucena, Liv. II., p. 263. Faber, p. 112.

[2] Vida de João de Castro. Por Andrade, 1651. Edit. por Bispo Francisco Leuz, Lisbòa, 1835, p. 51. "Carta d'el Rey a Don João de Castro."

temples destroyed, and every effort made to suppress idolatry.[1] The whole document, filling seven pages, is far too long to quote here, but we may cite one passage. "Above all, we charge you that in whatever occurs, you consult Father Francisco Xavier, and principally with reference to the growth of Christianity on the Fishery Coast." And we may further notice the benevolent provision made for succouring the newly-converted Indians, who had to endure great persecution on account of their change of faith. The historian quoted goes on to say that, "King John effected by this letter what his arms could not achieve," and that "Heaven blessed his exertions with distinguished success" in the Molucca islands.

Xavier, disgusted by the failure of his efforts to chastise with the sword the king who had massacred the converts of Manaar, or perhaps, seeing the hollowness of his so-called conversions, resolved to leave India. He went, however, for a short time to Meliapour or St. Thomé, near Madras, and there, according to the Roman Catholic writers, he underwent a series of most marvellous persecutions, being waylaid by devils on his way to church at night, and severely

[1] "Vos mandamos, que descrol rindo todos os Idolos por ministros diligentes os extinguais, et façais em pedeços em qualquer lugar onde forem achados, publicando rigorosas penas contra quæsquer pessvas que atreverem a lavrar, fundir, esculpir, debuxar, pintar, on tirar a'leoz qualquer figura de Idolo em metal, bronze, madeira, barro, on outra qualquer materia, &c., &c."—Vida de João de Castro, pp. 51-2.

beaten. We must refer the curious on this point to the writer already cited, who evidently believes the whole story.[1] He arrived at Malacca on the 25th of September, and there he found the Portuguese as depraved as their countrymen at Goa, though some efforts had been made by Antonia Galvao, a noble governor and zealous apostle to introduce Christianity amongst the Pagans. The Europeans, who, for more than thirty years had been successfully pursuing the spice trade, seemed to imagine that *the Christian faith was already theirs, and that missionary efforts were only required by surrounding heathenism.* Xavier, after many efforts, not always with good results, proceeded to Amboyna, and thence to the island of Ternate, the Isle del Moro, Java, and other places. On the return voyage, he arrived at Malacca in July, 1547, where he met with three priests, Beyra, Nunez, and Ribeira, who had come out as members of the Portuguese Missions, to test their qualifications, to point out defects in their plans, and to suggest greater attention being bestowed on the study of the native language. Space forbids our copying his address, but one cannot help admiring the wisdom and Christian love which seem to guide him in discoursing to these Jesuit missionaries. *Had such counsels been the ruling principles of the Portuguese missions in Southern India, the labourers of the sixteenth century would have been a*

[1] Faber's Translation, p. 121.

help, and not a hindrance to their followers in the nineteenth.

This great duty performed, he visited the Rajah of Jaffnapatam, whom his eloquence persuaded to treat the converts with humanity. Thence he went to Ramisarim and Ceylon, reaching Goa in March, 1548. He found his college prosperous, and the Japanese students not only diligent in their ordinary work, but so fully instructed in the Christian faith, that the bishop baptised him as Paulo da Santa Fè. Five more Jesuits had arrived from Portugal; native students had received the priesthood, and even a few of the pearl fishers were admitted as catechists. So that *the Portuguese missions, feebly started at the beginning of the century, and vigorously revived after forty years' torpor, were now beginning to put forth their energies.* Having sent Barzaeus as missionary to Ormuz, appointed Paulo de Camerina vicar-general, and Gomez warden of his new college, he set sail for Japan in 1549. His marvellous labours in that island, crowned with far greater success than his efforts in Southern India, would cause a digression from our theme. After two years' toil, he visited Goa for the last time in 1551. He then sailed for China; and when off the island of Sancian, feeling ill, he asked to be landed. Here he was left in a wretched shed, and died on the 2nd of December, 1552. The body was carried to Goa, and, being enclosed in a coffin enriched with silver and gems, was placed in a shrine of exquisite beauty, the resort and object of worship of numberless pilgrims.

Thus ended the life of Xavier. But the *effects* of his ten years in the East Indies are *felt for good and for evil to the present hour.* It is scarcely possible for the impartial student of history who toils through a mass of conflicting evidence in Latin, Spanish, French, and Portuguese, to arrive at a perfectly satisfactory conclusion on this subject. If he leans towards the supernatural, he will find abundance of support in the writings of nearly all the Jesuit Fathers, in the "processes," that is, the documents, authorising the canonization of Xavier, and in the recent works of Dryden, Faber, John Mason Neale, Strickland, Marshall, and others of the same school. If, on the contrary, he looks upon the narrative as a spiritual romance, or a tale of religious knight-errantry, he will find himself supported by sceptics from Gibbon to Buckle, by disappointed Romanists, like the Abbé Dubois, and by narrow-minded Protestants such as some of our modern missionaries to the east. Truth, in this instance, as in many others, lies between, and we cannot conclude this chapter better than by quoting the eloquent words of the author of "Christianity in India":—"Protestant zeal is only contemptible when it denies that Francis Xavier was a great man. Delusions he may have had, strong as ever yet wrought upon the human soul ; but the true nobility of his nature is not to be gainsaid. It would be the vilest injustice to fix upon the first Jesuit missionary, the charge of dishonesty and insincerity, because, among his followers have been liars and hypocrites of the worst class. He met the last summons with rapture, and beneath a miserable shed, he closed a life of agony and bliss, of humiliation and of triumph, with scarcely a parallel in the history of the world."

CHAPTER VII.

SUBSEQUENT MISSIONS IN THE XVIth. CENTURY.

"The history of modern Roman Catholic Missions to heathen countries forms an important subject of enquiry with all who take an interest in the progress of Christianity. One of the most remarkable periods is that which extends from the middle of the XVIth to the middle of the XVIIth century."—Venn's "Life of Xavier."

XAVIER fills so important a place in the Portuguese Missions of the XVIth Century, that one is apt to forget the efforts of others before and after his career. We have already noticed the very early movements connected with the voyages of Cabral and Da Gama, remarking that during the long period of forty years, the Portuguese had been too much occupied in conquest and commerce to pay attention even to their own Christianity, and, of course, they took no pains to secure its propagation amongst the surrounding heathen. We may now summarise the chief incidents of the Portuguese Missions, so far as the Pagans are concerned. In other chapters we shall speak of the influence exerted by the Jesuits on the Syrian Christians.

To go back a few years. In 1540, a preaching friar, Bernard de la Croix, of episcopal rank was sent by the Dominicans from Europe to Meliapour. This mission, with others of minor importance, affords proof of the zeal and perseverance of that Order in the cause of Indian Missions.[1] But a still more decided step was taken in 1545, when the Dominicans established "The Congregation of the Indies"—a missionary college for the training of young men, as apostolic labourers bound by solemn vows to dedicate themselves to the conversion of the heathen, and to shrink from no danger, privation, or toil, resisting even unto blood. The first fruits of this new "congregation" appeared in 1548, when twelve Portuguese Dominicans, under Father Bermudez, arrived in India. These new preachers were charged with the conversion of fifteen villages in the islands of Goa, wherein, it is said, they succeeded in erecting four churches. If we may credit the accounts given by Fontana, these missionaries saw their labours crowned with marvellous success within a year of their arrival. He speaks in the "Monumenta Domenicana" of eighteen churches and convents in Solor, Flores, Lamatta, and Malacca; and he computes their neophytes at 60,000. In the famous work from which we quote (a sort of Annual Report of the Order) minute particulars are given of the energy and eloquence of their preachers,

[1] Fontana, "Monumenta Domenicana," Ann. 1540.

especially of two, named Ignatius and Macedo, contempories of Xavier—and of the various expedients for securing and retaining the Indian converts. The zeal of the Dominicans was, however, by no means limited to Southern India; for we find that in 1555, Gaspard de la Croix, a native of Evora, one of the original twelve Portuguese who had landed in 1548, determined to set out for China; but his adventures there do not affect our present question. It is more to our purpose to notice that in the year 1557, three of the Missionaries of these Dominicans, or preaching friars, were promoted to the sees of Goa, Cochin, and Malacca. Attention is called to this circumstance, as it is a prevalent opinion that the Jesuits were almost the only missionaries in the East. So far, indeed, was this from being the case, that, towards the close of the XVIth. Century, the mission field of Portuguese India, was divided into three parts in order that there might be no interference of operations. To the Dominicans was assigned Ormuz, with its dependencies; to the Franciscans, Ceylon; while the Jésuits had, after a while, the chief superintendence of Goa and its environs.

Father Du Jarric, S.J., is our chief authority for this period of Missionary history, but his style is so prolix, his descriptions so minute, and his bias towards the Jesuits so decided, that it is impossible to do more than to give one brief specimen, not a translation, but a précis of his narrative. He says that the means employed to convert the Pagans were not solely or chiefly, as has been alleged, certain temporal advantages with promises of future happiness. All that the splendid ceremonial of the Roman Church could produce was employed to captivate the Gentiles. When the Jesuits had reason to believe that their missionary fields in the neighbouring villages were ripe for the sickle, they proceeded from Goa, not merely in Ecclesiastical pomp, but also escorted by a powerful military force, for the double purpose of ostentation and protection. Next day they were in the habit of forming a procession of neophytes in two columns; the first of men and boys, the second of women and girls. On their arrival at the Viceregal Metropolis, they were lodged in the House of the Catechumens, and carefully taught twice a day.[1] When duly prepared they were taken to Church on

[1] Hough and others deny that instruction as a rule preceded baptism. See "Christianity in India," Vol. I., p. 208. But the Roman Catholic writers positively assert that every care was taken, and it is but fair to hear their own words on this much disputed point:—"Une des choses qui contribue le plus à rendre la chrétienté de la côte de la Pecherie si distinguée entre toutes les autres, c'est le soin qu'on prend d'enseigner de trés bonne heure la doctrine chrétienne aux plus petits enfans. Cette sainte coutume s'est conservée inviolablement en ce pays la depuis le temps de S. François Xavier, il etait persuadé que la foi ne pouvait manquer de jeter de profondes racines dans le cœur des habitans, si dès la premierè enfance on les instruisait bien des mystèrés et des préceptes de notre religion."—Choix des "Lettres Edifiantes," Vol. IV., p. 554.

some great festival, flags, tapestry, flowers, and evergreens decorated the cathedral. The streets had banners and carpets hung from all the windows, and triumphal arches were erected along the line of procession. The Catechumens received new clothes, generally the gifts of the Viceroy, the Archbishop, and the leading officials. One interesting band, the Children of St. Xavier, robed in white, red crosses on their breasts, and green branches in their hands followed the Candidates. Next came the students of the College of St. Paul, of various races and complexions, the future labourers in the mission field. Lastly, the Brethren of the Society of Jesus marched two and two under the standard of the crucifix. On reaching the church the procession divided with that perfect regularity which is characteristic of Roman ceremonial, each falling into his proper place. The Viceroy, surrounded by a brilliant staff, in naval and military uniforms, the Archbishop and his clergy in all the splendour of gold jewels, and silk, with everything to enhance the spectacle which the wealth of luxurious Goa could produce, welcomed the poor bewildered Pagans to their new faith. Music, vocal and instrumental, prayers, ceremonies, statues, pictures, flowers, incense, all combined to render the baptism of the converts a sight never to be forgotten. After the administration, they proceeded in order to the "altar on which was exposed the Holy Sacrament," to render thanks to Christ that he had made them his children. The men and boys then went to the house of the Jesuits to dinner, the brethren acting as servants to their guests. The women and girls were kindly received and similarly entertained at the houses of pious ladies of high rank, who vied with each other in their attentions to the new Christians. Next day they returned to the same church, and received their first communion, going back to their native villages with joy. The good fathers took special care to visit them in their homes from time to time, in order to maintain their faith. This system of conversion, differing in many respects from others, appears to have worked well during the latter half of the XVIth Century; for, without speaking of the Franciscans and Dominicans, the Jesuits in Goa alone baptised at first a thousand, then nineteen hundred, then above three thousand, and lastly the astonishing number of twelve thousand every year.[1]

It must not however be supposed that the operations of the Propagandists were limited to the lowest of the people, or to those who might be fairly classed as idolaters. True to their principles, these missioners considered all beyond the pale of their Church, aliens to the faith, and, of course, needing conversion. Hence we find them, at one time working against

[1] Du Jarric "Hist. des Choises" plus mémorables, &c., Tom I., p. 315.

Hindoo idolatry, at another attacking Mahommedan deism, and at a third interfering with Syrian Christianity. Amongst the Moslems their success was not great, though, in 1557, they achieved a triumph in the baptism of the daughter of Sultan Meale of the Deccan.

From Goa, as a centre, missionary influence continued to radiate, and expeditions were undertaken for the destruction of idolatry, sometimes by moral force, often by physical. For example, the islands of Choran and Divar to the north of Goa were famed for a multitude of idols. In the second, there stood the temple of Genesa, a popular divinity, attracting pilgrims from all parts of India. The Jesuits considered this sacred spot a noble field, and advanced to the conflict with all the ardour, though happily without the cruelty of the old Teutonic knights, and success crowned their efforts.[1] Another instance may be found when Dom Constantino (twentieth Viceroy) besieged Daman, in Guzerat, in 1599. Convinced by a trifling incident of the superior sanctity of the Jesuits (at least so says du Jarric). he handed over the mosque of the captured city to the fathers to be purified and converted into a church ; and strange to tell, the wife of the Mohammedan Governor was suddenly seized with so strong a desire for baptism, that the rite was almost immediately administered.

[1] For a full account see Du Jarric, Tom I., p. 448, and Baron Herion's "Histoire des Missions."

We are further informed that the new Viceroy had the propagation of the faith so warmly at heart that he never ceased to exert himself in the Holy cause. Close to Goa lies the peninsula of Salsette, then containing 80,000 heathen in 66 villages, sunk in the grossest ignorance, and a prey to the cupidity of the crafty Brahmins. To this stronghold the Viceroy Constantine obtained an entrance by skilful diplomacy for the Jesuit missioners, and in a short time they could boast of two thousand converts as their first fruits. The Brahmins, frantic at the double loss of influence and trade, stirred up the heathen to persecute the neophytes ; and the Jesuits, in self-defence, built a hospital for the protection of their disciples. This measure, though absolutely necessary, still further irritated the Indian Priests and their followers to such an extent that they attacked the Jesuits, and beat them and their converts most cruelly. Whereupon the Viceroy, by landing a body of troops and destroying all the temples, proved to the natives that such interference with the propagation of Christianity would be severely chastised.

The reader may remember the cruelty of the Rajah of Jaffnapatam, and the disgust of Xavier at his escaping with impunity. The chastisement, however, was only deferred, for in 1560 the Viceroy Constantine attacked the Rajah. The results were the session of Manaar, the capture of the heir-apparent, the sack of the capital, and the seizure of the Royal treasury, the most valuable gem being the tooth of a white monkey named Anomna.[1] So highly was this ridiculous object venerated that the King of Pegu offered 300,000 crowns as a ransom! When this request reached Goa a council was held, and a long and serious debate took place as to whether or not the tooth should be restored and the money accepted. The result was a negative, and the Governor ordered the tooth to be pounded in a mortar and burnt in his presence.

Goa continued to be the focus of missionary enterprise, and the scene of numerous conversions, the harvest demanding more labourers, Alberto Laertio, an Italian Jesuit, set out from Goa for Rome, and brought back with him sixty-two missionaries of the "Company," who were soon afterwards followed by fifteen more.

But Goa was not the only centre. The Jesuits' College at Cochin had three dependent residences; that of St. James, a league from the town, where two Brethren had charge of three Churches—that of Murterhe, five leagues from Cochin, where there was no Church till 1581; that of Vaipacota, a league from Cranganor in the midst of the Christians of St. Thomas.

Towards the close of the XVIth Century, the Jesuit

[1] Abbè Dubois, Moeurs, &c., Tom. II., p. 430.

Francisco Ros, a man well skilled in Syriac and Tamil, carried on a successful mission in the kingdom of Calicut. The story is too long to tell here, but the outline is this. The Zamorin, fearing the power of Portugal on the one hand, and the extortions of a Moslem Corsair on the other, implored the good offices of the Jesuit Acosta, then a captive at Calicut, to negotiate a peace for him with Matias d'Albuquerque. The Viceroy sent Acosta back to the Zamorin with the Jesuit Ros, at that time engaged in converting the Syrian Christians in the Serra. The Indian Prince not only gave the missionaries a hearty welcome, but granted them every facility for preaching the Gospel. He, moreover, sent Ambassadors to Goa to request from the Provincial that a colony of Jesuits should be established at Calicut. The request was agreed to; the site of a Church was chosen close to the town; a Cross was erected to mark the sacred spot; and the Zamorin himself was the first to bend before the sign of our Redemption.

The Portuguese Missions during a hundred years had made little or no progress in the kingdom of Cochin, though the Sovereign had been one of the first allies of the Portuguese crown. Nevertheless, Christianity had crept in, as is proved by the violent persecution that raged during the last two years of

[1] Du Jarric, Tom I., p. 463.

the century. In Travancore the Jesuits De Veiga and Buccrio displayed great zeal, and in a short time succeeded in securing thousands of nominal converts. A violent persecution of the Christians soon followed, and it is asserted that twenty thousand were driven from their homes. After the Mission had been in abeyance for four years, it was restored by the energy of Father Spinola in 1607, and continued to flourish.

Turning to the fishery coast, the scene of Xavier's first success, we find the faithful Paravas bearing witness to the zeal of the missionaries who followed the Holy pioneer. Tutucurim, the chief town, was provided with an excellent hospital, Church and school. Eighteen Jesuits had charge of six stations, the entire population professed Christianity, and the capital itself was "si adonnée à la dévotion qu'on eut dit que c'était plutôt une maison religieuse qu'une communauté politique.[1]" The marvellous conversions begun by Xavier had been continued for fifty-three years by Father Henriquez, who died in 1600, leaving more than 135,000 converts as the results of his self-denying labours.[2]

The first step in the famous Madura Mission was taken in 1595 by Gonzala Fernandez, who founded a hospital and a school; but nothing effectual was

[1] Du Jarric, Tom III., p. 726.
[2] Du Jarric, Tom III., p. 744.

done till 1606, when Robert de Nobili joined the mission, and gave it new life. The reader who desires more information than this outline affords will find ample details in the ponderous volumes cited below.

BOOK III.

THE SUBJUGATION OF THE SYRIAN CHURCH.

CHAPTER I.

ROMAN CLAIM OF SUPREMACY.

"We are of the true faith, whatever you from the West may be; for we come from the place where the followers of Christ were first called Christians." Reply of the Syrians to the Portuguese.—"Buchanan's Researches."

SUCH of our readers as are thoroughly acquainted with the history of the pretensions of the Romish Church may safely pass over this chapter. But assuming that some may glance at our pages who are not familiar with the rise and progress of her claims to universal dominion, it may be necessary to give a brief sketch, introductory to the exertion of Romish tyranny over the Malabar Christians.

Prior to the sixth Century the Pope's jurisdiction was extremely limited. He asserted no secular authority; and his efforts were bent on promoting the extension of spiritual influence.[1] We read that in the fourth century, the Catholic Church contained fourteen Patriarchates,[2] whose rulers (Patriarchs or Archbishops) were equal and independent; and so far from "Pope" being a word indicating pre-eminence,

[1] Abbé Fleury "Ecc. Hist., Lib. XXII." N. 45.

[2] Bingham II. XVII. 20. "Theophilus Anglicanus," p. 112.

it was then the common designation of a Bishop, as "Mar" is in the Syrian Church. It is true that three of the Patriarchs, viz.: those of Rome, Alexandria, and Antioch, though not higher in order, had precedence of the others in place, but this precedence was liable to change, if a city rose or declined in civil power and importance.[1] None of these Bishops ever dreamed of claiming for himself, or admitting in his Brother Prelates any permanent supremacy; and Pope Gregory I. denounced the title of Universal Bishop as arrogant, wicked, schismatical, blasphemous, and anti-christian. "Qeusquis se universalem sacerdotem vocat, Anti-Christum prœcurrit."[2] "On account of the *civil* eminence of Rome, the Bishop of Rome anciently enjoyed precedence among Bishops by the Canons of the Catholic Church; but his jurisdiction as Bishop, Metropolitan, and Patriarch, was and is limited to his own diocese, province and patriarchate, in the same manner as that of every other Bishop, Metropolitan, and Patriarch."[3] It is therefore perfectly evident that the national churches were at this period independent of each other, and that there was no such thing as an admission of the supremacy of the Church of Rome.

In the year 533, the Emperor Justinian unfortu-

[1] "Theophilus Anglicanus," p. 116. Bingham IX., 17.

[2] Lib. VII., Epist., XXXIII., "Theoph., Anglicanus," p. 253.

[3] Crankanthorpe "Def. Eccl. Angl." p. 176. "Theoph. Angl." pp. 255-6.

nately admitted the claim of the Pontiff to be the head of all Christendom, and though after Justinian's death, the Patriarch of Constantinople threw off the yoke, and asserted his own right to the title of Universal Bishop, the usurpation of the Roman Bishop was confirmed in 1606. This first fatal step led to an immense increase of priestly influence during the middle ages. The little learning that existed was entirely in the hands of the clergy, who thus acquired not only religious, but social and political power. In course of time Papal arrogance had reached such a pitch that Gregory VII. asserted his supremacy, not merely over Bishops and Priests, but also above Emperors and Kings. He boldly declared that crowns were held of the Pope, and that therefore all Christian sovereigns were his vassals, bound to pay him tribute, and yield him entire obedience. We need not pause here to tell the well-known story of "the Decretals of Isidor," falsely asserted to be ancient documents (conventions, acts of councils, &c.), proving that from the first periods of the Church the Popes were invested with the same supremacy which they have since asserted. These "decretals," being in reality forgeries of the seventh, eighth or ninth century, have been long ago shown to be utterly worthless as evidence on the point in question.[1]

[1] Mosheim's "Ecc. Hist." Cent. IX., CII. Sec. 8. Geddes on the "Supremacy," p. 46. Hough's "Christianity," Vol. I., p. 141.

The structure thus founded in error was strengthened by additional frauds as time rolled on. The VIIIth Century introduced image worship under Papal sanction. The IXth furnished long lives of Saints full of the wildest inventions, all tending to the assertion of the unlimited sway of the Pope. Closely connected with this was that wonderful device, the Canonisation of Saints, to which we have alluded in the chapter on Xavier. The Xth Century could boast of important additions, the institution of the rosary, the baptism of bells, and many superstitions of the same character; but the XIth eclipsed its predecessors and seemed to soar to the climax of assumption for we find that the Pope, not satisfied with the lofty title of Pontifex Maximus, blasphemously assumed the designation of divinity, "King of Kings and Lord of Lords," laying claim to absolute infallibility, and declaring that the Church of Rome never had erred, and was incapable of erring.

The Roman Pontiff's assumption of temporal power and jurisdiction in the various kingdoms of Europe, naturally provoked resistance from those who felt their authority invaded and undermined. While the Sovereigns of Germany, France, and England opposed the Pope chiefly on political grounds, the national churches, if not in a corporate capacity, at least through their individual members struggled hard, and often successfully, for religious freedom. To crush these attempts the Roman Church established the Inquisition, which has been justly characterised as the "depth of Satan, for Satanical it is by the conjunction of three qualities, indefatigable diligence, profound subtlety, and inhuman cruelty."[1] The XIIth and XIIIth Centuries had introduced or sanctioned many superstitions in relation to the Holy Communion such as Transubstantiation, and the adoration of the Host. The Confessional too, began to exert its baneful influence, and, at a later period, became a powerful instrument in the hands of the Jesuits.

Historians generally consider the XIVth century as the acmé of Papal greatness. The remarkable events were the open war between Philip the Fair and Boniface VIIIth, the existence of rival Popes at Rome and Avignon, the preaching of John Wickliffe in England, and, above all, the translation of the Bible. But in the next century the spirit of religious freedom fought more vigorously than ever against the encroachments of Rome; and, though Huss and Jerome perished at the stake, though the laity were deprived of the cup in the Communion, though the Council of Constance declared that no faith was to be kept with heretics, though, in short, the Papacy made the most desperate efforts to extinguish the light of the Reformation, all its opposition signally failed.

Superficial as this summary is, it will at least serve

[1] Trappe's "Popery Stated," p. 2. Sect. XII.

to refresh the reader's memory, and to afford him a key to the principles of that formidable Ecclesiastical Power, which, by means of the *Portuguese Missions was to influence Southern India in the XVIth century.* Luther was a lad at college while the Portuguese vessels were doubling the Cape of Good Hope ; and, twenty years later, when he inaugurated the Reformation, and deprived Rome of many of her subjects, the Pontiffs found consolation in the foreign dominions which maritime discovery had brought under the sway of the Church. It was an age of struggles, and a comparison of dates would exhibit some striking coincidences. Thus, for example, in 1521, while the German champion at the Diet of Worms was boldly acknowledging all his public opinions, and firmly establishing the Reformation, the Spanish soldier was lying wounded at the Pampeluna, and devoting himself to that long course of dreaming and planning which led to the establishment of the most powerful counteraction to Protestantism—the Order of the Jesuits.

It is thus abundantly evident from the whole history of the rise and progress of the Papacy, that Rome asserted an unqualified supremacy over other Churches throughout the world. How this *theory influenced her treatment of the Syrian Christians in Malabar will appear in the following pages.*

CHAPTER II.

FIRST ATTEMPT BY THE FRANCISCANS.

"'These Churches,' said the Portuguese, 'belong to the Pope.' 'Who is the Pope?' said the Syrians, 'we never heard of him.'"—Buchanan's "Christian Researches," p. 89.

As a natural sequence to the claims of the Romish Church, narrated in our last chapter, the Portuguese missionaries proclaimed their undoubted right to subdue the Christians of St. Thomas. A glance at the history of the early Church in Malabar, whether founded by the Apostle himself or by another of the same name at a later period, will clearly prove to the impartial student that there never had been the slightest connection between the Italian and the Indian branches. Of course, on the theory of Papal supremacy just described, the attempts made by the Portuguese "Missioners" were not only allowable, but highly praiseworthy; for, on that theory due subordination to the Roman centre must not only be asserted, but vigorously enforced at whatever cost. The proof of this dogma failing, as all history shows that it does, there is no more evidence for the early subordination of the Christians of Malabar to the See of Rome, than for the subjection of the Church of England at the dawn of her existence, or at the present day.

In our former pages it has been made evident that the true ecclesiastical head of the Christians of St. Thomas was the Patriarch of Mosul, resident at Seleucia, on the distant banks of the Tigris. An examination of the testimony so laboriously collected by Gouvea, Asseman, Renaudot, La Croze, and others, clearly proves that these Christians had, from the earliest ages, acknowledged the Bishops of the Church in Persia as their Primates. And, though two of the writers just named are, as Romanists, most anxious to show a different origin for the Church of Malabar, they have utterly failed in establishing the desired resemblance in doctrine, discipline, and ceremony to the *distinctive* pecularities of the Romish Church. For instance, the Roman service has always been in the Latin language, whereas the Malabar prayers were constantly recited in the Syriac tongue. Of the Pope they had never heard; and all their traditions pointed to the Tigris, not to the Tiber, as the source of their ecclesiastical system. Driven from their first position, some unscrupulous advocates have attempted to show that the parent Church of Babylon itself owed allegiance to the Roman Pontiff, and that, therefore, the daughter Church of Malabar was necessarily bound to yield obedience to the central power. This strange assumption is founded on the following legend. In the year 1552, one Tum Sind, or Simon Salacan, a monk of the Order of St. Pachomius, who pretended to be the Patriarch of Mosul (or Seleucia, or Babylon), came to Rome and submitted himself to the Pope. His Holiness received him graciously, and made him a Bishop; though, according to others, his former consecration was reputed valid, and the Pallium was conferred The said Simon delivered letters and a confession of faith, which he pretended all the Eastern Bishops had commissioned him to present to the Pontiff. In these letters the very point in dispute—the Papal supremacy—was as plainly set forth as if they had been written by the most bigoted Canonist. This Pseudo-missionary also asserted that he had been attended by a cortège of seventy distinguished persons as far as Jerusalem, but that only three had resumed the journey, of whom one had died, another had stayed behind ill, and the third alone was with him. This very questionable Patriarch, on leaving the Vatican, instead of returning to Babylon, retired to Charamet, where he was slain by the Moslems—the Christians rather rejoicing than grieving, for they evidently considered him an impostor, like the Bishop of Iona, and others of the same stamp in our own day. The fate of Simon did not deter Abed Jesu from making a similar attempt.

This monk, author of several defences of Nestorianism, on arriving at Rome in 1562, was eagerly seized upon, and sent with great solemnity to the Council of Trent, as the duly accredited representative of the Chaldean Church. Of course, the great object was to make use of this adventurer as a living proof that *this branch of the Eastern Church had, in its corporate capacity, yielded entire obedience to the Pope.* A third actor appears in this strange performance, one Elias, a mock Patriarch of Babylon. We read that he sent several special Nuncios to the Pope with more letters of submission; but these emissaries rather overacted their part; for, in order to prove the identity of the two Churches, they tore several pages out of their office book. The transparent fraud being at once discovered, they were dismissed with disgrace; but, nothing daunted, Elias sent an Archdeacon in 1570 to deliver personally to Paul V. a treatise on the "Reconciliation of Chaldea" with Rome. We may quote one passage from his letter :—"Let heretics do what they will, I, for my part, am resolved never to go against the holy precepts of the Apostles and Orthodox Fathers, who have all affirmed the See of Rome to be the head of all other Sees, but would always confess that the Roman Church was the mother of all the other Churches in the world, and that all that did not own her to be so are accursed.[1] Elias went rather further, for he

[1] Geddes's "Church of Malabar," p. 15.

assured the Pontiff that all the Chaldean Clergy derived their orders in former times immediately from Rome; but that as many candidates perished on their way to the Holy See, the Pope graciously consecrated a Patriarch, that thenceforward these perils might be avoided, and the clergy ordained at home. "And thus," reasoned Elias, "we received all our authority from the Roman source." On no better foundation than such childish fictions do the defenders of Papal supremacy try to prove that the Chaldean prelates have unreservedly admitted the derivation of their orders from St. Peter's, and that, therefore, all canonical obedience is due to the head of the Roman Catholic Church.

A full refutation of these idle tales is foreign to our purpose. Suffice it to say that all authorities, worthy of credit, clearly prove that the Church of Seleucia, the mother of the Malabar church, was formerly subject to the Patriarch of Antioch. One of many testimonies may be found in the thirty-third canon of the Council of Nice:—"Let the See of Seleucia which is one of the eastern cities, be honoured likewise, and have the title of Catholicon; and let the Prelate thereof ordain Archbishops as the other Patriarchs do, that so the eastern Christians who live under heathens, may not be wronged by waiting the Patriarch of Antioch's leisure, or by going to him, but may have a way opened to them to supply their own necessities; neither will any injury be done to the Patriarch of Antioch thereby, seeing he has consented to its being thus, upon the Synod's having desired it of him."[1]

Having attempted to show the importance attached by the Romish Church to the question of universal dominion and the expedients adopted to make out a case in reference to the Church of India, we may proceed to sketch the first attempt to convert theory into practice.

The reader will recollect the surprise and gratification of Vasco da Gama and his officers when they were visited in 1502, at Cochin, by the representatives of the Christians of St. Thomas. The religion professed by these visitors won for them the cordial support of the Europeans, and the Portuguese missionaries who, years afterwards, formed a more intimate acquaintance with this interesting people, would have received them into Christian fellowship, but for the discovery of two unpardonable offences—the heresy of Nestorius, and the sin of schism, in not acknowledging the Roman Pontiff. They immediately made the greatest efforts to induce the Malabar Christians to turn from Nestorianism to what they believed to be the Catholic faith, and to swear allegiance to the wearer of the triple crown. To accomplish these objects they adopted various lines of policy. Follow-

[1] This version is from the *Arabic* Canons of the Council.

ing the example of Xavier, they preached to the Christians, as he had done to the heathens, they established mission stations, and held discussions with the Syrian clergy, publicly and privately, and founded missionary colleges as the means of training a native ministry, to supplant the Syrian priests. Moral means failing to produce the desired effect, they employed alternately fraud and force during a long series of years, ending with the Synod of Diamper, which extinguished for a time the independence of the church of St. Thomas. A still more decided form of compulsion was the Inquisition established at Goa, in the year 1560, which soon made itself felt by its terrible and mysterious punishments, as the most effectual instrument in the conversion of "Jews, Turks, and Infidels," and in the subjugation of Christian brethren.

The first decided attempt in which persuasion only was employed, was made by the Franciscans in the year 1545, under the second Bishop, but first Archbishop of Goa, Dom João de Albuquerque. He had heard of this singular body of Christians dwelling in and near the mountains far to the south of Goa, and he felt it to be a reproach alike to Portuguese power and Romish authority, that these stray sheep had not long before been restored to the true fold. He accordingly selected Father Vincent, a brother Franciscan, and sent him to Cranganor to inquire into the condition of the Syrian Church, and to use his utmost eloquence in trying to reduce it to obedience. In reading the history of his labours, as given by Gouvea, one is at a loss to distinguish between historical truth and "pious fraud." It seems scarcely possible that one man could accomplish the enormous amount of work attributed to him by his biographer. From morning till night, publicly and privately, on the roadside, in bazaars, under trees, in churches, he talked, exhorted, argued, preached "without ceasing"—at least so we are told. But a question arises as to the possibility of this wonderful command of a foreign tongue. The worthy Franciscan had been but a year in India, during the greater part of which he had been at Goa, with little or no opportunity of studying Tamil; and yet we find him all at once, without any miraculous gift, in full possession of this marvellous fluency. It seems impossible to admit the truth of a narrative which contains within it so damaging an element as this apocryphal story. Yet we glean that, after all, the good Friar was no Mezzofanti; for his imperfect attempts were almost, if not quite, unintelligible. He candidly admitted that no success had attended his preaching, that the Cattanars (*i.e.*, priests) were obdurate, and that, without their hearty co-operation, there was no hope of influencing the laity. He therefore wrote to the Viceroy and to the Archbishop of Goa for their sanction to the erection at Cranganor of a college.[1] Both officials gave their consent and supplied funds, and the new Seminary was ready within the year (1546) for the instruction of Syrian boys in the Roman tongue and ritual. Thus far the scheme had been prosperous. But when the young Syrians were ordained by the Romish priests, the Cattanars positively refused to allow them to officiate in their churches. They considered these youths as the dupes and tools of Rome, as renegades from the faith, and as revolutionists eager to destroy the Church of their fathers. The Syrian Christians had, up to this time, given the Romish emissaries the most friendly reception. But now, thoroughly roused, and clearly perceiving the real object of the Portuguese missionaries, they broke off all friendly intercourse, and shut the doors of their churches, not only against the European priests, but also against their own apostate sons.

Thus the Franciscan attempt utterly failed, and here the first act of this singular drama closes.

[1] Raulin, "Hist. Ecc. Malab." La Croze, p 55. Du Jarric, III., p. 552.

CHAPTER III.

SECOND ATTEMPT BY THE JESUITS.

"A strange and melancholy chapter in the annals of the world are these same missions in India, and not tending, it must be confessed, to lessen the feeling of distrust so universally inspired by the Society of Jesus, in spite of the zeal, learning, and splendid abilities of many of its members."—W. S. MACKAY in "Calcutta Review," Vol. II.

NEARLY twenty years elapsed between the failure of the Franciscans and the aggression of the Jesuits, during which the Syrian pastors were allowed to feed their flocks in peace. No doubt, during this lull, there were many minor efforts which history has not thought it worth while to record; and, unquestionably, much soreness existed between the oppressor and the oppressed. The crusade, however, was suspended, not abandoned; for the Jesuits were not the men to be driven from their purpose by disaster or failure. Reflecting upon the causes of Father Vincent's defeat, the Provincial believed that he had discovered it in the contempt with which the Franciscan College at Cranganor had treated the Syriac language. This tongue the Malabar Christians held sacred as that in which our blessed Lord preached the glad tidings of salvation, as that which He probably used in ordinary converse, and certainly employed on several remarkable occasions.[1] They therefore made it the vehicle of all the offices of their Church, though by many of the Cattanars it was imperfectly understood; and they naturally resented every attempt on the part of the Portuguese missionaries to ignore its existence or to expel it from the services of the Church. The Jesuits, admitting the force of these sentiments, varied their mode of attack. They resolved to erect a new college; and, in order to destroy unpleasant associations, three miles from Cranganor, the scene of the former conflict.[2] They applied to Philip II. of Spain (who had usurped the Crown of Portugal) and received a large contribution, though he was then preparing his famous Armada for the invasion of England. The Rajah of Cochin, too, gave his sanction, though not a convert. In 1587, the buildings were erected and the work of education commenced under Antonio Morales—as Principal. In the other school at Cranganor, the students had been taunted by their countrymen for adopting the language and dress of the Portuguese, and thus casting contempt

[1] "It appears that He spoke Syriac when He walked by the way (Ephphatha) and when He sat in the house (Talitha Cumi) and when He was upon the Cross (Eli, Eli, lama sabacthani)."—Buchanan, p. 96.

[2] Raulin, "Hist. Ecc. Malab.." p. 11. La Croze, Hist., p. 56. Du Jarric, Tom. III., p. 552. Gouvea, "Jornada," p. 7.

upon their own. The policy of the Propagandists easily overcame these objections. They not only permitted the use of the Syriac or Chaldee, but made it a compulsory part of the curriculum, teaching it more accurately than the Syrians themselves. They conceded also the question of costume; and hence the new college began its career with the fairest prospect of uniting adverse elements on its neutral ground. But under this specious appearance of impartiality the Jesuits concealed their deep-laid scheme. *They never lost sight of the necessity of training the students in the Latin language, of shaking their faith in their native Church, and of indoctrinating them, slowly but surely, in the principles of Rome.* But again the aggressors were doomed to disappointment. The pupils, who had been sedulously prepared for years, whose allegiance had been, to all appearance, firmly secured, were no sooner ordained than they asserted their independence. Nothing that the Jesuits could do, by threats or promises, could induce these young men to forsake the faith of their fathers, to preach against the Syrian Bishop, to alter their Prayer Books, or to omit the name of the Patriarch of Seleucia.

The missionaries of Vaipacotta, thus once more baffled, met to determine the next line of action. They no doubt consulted the Provincial at Goa, who in turn submitted the question to the General in one of those reports already noticed. The result was the adoption of a much more decided policy. Education failing, they desperately resolved to resort to an unscrupulous combination of craft and violence which outraged every principle of justice. The object of the Society being to check new heresies in Europe and to crush old ones in Asia, they acted on the conviction that the end would justify the means, and they therefore resolved to remove the only obstacle which impeded their onward march.

The Bishop who at that time filled the See of St. Thomas, if it may be so called, was named Joseph, or, according to their custom, Mar[1]-Joseph. There are conflicting accounts of his consecration; one speaking of him as having been sent to Malabar by Andixa, another giving the Patriarch's name as Abdichio, and a third calling him Abba, or Hebed-Jesus.[2] The Portuguese historian, Gouvea, to whom we owe the account of these transactions, speaks in high terms of the Syrian Bishop. He commends him for his personal piety, his enlightened understanding, and his reforming zeal in certain doctrines of his Church. But we must read this commendation in the light of our knowledge of the antecedents of the Patriarch Hebed-Jesus, and his disciple Mar-Joseph. Of the

[1] Mar is the Syriac for Lord, or Lord Bishop.

[2] Gouvea's "Jornada," p. 7. Asseman, Tom. I., pp. 536-542. Geddes's "Church of Malabar," p. 11. Hough's "Christianity," Vol. I., p. 351.

former we have already heard, as making certain important concessions at the Council of Trent. Supposing this statement correct, we can easily account for Gouvea's applause; for, if Joseph was influenced by his Patriarch's subserviency, he was already more than half way to Rome. Nevertheless, his temporising conduct did not save him. He was still a Nestorian at heart, though he wished to be thought favourable to Romanism. To promote this idea he entered freely into Portuguese society; yet he failed to impress his new friends with an opinion of his honesty. Determined to bring the matter to a crisis, the crafty Jesuits set a trap for the poor Bishop. One day when teaching some Portuguese boys (probably spies) he cautioned them against praying to the Virgin Mary as the Mother of God. This was instantly reported to the Bishop of Cochin, who, delighted to catch his brother in so dreadful a heresy, immediately wrote to the Archbishop. An order came from headquarters for the arrest of Mar-Joseph, who was put on board a ship and dispatched to Goa. The Viceroy, perplexed and unwilling to adopt extreme measures, sent the Bishop to Europe; and thus, the shepherd being removed, the Jesuits at Cochin hoped to make short work with the flock. That the whole affair was a deeply-laid plot is frankly admitted, the old watchword stifling all scruples of conscience.[1]

[1] Gouvea's "Jornada," Cap. III. La Croze, Hist., Liv. I., p. 58.

On his arrival at Lisbon, he seems to have assumed an appearance of extraordinary sanctity. He thereby won the favour of the Queen Regent, Catarina, by whom he was sent back to Goa with royal letters to the Viceroy to see that he was instantly restored to his Bishopric. The reason of this sudden change in his favour is at once apparent, when we learn that he had given a solemn promise to the Cardinal Dom Henrique, then inquisitor-general, to do all in his power on his return to purify his Church from Nestorian heresy and to secure its full submission to the Roman See.

To return to the deserted Church. As soon as the Syrian Christians saw their Bishop thus suddenly seized and shipped off without trial, they sent a secret message to the Patriarch of Babylon, imploring him to consecrate, without loss of time, a new prelate to guard them against the assaults of the Portuguese missionaries. These had managed to penetrate the secret, and took every precaution by searching the ships and guarding the passes to prevent the new shepherd from reaching his mountain diocese.[1] But Mar-Abraham, in his turn, was duly informed of the snares, and travelling in disguise, arrived at the Serra in safety, where he was received with frantic joy. He had hardly made the acquaintance of his flock, when

[1] Gouvea, "Jornada." Geddes's Hist., p. 18. La Croze. Hough, Vol. I.

news came to him of the return of the Bishop Joseph to Goa, where his presence was as embarrassing to the authorities, civil and ecclesiastical, as it would prove to be in Malabar. Both Viceroy and Archbishop were bound to obey the royal letters, but they craftily requested Bishop Joseph to take back with him to Cochin several missionaries to instruct his flock in the Roman doctrine, language, and ritual. The vacillating Syrian craved time to consider the question; and next morning gravely informed the Archbishop that a vision had appeared to him in the night, forbidding his compliance. The Roman prelate, quickly detecting the imposture, exclaimed, "And I, too, have had a revelation far better than yours. Mine is in the Bible, in the words, 'Ye shall know them by their fruits.' You are a wolf in sheep's clothing, and I shall take good care to expose you to the royal family at Lisbon, on whose kindness you have imposed."[1] The Archbishop, however, offered no impediment to Bishop Joseph's return to his diocese, for he sagaciously perceived the great advantage to the Roman cause afforded by the presence of rival prelates. The creation of a schism would, he foresaw, be a golden opportunity for Papal aggression. The event proved the correctness of his judgment, for no sooner did Mar-Joseph appear on the scene, than the mountaineers were divided into two contending factions. Of

[1] Geddes's "Ch. of Malabar," p. 19.

course the old friends of the first Bishop naturally supported their early pastor; but he had evidently lost caste with the influential portion of the Church, who looked on him as at least tainted by Romish sympathies. Finding himself thus deserted by the majority of his co-religionists, he was compelled to seek for support from the very Church whose dearest aspirations were for the subjugation of his own. He wrote a violent letter to the Archbishop of Goa, denouncing his popular rival, not merely as a usurper, but as an implacable enemy to the Roman Church. The Viceroy, influenced by the prelate, was only too glad to avail himself of an opportunity so long desired. A dispatch was immediately sent to the Portuguese governor, ordering the arrest of Bishop Abraham. As the troops of the Rajah were combined with those of the Governor, no effectual resistance could be offered by the Christians of the Serra. Bishop Abraham was therefore torn from his flock, sent first to Goa, and then to Lisbon, whence he was to proceed to Rome, to be tried by the Pope himself. A gale of wind, however, changed all this. The ship was driven into Mozambique, and Bishop Abraham effected his escape, reaching Mosul in safety. The Patriarch of Babylon conferred on him new briefs to strengthen his claim, and urged him to return to his diocese. Mar-Abraham considered "discretion the better part of valour," and foresaw that "without the

Pope's order, the Portuguezes would quickly make the Serra too hot for him."[1] Instead of returning to Malabar, he set out for Italy, and on reaching the capital, he abjured Nestorianism, professed obedience to Rome, and promised to bring his Indian flock to the true faith. Pope Pius IV. then gave him all the necessary credentials, with the title of Archbishop. Another version of this story exists. The original ordination of Mar-Abraham being invalid, the Pope determined that he should receive all the orders from the tonsure to the priesthood. This done, he was sent to the Patriarch of Venice, and consecrated by the Archbishop to the see of Malabar. The object of his visit to Rome being thus gained, he landed in India under the imposing title of Archbishop of Angamale.[2]

While these things were going on in Italy, the other bishop, Mar-Joseph, resumed his public functions, and preached the very doctrines which he had abjured at Lisbon. The report soon flew to the Archbishop of Goa, who wrote to the Regent, Dom Henrique, who in his turn, appealed to the Pope. Pius V. immediately issued an order, dated 15th January, 1567, for the apprehension of the Bishop. He was arrested at Cochin, and sent off to Portugal, without any examination. He ended his life at Rome,[3] but when, or

[1] Geddes's Hist., p. 21.

[2] Gouvea, "Hist. Orient." Chap. III.

[3] Gouvea, p. 8. La Croze, p. 62. Raulin, p. 14. Du Jarric, p. 558.

how, we know not. Gouvea, our chief authority, is ominously silent ; and La Croze says, " We can have little doubt that this unhappy prelate became, at Rome, the victim of the Portuguese superstition, and of the Pope's inhumanity." [1]

The leading incidents in the thirty years' struggle will be sketched in the next chapter.

[1] La Croze, Lib. I., pp. 62-3.

CHAPTER IV.

THE STRUGGLE AGAINST ROME.

"Soon the overbearing policy of Rome began openly to assert itself, and the Christians of St. Thomas saw their independence threatened by men whom they regarded as little better than idolators in religion, and buccaneers in after life."—Kaye's "Christianity," p. 23.

"THESE repeated tyrannies of the Portuguezes in the Indies of dragging ancient Bishops thus out of their own country and diocese, and tumbling them so about the world, I cannot but reckon among those violent injustices for which God has punished them so visibly."[1] These are the quaint words in which the translator, or rather paraphraser, of Gouvea's "Jornada" expresses his opinion of the conduct of the Portuguese to their Christian brethren; and the reader will find this judgment corroborated by another well-known historian.[2] Similar violence was exercised in their method of converting the heathen. Insatiable in their thirst for gold, and not satisfied with the numerous concessions they had obtained from the

[1] Geddes's History, p. 22.

[2] Manoel De Faria, "Asia Portuguesa," Vol. III., last chapter.

native princes, they were perpetually encroaching on the surrounding states, their arrogance and rapacity augmenting with their prosperity. The result was a deeply-rooted and widely-spread feeling of resentment against men who, professing to be the possessors and propagators of a pure faith, were everywhere conspicuous for avarice and tyranny, robbery and insolence. Portuguese and native testimony concur to place this beyond dispute. In the Asiatic researches there is an interesting article showing the Mohammedan view of these compulsory conversions, in which the following passage occurs :—"They did also put Hajes and other Mussulmans to a variety of cruel deaths, and they reviled and abused with unworthy epithets the Prophet of Goa; and confined the Mohammedans, and loaded them with heavy irons, carrying them about for sale from shop to shop as slaves; enhancing their ill-usage on these occasions in order to extort the larger sum for their release. They confined them also in dark, noisome, and hideous dungeons, torturing them also with fire,"[1] and much more to the same effect. Further proof of the impression produced by the Portuguese may be found in the letters and speeches of a Mohammedan prince named Hidalcon, who besieged Goa in 1570. In one of his letters to the Viceroy he says :—"I am con-

[1] "Asiatic Researches," Vol. V., p. 20. Hough's History, Vol. I. p. 264.

fident the King of Portugal will not thank any that shall be instrumental in making a breach between me and him by compelling my subjects against their wills to turn Christians, a practice that is abominable in the sight of all the world ; nay, I am confident that Jesus Christ himself, the God whom you adore, cannot be well pleased with such service as this ; force and compulsion in all such cases being what God, Kings, and all the people of the world do abominate." In another letter the Prince thanks the Portuguese Governor for having issued an order to repress these violent measures, but complains that it was ineffectual, adding, "as I know that neither God nor wise Kings take any delight in discord, so I am certain that there is no religion in the world that justifies the forcing of people from one religion to another." Commenting on these remarkable transactions, Chancellor Geddes says: "In this affair the Christian and Mahometan, of which sect this Hidalcon was, seemed to have changed parts, the Mahometan writing therein like a Christian, and the Christians behaving themselves like Mahometans."[1] The reader must not suppose that these atrocities were restricted to the civil and military powers, or the pirates who, under the name of merchants, robbed as often as they traded. The chronicles of the time afford abundant proof that Ecclesiastics were no longer the imitators of the

[1] Geddes's "Hist. Mal.," p. 27.

gentle Xavier. A few years of conquest had sufficed to convince them that the arm of the civil power was a far more effectual instrument of conversion than the tongue or bell of the missionary. The Dominicans, for example, pretending to erect a convent, built a fortress on the island of Solor, which was soon garrisoned by a strong body of Portuguese. The unsuspecting natives were enraged at this deception; constant skirmishes took place between the intruders and themselves, and not a few of the monks fell, sword in hand, obtaining what they were pleased to call the crown of martyrdom in this singular method of converting the heathen. Another instance may be quoted. One of the missionaries, appropriately named Vinagre, actually commanded a fleet, sent by Portugal to aid its ally, the Rajah of Tidore, in the Moluccas. He is said to have been quite as successful in the art of war as in the propagation of the Gospel, at one time in full armour, at another in full canonicals. And, if the historian does not over-colour the narrative, the soldier-monk was in such haste to baptise his converts that he put the surplice over the breast-plate. Antonio Galvão, an eminent Portuguese navigator, is said to have assisted Vinagre in this work; but they appear to have professionally changed places; for Galvão, though he introduced Christianity as a means of civilisation, made himself so beloved by the conquered people at Tidore and Ternate, that popular songs were composed in his honour. No doubt there were many pious Christians amongst the Portuguese, and to such we would render all praise, but after a careful examination of evidence on both sides, we are forced to the conclusion, fully justified by the History of the Inquisition at Goa,[1] that Christian persuasion was quite the exception in the Portuguese system of conversion, and persecution the almost universal rule.

This digression from our main subject is more apparent than real, our object being to show the spirit of the age, and especially that of the Portuguese nation. The people of India live upon traditions. An impression once made is rarely effaced. The terrible tales of Portuguese atrocities have been handed down from father to son in the mountains and valleys of India for the last three centuries. Conquest and Christianity, cruelty and conversion, are linked together indissolubly in the Hindoo mind. And if these traditions inspire the native heart with abhorrence and disgust, the lamentable exposure of the frauds connected with the Madura mission in the XVIIth Century produced unmitigated contempt. The considerations cannot be omitted in estimating the influence which the Portuguese missions exerted in Southern India, not only on the Syrian Christians,

[1] Geddes's "View of the Inquisition in Portugal;" Dellon's "Relation de l'Inquisition de Goa." Buchanan's "Christian Researches," p. 166. Canon Trevor's "India," p. 151. Hough's "Christ," Vol. I., p. 212.

but on all classes of the native population and on modern missionary efforts throughout our Eastern Empire.

We need not therefore feel surprised that the universal indignation found vent in prophecies of the downfall of Portuguese power. "Let them alone, said a Hindoo, for they will quickly come to lose that, as covetous merchants, which they have gained as admirable soldiers; they now conquer Asia, but it will not be long before Asia conquers them."[1] Nor was it long ere these predictions began to be fulfilled, as the natives of Ito succeeded in expelling the Portuguese from their island, the first check to their hitherto victorious career, and the first step in the downward path to the present melancholy condition of their dominions in the East.

We must now return to Mar-Abraham, whom we left just after his re-consecration as Bishop, or Archbishop, of Augamale. On arriving at Goa, he was happy to find his rival Mar-Joseph "shipped off for Portugal"; and he therefore flattered himself that he would be able to pass the remainder of his life in the quiet possession of his see. This, however, was no such easy matter. The Portuguese no longer had any use for him as an instrument in maintaining a schism. So, in spite of his credentials, they detained him at Goa, on pretence of examining the Papal

[1] Geddes, p. 28.

briefs. The crafty canonists, though unable to deny the validity of the documents, were at no loss to detect certain flaws, and the Archbishop decided that his appointment was null and void. Mar-Abraham, instead of being welcomed by his Cattanars and his flocks amid the green hills of Malayalim was put under arrest in the Dominican convent, there to await the Pope's reply to the Archbishop's report of the case. Fully aware that this was only another form of imprisonment for life, he took the law into his own hands; and one night while the Dominicans were in chapel, he escaped and reached his diocese in safety.[1] Consternation prevailed at Goa. All the authorities on the coast were informed of the flight and ordered to secure the Bishop, dead or alive. But he took good care never to venture near any of the Portuguese settlements. His conduct as a Bishop seems to have been as undecided as that of his predecessor. On the one hand he professed himself a Romanist, and re-ordained all the Syrian priests. On the other hand he not only preached the Nestorian doctrines, but publicly prayed for the Bishop of Babylon as the Head of his Church. Intelligence of this state of affairs soon reached Gregory XIII.,[2] who, in 1578, commanded the Syrian Bishop to attend the next Provincial Council at Goa, and to be governed by its

[1] Gouvea, p. 8. La Croze, p. 63. Raulin, p. 15. Du Jarric, p. 558.
[2] Raulin, "Hist. Ecc. Malab.," p. 15.

decrees. Whereupon, the fifth Archbishop of Goa, Vincente de Fouseca, called a council, and commanded the attendance of Mar-Abraham under letters of safe conduct.[1] The poor Bishop felt that he had no alternative; for, if he resisted, Portuguese troops would lay waste his diocese. He therefore attended the council, abjured his faith, swore to Romanism and to the punctual execution of the decrees of the Synod. He further promised to alter or burn all the heretical books, and to re-ordain all his clergy, thus making the fatal admission that the Orders of the Syrian Church were invalid.[2] This done, his next perplexity was how to justify himself before his own Patriarch. He wrote a sad letter, exhibiting the straits to which he was reduced, "the Portuguese hanging over his head as a hammer over an anvil."[3] He alleged that the Profession of Faith which he had made was not understood (from the difference of language) by the council at Goa, and that he was as firm as ever in his fidelity to the Syrian Church. He added that "being grown ancient, and very much broke by the long and unintermitting persecutions of the Portuguezes," he desired the assistance of a coadjutor.

[1] La Croze, p. 65. Geddes, p. 32.

[2] The reasons given by the Romanists for forcing Bishop Abraham to take this step are stated at length from p. 33 to p. 37 of Geddes's "Church of Malabar."

[3] "Os Portugueses estavão sobre sua cabeça como malhos sobre bigorna."—Gouvea, p. 9. Raulin, p. 16.

The Suffragan, Mar-Simeon, soon became so popular with the Syrian Christians, on account of his freedom from Romish contamination, that he felt himself strong enough to declare his independence of his superior, and to set up a rival See at Carturte.[1] Again a schism arose. Anathemas were reciprocated. The whole diocese was in a ferment; and Abraham, losing ground, complained of Simeon as a usurper and a heretic.[2] The Viceroy, though by no means a friend of Mar-Abraham's, was forced to acknowledge him as Bishop of Augamale in virtue of the Papal appointment; and therefore determined to take his part against Mar-Simeon. Feeling, however, that it would be difficult, if not dangerous, to employ force, he induced some Franciscans to excite in Mar-Simeon's mind a doubt of his Ecclesiastical position, so as to render a journey to Rome necessary for security and peace. He went with the Friars to Cochin; and thence to Goa, Lisbon, and Rome, where, to his intense astonishment, Sixtus V. declared him not to be in Holy Orders at all! Thus sentenced, or deprived, he was forwarded to Philip II., at that time King of Spain and Portugal, who committed him to Alexis de Menezes, then starting for Goa as Archbishop. The Syrian Prelate, however, instead of

[1] Raulin, "Hist. Ecc. Mal.," p. 16. Du Jarric, p. 561.

[2] "Excommunicationes inde ac anathœmeta (res ridicula quasi missilia, alter in alterum mutuo intorquet."—Raulin, "Hist. Ecc. Mal.," p. 11.

accompanying the Portuguese Metropolitan, was thrown into the Franciscan convent in Lisbon. From his prison he wrote to his Vicar-General, Jacob, by every fleet that went to India, professing fidelity to the faith of his fathers and claiming his Episcopal rank. Years afterwards these letters fell into the hands of Archbishop Menezes, by whom they were sent to the Inquisitor-General of Portugal. The result is not recorded. But the unfortunate Syrian's fate was, no doubt, hastened by the arrival of these letters, the dungeons of the Inquisition finishing what the Franciscan convents had begun.

Following this complicated history we must return to Goa, where, in 1590, another Provincial Council was convened, and Bishop Abraham summoned to attend. But the aged Prelate, taught by experience, refused to trust the Portuguese. He was possibly influenced in his determination by some feeling of remorse for his former conduct, and for the ruin that he had brought on Joseph and Simeon. Be the cause what it may, he stood firm, maintained the Chaldean faith and defied the Roman power. Clement VIII., duly informed of this contumacy, commanded the Archbishop, in 1595, to enquire into the crimes of the rebellious Prelate, and, if guilty, to commit him to prison.[1] The Papal brief further ordered that a

[1] This mandate of Clement VIII., dated 27th January, 1595, is quoted at length in Gouvea's "Jornada," p. 10,

Vicar-Apostolic should be placed over the diocese, and that no Chaldean bishop should be suffered to enter Malabar. Archbishop Menezes obeyed, found Mar-Abraham guilty, without going through the useless form of summoning the bed-ridden victim to appear at Goa; and having learnt that application had been made to Babylon for a Suffragan and successor, he ordered all the passes to be guarded, so that no Chaldean priest should enter. Every expedient was adopted to elude his vigilance. Disguised as Indians they came by land, as sailors they entered the Port of Cochin, but were always stopped, sent home or imprisoned, and thus the diocese remained without a head.

The Archbishop, delighted by this success, pursued his enterprise with zeal. He first addressed himself to Mar-Simeon's Vicar-General, imploring him to submit and promising him the most ample rewards. But Jacob was deaf to all his entreaties, refused to throw away his commission, and inflamed still more his excited flock against their relentless tormentors. Menezes was equally urgent with the other side, entreating the aged Mar-Abraham and his energetic representative, the Archdeacon, to reduce the diocese to the Roman obedience, but with no better success than in the other case.

Two deaths now cleared the way for the Archbishop's triumph. The first was that of Jacob,

Simeon's Vicar-General, whose sudden decease, under singular circumstances, was interpreted as a judgment on him for resistance to the true faith.[1] The second was that of the Syrian Bishop Abraham, in February, 1597. Worn out by controversy, but still firm in his religion, he refused the rites of the Romish Church, forced upon him in his dying moments by two Jesuits from Vaipacotta, and to remove all doubts of his position, he left express orders that he should be buried in the modest cathedral which he had built amongst the woods at Augamale.

Thus ended the first part of the struggle.

[1] Gouvea, "Hist. Jornada."

CHAPTER V.

THE ARCHBISHOP OF GOA.

"Dom Alexis de Menezes was appointed Archbishop of Goa. It was his mission less to make new converts than to reduce old ones to subjection; and he flung himself into the work of persecution with an amount of zeal and heroism that must have greatly endeared him to Rome."—KAYE.

DOM ALEXIS DE MENEZES, whose actions form the principal subject of this chapter, was an Austin Friar, and was the seventh Archbishop of Goa, a see founded by Paul III. in 1537. He was Governor-General of India for three years, was afterwards translated to the Primacy of Braga, was Governor of Portugal for two years, and after that was President of the Council of State of Portugal at Madrid, where he died. It would be foreign to our purpose to give his biography here; and his character, no ordinary one, will be gleaned by the intelligent reader from our brief sketch of his trenchant decision, consummate craft, and dauntless courage in overthrowing the Church of St. Thomas, and raising that of St. Peter on its ruins.

On the very day that Archbishop Menezes received

at Damaon the news of Mar-Abraham's death, he appointed the Jesuit, Francisco Ros, Governor and Vicar-Apostolical of the vacant see. Three months afterwards, the Archbishop held a meeting at Goa concerning the Syrian Church, and the result was that, in spite of the Pope's orders that none but a Roman Catholic should be appointed, it was deemed expedient to nominate the Archdeacon.[1] To please all parties, the office was put in commission, the three officials being the Archdeacon, the Jesuit Ros, and the Rector of Vaipacotta. But when the Archdeacon was required to subscribe to the creed of Pius IV., he declined, alleging that he objected to the other commissioners. And Menezes, though detecting the pretext, dissembled for the present, and made him sole governor. The Archdeacon, pursuing a temporary policy, accepted his patent, though under protest that it gave him no more authority than what he previously possessed, and still declined subscription, hoping for a Bishop from the Patriarch. Pressed still further by the Romanists, he declared positively that he would

[1] The Archdeacon who plays so conspicuous a part in the following chapters was named George, and is thus spoken of by Raulin :—"Georgius homo dolis instructus, et vulpern in pectore servans."—Raulin, "Hist. Ecc. Mal.," p. 20. There was but one of this title amongst the Malabar Christians, and he seems to have exercised the office of a sort of deputy during the life of the Bishop, and that of substitute or representative when the see was vacant. Archdeacon George was a man of the highest family, and had exercised quasi-episcopal functions during the declining years of Mar-Abraham, who, when dying, committed the Church of the Syrian Christians to his care.

not submit to the Pontiff, for that the Church of St. Thomas always had been, and always should be, independent of Rome. To strengthen his resistance, he convened a Synod at Augamale. There Cattanars and laymen alike swore to defend the faith of their fathers, to accept none but a Bishop of their own Church, and to maintain this solemn league and covenant to the death.

Popular excitement was now at its height. The poor mountaineers, who had at first welcomed their Roman fellow-Christians so warmly, were thoroughly excited against their oppressors. They looked upon the Portuguese as the relentless enemies of their ancient faith, and as the barbarous persecutors of their beloved bishops and priests. They therefore rose in arms, expelled the Jesuits from their country, and in two instances were barely restrained from putting them to death. The news of this terrible outbreak, though it frightened the ordinary "Soldiers of the Pope," served but to stimulate the resolute Archbishop, who determined to crush this rebellion by his personal presence. In vain did the Archbishop and the whole clergy of Goa implore him to refrain from so perilous an enterprise. He resolved, as soon as the war between Mangate and Paru (two small Malabar states) had ceased, to subdue the storm which he had raised, contenting himself meantime with an appeal to the Archdeacon. That dignitary, alarmed at the Archbishop's announcement, pretended that he had refused subscription because the Rector of Vaipacotta was commanded to receive it, but that he would sign before any other priest (not a Jesuit) duly commissioned. But Menezes, considering this an attempt to render the Jesuits unpopular, because they were the most active proselytisers, refused to comply. This refusal gave great and just offence, not only to the Syrians, but also to the Romanists; for the other orders loudly declared that the Archbishop was so infatuated with the Jesuits that he would rather lose the Syrian Church than offend the Order. The brethren, it seems, did not reciprocate the Archbishop's affection, at least they had done their best (in a work which we often quote in this history) to deprive him of what he believed his chief honour, the conversion of the Syrian Christians, or rather, the reduction of their Church to the Roman obedience.[1] In this historical romance we have an entirely new version of the story (a Jesuit's, be it remembered) to the effect that Mar-Abraham loved the Jesuits, was governed by them in all things, invited the Rector to his death-bed, committed his flock to the care of the Pope, commanded all his clergy to obey the Brethren of the Society, and to accept as truth all that they taught. Furthermore, this veracious

[1] "History of the Jesuits in India." By Pierre du Jarric, Bordeaux, 1608.

narrative asserts that the Syrian Church was so completely reconciled, that in 1596 they celebrated with joy the Jubilee of Clement VIII., crowding the churches till midnight. The Archbishop of Goa had therefore no conflict, but simply enjoyed a triumph where the Jesuits had won the battle.[1]

Trifles often lead to great events; and an incident occurred at this time which plainly proved that the Syrian clergy were not yet the slaves of the Pope. One of the boys of the Jesuits' College had been taught to pray for the Pope before the Patriarch. The Cattanars, overhearing this one day in church, beat him and turned him out. They spoke also to his father to repeat the chastisement. The Archbishop, hearing of this, wrote to Archdeacon George, ordering him to punish those impudent heretics, but, so far from obeying the Roman Prelate, he commended the zeal of his own priests. A Franciscan Friar was therefore sent from Goa to request once more the Archdeacon's subscription, and to insist on his punishing the Cattanars. The Syrian, anxious, at any price, to keep the Archbishop out of the Serra, at last subscribed *a* confession, though not that of Pius IV., professing himself a Catholic, but avoiding the word Roman. It is, however, affirmed that he afterwards gave his assent publicly to the creed of Pius IV., read to him in Portuguese, of which he

[1] Geddes's "Hist. Ch. Mal.," p. 49.

knew nothing. Be that as it may, he everywhere taught that though the Pope was Head of the Roman Church, he had nothing whatever to do with the Syrian. Irritated by these vexatious delays, the indomitable Prelate fixed a day for his personal visit to the headquarters of these rebellious Christians. The Viceroy's remonstrance was answered thus:—"My life is but too secure, as I have never done enough to win the martyr's crown."[1] Still he did not rely too much on his want of merit, and therefore travelled with an armed escort. His journey, too, was partly political, as the Viceroy wished to secure the co-operation of the Zamorin in destroying a nest of pirates at Cunhale. On the 27th September, 1598, the Archbishop embarked in a war galley, and on Epiphany was saluted at Cunhale by the guns and music of the Portuguese Fleet. Here he held a Council of War, sent dispatches to Goa, inspected the siege works, and, after these Apostolical proceedings, set sail for Cananore, and thence to Cochin. The grandest preparations had been made for his reception, richly carpeted stairs had been expressly constructed; the Governor and a brilliant staff were at the landing place, and the Prince of the Church disembarked amid the waving of flags, the clang of martial music, the shouts of the people, and the thunder of artillery.

[1] Gouvea, "Jornada," Cap. IX., p. 26. Raulin, "Hist. Ecc. Mal.," p. 22. La Croze, p. 101. Du Jarric, p. 574.

Gouvea, with his characteristic prolixity, enters into the most minute details of councils, negotiations, intrigues, in which the Archbishop, the King of Cochin, and the Zamorin are the principal actors. But they are totally uninteresting to the general reader, and have little or no relation to our subject.[1]

The Roman Prelate, having discharged his political and military duties, thought himself bound to devote some attention to the ostensible object of his mission. He therefore sent for Archdeacon George; and, as no notice was taken, he wrote again, enclosing a letter of safe conduct. The perplexed Syrian assembled his Presbyters. After a long discussion, they were forced to admit that they were at last reduced to a most painful position. They saw clearly that the wily Archbishop had laid his measures well, and that the game was now in his own hands; for, as the Rajahs, in whose dominions the Syrian Churches were, had formed an alliance with the Portuguese, there could be no difficulty in inducing the native Princes to destroy their Christian subjects if they attempted to resist their oppressors. They therefore resolved to send their President with instructions to consent to the Archbishop's saying Mass, and preaching in their churches, but to resist all his claims to exercise

[1] The curious student will find full particulars in Gouvea, and in La Croze; in Geddes, an abridgment, pp. 54-5-6; and in Hughes's "Christ.," Vol. I., p. 336.

Episcopal functions. They further determined that if he insisted on such acts, they should temporise until they exhausted his patience, and forced him back to Goa. They then sent messengers through the mountains, and soon mustered a force of three thousand skilled marksmen for the defence of their Archdeacon and their faith. The Archbishop, too, appealed to force, for he requested the presence of the Paniquais,[1] chiefs who could bring four thousand men into the field, but they, instead of going to Cochin, took the oath of Amonços,[2] *i.e.*, they solemnly swore to defend their Archdeacon, if they died in his cause. Guarded right and left by two of these champions, and at the head of an imposing force of well-armed mountaineers, the Archdeacon appeared before Cochin. The Portuguese Governor, with a splendid retinue, courteously received the Syrians outside the gates, and conducted them with great ceremony to the Episcopal Palace. The scene must

[1] Hough explains the name to signify "Captains not unlike feudal lords, or independent chieftains," Vol. I., p. 341. But the original authorities give a different account. Gouvea ("Jornada," Chap. X., p. 29) gives a long description of this singular institution, the substance of which is that these Paniquais were a caste of fencing masters, whose pupils became their vassals or retainers, and whom they could command by thousands. "Les Malabars appellent Paniquals, les maistres d'escrime auxquels ils portent un si grand respect que tous ceux qui ont este leurs éleves, leur obeyissent durant toute leur vie."—Du Jarric, p. 575.

[2] "Amonços entre les Malabars sont des gens desesperez qui jurét de mourir en ce qu'ils enteprenné."—Du Jarric.

have been very striking. The Primate of India, seated on his throne, rose to receive the Archdeacon, who knelt and kissed his hand. The long train of Syrian priests followed his example. The principal laity, including the two Paniquais guards, were in turn also presented. Faithful to their oath, these officers stood with naked broadswords, close to their Archdeacon, on the watch for the slightest indication of treachery. An accident had nearly led to fatal consequences, for, the door of the audience-chamber closing, the three thousand Syrians who crowded round the building shouted "To arms! to arms!" thinking that their Archdeacon was taken prisoner. Swords were drawn, arquebuses loaded, matches lighted, and the doors assailed with cries of "Let us die for the Archdeacon and the Church of St. Thomas," when a stentorian voice of a Latin priest, who understood Tamil, succeeded in convincing them that the Archdeacon was safe and incurred no danger whatever. This stormy episode ended, the conference went on by means of interpreters, much as in a modern durbar; and it was finally agreed that the Metropolitan should begin his visitation at Vaipacotta, and that the Assyrian ecclesiastics should meet him there. On the day appointed, a procession of Jesuit professors and students conducted the Archbishop, mitre on head and crozier in hand, to the church, where he preached from John x., 1.: "He that entereth not by the door," &c.[1] His object, of course, was to prove that the Roman Church was the only true one, and that, therefore, the bishops and priests of the Syrian Faith were thieves and robbers, that the whole Church was in deadly schism, and doomed to perdition if they did not accept the salvation now offered. Archdeacon George, for obvious reasons, did not appear till two days after these proceedings, yet he was most courteously received by the dissembling Prelate. During the Archbishop's stay at the College of the Jesuit missionaries, he of course attended Matins and Vespers, but these being sung in Chaldee were unintelligible to him. Learning, however, that the Patriarch of Babylon was mentioned in the prayers by the title of Universal Pastor of the Church,—a stroke of conciliatory policy on the part of the Jesuits—he was perfectly horrified, and summoned the professors and students, the Archdeacon and Cattanars, into his presence. Addressing them with great vehemence, he declared that the Pope alone was supreme, and the Patriarch of Babylon a heretic and schismatic. Then, producing a formal excommunication, he commanded his secretary to read it aloud, and his interpreter to translate it, enjoining

[1] Gouvea, "Jornada," Cap. X., p. 29. Raulin, "Hist. Ecc. Mal.," p. 23. La Croze, "Hist. Du Christ.," p. 103. Du Jarric, Hist., p. 578.

that no person do henceforward presume to pray for the Patriarch of Babylon. He then turned sharply round to the Archdeacon with the brief command, "Sign it." The terrified Syrian stood aghast and wavered. Seizing the moment of hesitation, the resolute Primate pressed his advantage—"Sign it, Father, for it is full time the axe were laid to the root of the tree." The Archdeacon was speechless. He quailed beneath the stern eye and sharp voice of the Roman Primate. Slowly and silently he took the pen, signed the deed, and with it the doom of his Church.[1]

The report of this cowardly concession spread like wild-fire through the village. At first the rumour was utterly disbelieved, but when the excited crowd saw the fatal document fixed on the gates of the church, there was no longer room for doubt. They rushed frantically to the Archdeacon's house, when they cried out that the Archbishop of Goa and his Portuguese had come to destroy their religion and to insult their Patriarch. Railing against the Archdeacon as a traitor, they implored their Cattanars to let them fight for their faith and take vengeance on its enemies. But, on his raising his hand, they were instantly silent. "There was a time for all things," he said, "but this was the time for dissimulation, not revenge; that he

[1] Gouvea, "Jornada, Cap. X., p. 30. La Croze, "Hist. Du Christ.," p. 106. Du Jarric, Hist., p. 580. Raulin, "Hist., Ecc. Mal.," p. 24.

had signed the excommunication through fear of the joint revenge of the Archbishop and the Rajah of Cochin, but that he would rather die than consent to change his old religion for Popery, that he clearly saw that the Archbishop of Goa wished to make himself Primate of all India, but that he hoped all the Syrian Christians would resist even to the death." A tremulous shout was the answer to this address. "We would die sooner than yield" rang a thousand times in the air, and struck terror into the hearts of all the Portuguese, except the Archbishop himself. His panic-stricken attendants implored him to seek safety in flight, upbraiding him with his rashness; but he calmly replied that he did not repent of a single step, and that so far from retreating to Cochin he would advance to Paru. At this little metropolis, the Christian nobility had made great preparations for the reception of the Portuguese Primate, but, hearing of his conduct at Vaipacotta, their rage knew no bounds; they tore down their triumphal arches, and received him with stern looks and fully armed. Alexis de Menezes was equal to the occasion. Affecting not to see the sullen aspect of the citizens, he went straight to the church, his Cross borne before him. There an extraordinary sight presented itself. The sacred edifice was crowded to excess, but not a woman was to be seen. Men only, armed to the teeth, sternly awaited the appearance of their oppressor. Nothing daunted, the Archbishop, to prevent a collision, sent all his guards on board, retaining but two priests to assist in the service. Then, calmly robing himself in his pontificals, he blessed the congregation, and preached for an hour and a half. All listened in respectful silence, till he invited them to submit to confirmation. Then their suppressed fury burst forth, and they called out tumultuously, "We will never be confirmed by you—confirmation is no Sacrament of Christ's—we will not be slaves—you shall never touch our beards or our wife's faces. Go home to your Portuguese and let us alone, if you continue to plague us, it will cost you dear," and much more to the same purpose. This storm produced no effect on the preacher. Quietly sitting down, he pursued his subject; but when they refused to listen he rose up, and, advancing firmly, crozier in hand, he exclaimed, with great vehemence, that the doctrine he preached was the Faith of Christ and of St. Thomas, that it was believed by all Christians, and that he was ready to die in confirmation of its truth. After much more discussion, the time-serving Archdeacon left the church, picked up ten boys in the streets, and presented them for confirmation. This noisy service over, the Archbishop was forced to content himself with this paltry triumph, and retreated angrily to his galleys.[1]

[1] Gouvea, "Jornada," Cap. X. La Croze, Hist., p. 108. Raulin, "Hist. Ecc. Mal.," p. 24. Du Jarric, p. 582.

We should utterly exhaust the patience of the reader if we were to insist on his following the Archbishop through his visitation. The pages of Gouvea are filled with minute accounts of perpetual fencing between the Primate and the Syrian Archdeacon, each endeavouring to outwit the other. The Asiatic, in this case, as in many others, was no match for the European, and the whole history reminds one of the ineffectual flutterings of the poor bird to escape from the fascinating gaze of the serpent.

The historian of the "Jornada" is, however, worthy of consultation by the student who wishes to enjoy a picturesque narrative in the curious Portuguese of the XVIth Century. The English reader may consult Chancellor Geddes's equally curious translation, or the more polished English of Hough's Paraphrase of Geddes.

We shall therefore hasten to give the barest possible outline of the events that preceded the Synod of Diamper, noticing only such incidents as serve to indicate the irrepressible determination of the Primate, the ever varying means that he employed to effect his purpose, and the dangers that he encountered in subduing the Syrians to the Roman obedience. Failing, as we have seen, at Paru,[1] he set out for Mangate, and incurred, on two occasions, great danger from attempts at assassination, at least according to Gouvea

[1] Often spelt Parour, close to Cranganor.

and his Jesuit copyists;[1] but La Croze doubts the stories as inconsistent with the character of the Christians, who could easily have dispatched the Archbishop on many occasions, had they felt so disposed. During the night, the Primate's barge conducted him to Chegurce in the kingdom of Cochin, where he found the church door shut against him.[2] He waited patiently till sunset, and then ordered his servants to force open the doors that he might pray at the altar. His visit to Chegurce being thus fruitless, his friends implored him to proceed no further in his visitation, but he answered resolutely "That their remonstrance, though kindly meant, was in vain, that he was determined to complete his visitation, even if he should travel alone throughout the diocese; that he was not only Metropolitan of India, but the successor of St. Thomas, in whose powerful intercession he placed all his hopes." Violent measures had thus been attended with but slight success; and Menezes thought it prudent to make some attempt at conciliation. Retiring to his cabin, he wrote a long letter to Archdeacon George, inviting him to a conference, and promising forgiveness of the past, and rewards in the future. Then followed a public discussion, between the Archbishop and the Archdeacon, in which the whole controversy of Nestorianism was

[1] Gouvea, Cap. XI.

[2] Gouvea, "Jornada," Chap. X., p. 34. Du Jarric "Hist. Ecc. Mal.," p. 587.

passed under review.[1] Of course, the infallibility and supremacy of the Roman Pontiff were stoutly maintained by one side, and as stoutly denied by the other. The disputants came at last to this agreement, that as soon as possible a Synod should be convened to settle the points under discussion, that meantime Archbishop Menezes should be courteously received in their churches and allowed to preach, but that he should not perform any episcopal act; that, further, Archdeacon George should refrain from exciting the people, and should dismiss his armed escort. This concordat being signed, the rivals parted at Canhur, and the Archbishop proceeded to the south on March 1st. On his way, at a castle near Cochin, he received a visit from the Rajah late at night in the house of the village priest. The Indian prince came in great state, with a large retinue in shining armour, attended by bearers of lanterns and torches. The King himself naked to the waist, with a skirt of gorgeous silk, his head, neck, wrists and ankles in golden chains studded with the richest jewels.[2] All this display of magnificence had an object, the claim to be called brother-in-arms of the King of Portugal, like his neighbour the Rajah of Cochin. The Primate quickly saw that this was another instrument ready

[1] Gouvea, Cap. XII. Du Jarric, Hist., p. 589. La Croze Hist., p. 118. Hough, Vol. I., p. 366. Geddes, Hist., p. 68.

[2] Gouvea, "Jornada," p. 36. Du Jarric Hist., p. 592. Raulin, "Hist. Ecc. Mal.," p. 527. Geddes, "Hist. Ch. Mal.," p. 72.

for use when wanted, and he promised to obtain the title in return for service rendered. Next day Menezes went to church, where he took the first opportunity of breaking the agreement, for he not only said Mass, but confirmed the whole congregation.[1] At Molandurte the Syrian Christians received him so kindly that he again broke the convention of Chegurce by confirming and performing other episcopal acts. This naturally irritated the Archdeacon, who, justly considering the compact broken, sent circulars to all the churches to hold no communion with the Primate. He wrote also to the Rajahs, warning them of the design of Menezes to take away their subjects, and make them Portuguese vassals. The King of Cochin took the alarm, punished the Christians of Molandurte for their hospitality to Menezes, and ordered them to go to their Archdeacon at Augamale. We next find the crusading Archbishop at Diamper,[2] where, learning that there had been no ordination in the diocese for

[1] This wholesale style of confirmation implies a mere opus operatum; for, of course, there could not possibly be the slightest opportunity of ascertaining the fitness of the recipients Yet there can be no doubt of the fact, for Gouvea repeatedly uses such expressions as this, "Chrismon *todo* o povo sem contradicção alquã," p. 29. And the Jesuit compiler Du Jarric says, "Apres le serment, il leur commandait de retourner le lendemain à l'eglise pour recevoir le S. Sacrament de la confirmation. Ce qu 'ils firent, sans contredit, tellement qu'il donna á tous le tel Sacrament."—Hist., p. 579.

[2] Geddes is evidently at fault in his geography when, at p. 78, he says the Archbishop "*set sail for Diamper*," inasmuch as this famous little town is fourteen miles inland.

more than two years, he announced his intention of ordaining on the Saturday before the fifth Sunday in Lent.[1] The Archdeacon was naturally astounded at this intelligence, and wrote to the Primate in the strongest terms protesting against this flagrant violation of their compact, and declaring that if he persevered in his intention, there was not the slightest use in convening the Synod. The artful Portuguese, suspecting the Archdeacon to be as great a hypocrite as himself, replied that nothing should prevent him from ordaining at the time named, nay more, that he would perform all the other functions of a Bishop in obedience to the Papal briefs. The Archdeacon rejoined entreating him to limit the ordination to the Latins.[2] The Archbishop's answer was short, sharp, and decisive: "I will ordain both Latins and Syrians, for it is my duty to abolish such distinctions, and make one fold under one shepherd, the Pope." The Archdeacon, in desperation, wrote again to the Rajahs of Cochin, and other states, conjuring them to prevent this monstrous aggression on civil as well as ecclesiastical liberty. The Prince of Cochin, in whose dominions Diamper is, especially requested the Primate to refrain, but Menezes haughtily replied, "That though

[1] Hough calls this Palm Sunday—History, Vol. I., p. 385.

[2] *i.e.*, the students of the Jesuits' College whether Portuguese or natives; "for so they called not only the Portuguezes but all the Malabars who were bred under the Jesuites."—Geddes, "Hist. Ch. Mal.," p. 78.

he should obey them as sovereigns, he would brook no interference from infidels in matters of faith." The Archdeacon also published an edict prohibiting candidates from receiving Roman Orders, and forbidding the parish priests to hold communion with the Primate. He sent a special olla[1] to the Cattanars of Diamper, ordering them to prevent the threatened ordination. A popular tumult was the immediate result. The Chief Priest went to the Archbishop, and commanded him instantly to leave the town. The Primate, unshaken in his resolution, smiled at the demonstration, and continued his work as if nothing had been said. The Rajah of Cochin sent a peremptory order to the Governor of Diamper, to interrupt the service if attempted; and the Nairs[2] marched up to the church, and dashed their shields against the doors as a declaration of war. These threats alarmed the Portuguese, who implored their leader to save his life by flight. As usual, he was firm, and next morning he determined to proceed with the ordination in spite of the Rajah's prohibition. At daybreak he found that an order had been issued that no one was to leave his house, enter the church, or have any communication with the Portuguese. A singular Malabar custom accompanied this edict, for branches of trees were

[1] *i.e.*, leaf. The natives of Malabar and other parts of India write upon palm leaves with an iron pen.

[2] The soldier caste or fighting men. Gouvea, "Jornada," Chap. XII., p. 39.

placed across the threshold of the doors, and a barrier of bushes formed all around the church.[1] These measures were just a day too late. Menezes, ever on the alert, suspected the trick, or perhaps had received private information, for he had collected all the candidates in the church the night before, and next morning ordained thirty-seven or thirty-eight of them after subscription to the creed of Pius IV., and an oath of obedience to the Pope.[2] This masterpiece of policy accomplished, he left Diamper, visited several churches in the small kingdom of Pimenta; at Mangalan was in danger, it is said, from the matchlocks of the Nairs, and reached Carturte, on April 1st, the Friday before Palm Sunday. On Saturday he said Mass and preached. In the afternoon he sent for choristers from Cochin, and on Palm Sunday had High Mass performed with all the magnificence of a Cathedral service. But the impression produced was not admiration but aversion, and the popular resentment was increased by the ejection of the regular Syrian service to make way for the Roman, by his stopping the customary offerings, and by his attempt to introduce auricular confession. A popular tumult was the result. The Portuguese were insulted in the

[1] La Croze, p. 131. Du Jarric, p. 598. Raulin, "Hist. Ecc, Mal," p. 29.

[2] Gouvea, "Jornada," p. 40. Du Jarric, Hist., p. 598. La Croze, p. 133. Raulin, "Hist. Ecc. Mal.," p. 29. Hough's "Hist. of Christ.," Vol. I., p, 391. Geddes, "Hist. Mal." p. 79.

streets, and the Archbishop was obliged to shut himself up till the storm passed over. One body of the patriots marched off to the Archdeacon at Augamale, another went to the Queen's Palace, six miles off, to rouse their Sovereign's indignation against the invaders. The Rannee immediately sent an officer to order the Archbishop out of the kingdom in three days on pain of death. As she could command 30,000 men, the Prelate thought it expedient to send away part of his train, and by dint of representing himself as one of the Syrian Prelates who had, for 1,500 years, enjoyed the protection of her ancestors, he felt certain that she would not carry her threat into execution. He did not, however, place all his trust in this masterpiece of dissimulation, but bribed the Governor of Carturte with a bag of gold to keep a watch round his house. On Wednesday, in the presence of the Cattanars, he surprised them by consecrating the holy oils, and still more by enclosing the Host in a pyx. Robed in his pontificals, crowned with his mitre, he knelt on the ground, washed the feet of the Cattanars, wiped them with a towel, and then kissed them. This act of humiliation affected the beholders to tears, excited the warmest devotion, and won more adherents than all that the pomp and music had secured. The adoration of the Cross followed on Good Friday, and several of the Cattanars, deeply impressed, threw themselves at his feet, and volunteered to swear allegiance to the

Roman Church. On Easter Eve, the Primate held a second ordination, and the same day, Francisco Rodriguez (contracted Ros), afterwards Bishop of the Serra, came to pay his respects and preached in the Malabar language. The services of Easter Day were celebrated with the greatest pomp—processions, torches, dances, and every sort of display, sacred and profane, of which a long account is to be found in the Chapter XV. of Gouvea's "Jornada." On the evening of the day, the indefatigable Archbishop walked through the straggling streets of Carturte, visiting the sick, and relieving the poor. This completed the victory, and the author of the "Jornada" might well say, "Este foy o principio do bem de toda esta Christandade, porque foy o primeyro povo que se sogeyton ao Arcebispo e à Santa Igreja Romana."[1]

We may dismiss the rest of the Archbishop's visitation in a few sentences. He re-visited Malandurte and was so coldly received that the church doors were shut against him.[2] After complaining of the conduct of the people, and of that of the Rajah of Cochin, he succeeded in securing the allegiance of the inhabitants. The Archdeacon still held out, and more correspondence took place with much the same result.[3] Menezes then went a second time to

[1] Gouvea, p. 46.
[2] Gouvea. Du Jarric, p. 610. La Croze, p. 149.
[3] Gouvea. La Croze, p. 152.

Diamper, and had a violent altercation with the Premier of Cochin, under the porch of the little church now so famous. His next determination was to excommunicate the Archdeacon, whose irresolution but little fitted him to be the champion of his falling Church against so powerful an opponent. At last the Portuguese Prelate received a submissive letter from the poor Archdeacon, and sent him in reply ten articles for his subscription. The reader will find this document fully quoted, but the substance was, of course, implicit obedience to the Pope and admission of his infallibility. Twenty days were granted for consideration of these articles, which the Archbishop employed in negotiations with the Rajah for troops to assist him in crushing the Syrians if necessity should arise.

The result of all this discussion was that the Archdeacon went to the Archbishop's house at Vaipacotta, knelt down before a crucifix, and swore on the missal to the ten articles and the Profession of Faith. It was then resolved to hold the Synod at Diamper on the 20th June, 1599, the third Sunday after Pentecost. The Archbishop then retired to Cranganor, where, assisted by Francisco Roz, he composed the celebrated decrees for the Synod. He next secured the co-operation of all the neighbouring Rajahs, and in order to make quite certain of a majority, he ordained fifty more priests on Trinity Sunday.

We have done our best to condense many a long chapter in Gouvea, the only original authority, so as to give the reader a connected view of this remarkable visitation, that he may be incited to imbibe more either at the fountain head, or in the various translations, compilations, and paraphrases derived from that source.

CHAPTER VI.

THE SYNOD OF DIAMPER.

"Alexius Menezius Goae Archiepiscopus Malabarium visitavit; Synodum Diamperensem habiut liturgium aliosque Chaldeorum libros ab erroribus purgavit; Georgium Archidiaconum, aliosque sive Presbyteros, sive nobiles viros Chaldaeos Nestorianiœ hœresi abremuntiare coegit; ac prœcipue Babyloniœ Patriarcham anathematizare; Romanum autem pontificem, Christi Vicarium et Ecclesiœ caput agnoscere; eique obedientiam promittere."—ASSEMANUS.

ON the banks of a small stream issuing from the lofty Ghauts which divide the Carnatic from Malayala, stands the little but now celebrated town, or rather village, of Diamper.[1] The surrounding country is extremely beautiful, exhibiting varied scenery of hill and dale, and winding rivers. The valleys are clothed

[1] Diamper is called Udiamper by the natives. It is omitted in Mr. Culloch's "Geographical Dictionary," 1866, but is noticed briefly in Wright's "Gazetteer" "We pass the Church of Udiamper," our Syrian friend Marcus observed, "that a divine judgment seemed ever since to rest upon the place, for they had now no worship at all; the inhabitants professed Romanism, but the church is in ruins, and they have no priest." "The justice of Marcus's observation is not to be defended, but it is curious as showing the light in which the Syrians still regard the transactions of those days."—Major Mackworth's visit to the Syrian Christians in 1821.

with perpetual verdure, and the mountains are not barren, but covered with forests of pine timber trees, the teak, jack tree, and others.[1] These woods are filled with the most beautiful creepers, such as the pepper vine, which adds so largely to the commerce of the country. Cardamums and cassia, frankincense and aromatic gums, grow abundantly on all sides, while the graceful coca-nut palms, the areca palm, the sago palm, add beauty to the picture, and form the pride of these tropical groves. The view is bounded on the east by pinnacles of granite, six thousand feet high, running northward to the Neilgherries, and southward to Cape Comorin. Diamper lies about fourteen miles east from Cochin on the road to Madura. It was formerly of much greater importance than it is at present, having been the metropolis of the Syrian Christians, the residence of Beliarté, the last of their kings, and containing also the palace of the Bishops of the Serra.[2] A town of this description in the South of India has little to distinguish it from others in the same region. The central feature is the bazar, or market place, surrounded by narrow bye-lanes, little alleys enclosed with mud walls, and often more like water-courses than roads.

[1] Buchanan's "Christian Researches," p. 88. Howard's "Christians of St. Thomas," p. 4.

[2] "Diamper outrosi lugardos mais principaes dos Christaõs de Sam Thome e que antigamente ania sido residencia de algos Bispos da Serra."—Gouvea, "Jornada," p. 38.

The Church of All Saints, to which we wish to conduct the reader, stands within a large enclosure of "compound" surrounded by a high, dingy, mud wall. The sacred edifice is large, substantial, and built of a reddish stone, squared and polished at the quarry, the front wall being six feet thick.[1] There is but little to attract the admirer of church architecture, but the general effect is good. The roof is high-pitched, the windows arched, and buttresses support the walls, the west front has three storeys, an arched door-way in the centre, three recesses, like built-up windows in the tier above, and the gables are generally surmounted by beautiful stone crosses. We may now look at the interior. We find a nave and chancel without transepts, the eastern portion being separated by railings about ten feet from the chancel arch. Within the rail the floor is raised, and near the wall on the south side stands the baptistery. The beams of the roof are highly ornamented, and the ceiling of the choir is circular and fretted. A splendid brass lamp hangs over the chancel steps; and as this was the Cathedral of the diocese, the shrines of the departed bishops are on each side of the altars. The nave, which has an earthen floor, is without seats or furniture of any kind, and therefore the whole beauty

[1] This description is founded on personal observation. See Buchanan's "Researches." Howard's "Syrians of St. Thomas," and Day's "Land of the Permauls."

of the church centres in the chancel, containing one principal altar and two minor ones.[1] The great altar is ornamented by an exquisitely carved frame-work, picked out in colours and gold, and surmounted by a cross. The church has two bells, hung within the building. These are cast in the foundries of the country, are of a great size, and lettered in Syriac and Malayalim. "In approaching a town in the evening, I once heard the sound of the bells among the hills; a circumstance which made me forget for a moment that I was in Hindostan, and reminded me of another country."[1] Such was the scene of this Synod, so fatal to the Church of St. Thomas, so influential for good and evil on succeeding missionary enterprises in Southern India.

On the 9th of June, eleven days before the time named for the meeting, the Archbishop of Goa, attended by six Jesuits, and several of the Syrian clergy, entered Diamper. His first act was to hold a Junto of the most enlightened and popular Cattanars, to revise, and, if necessary, amend the decrees which he was about to lay before the Assembly. A few suggestions were timidly hinted, and a very few trifling alterations made, but the Primate's resolutions

[1] "I am not at all clear as to the use of these quasi altars. Two of them may possibly be protheses or credence tables."—Benaudot, Lilor, II. 54. "Madras Ch. Miss. Rec.," Vol. III., p. 35: Howard's "Christians of St. Thomas."

[2] Buchanan's "Researches," p. 85.

were all carefully made, his consultation with the Cattanars was little else than a complimentary form, and yet the decrees were brought before the Senate as the result of a meeting at which the representatives of the Syrian Church were invited to full and free deliberation.

The morning of the 20th of June[1] dawned upon a crowded and excited town. The Governor of Cochin, with a large staff of officers, in the rich costume of the XVIth Century, silk, velvet, and lace, blending in dazzling colours with polished mail and plumed helmets, had arrived the evening before. The Dean, Chapter, and Choir of the Portuguese Church at Cochin came in the cool of the morning, some on foot, and some in the well-known palanquin of the country. All the civil authorities, the Camera, or Town Council, felt it their duty to attend, and even merchants, captains of ships in the ports, all, in fact, within travelling distance, forsook their ordinary avocations in order to be present on the opening day.[2] On the part of the Syrian Christians, too, there was at least a

[1] There is much contradiction as to this date. Gouvea says in one place (Fol. 56) "20 de Julho o Domnigo 3 depois de Pontecoste," and in another (Fol. 64) "O Domingo terceiro depois de Pentecoste 20 de Junho." La Croze has "20 de Juin, 1599," p. 184; and Geddes, with characteristic inaccuracy, has not only the 20th of June at p. 108 of the History, contradicting 20th of July in the Preface to the Diocesan Synod, but positively, by one of the numerous blunders of the Press, gives 1199 for 1599.

[2] Gouvea, "Jornada," Chap. XX.

corresponding interest. The Archdeacon, as the chief dignitary of his Church, came, robed in a splendid vestment of dark red silk, a large golden cross hanging from his neck, and his beard reaching below his girdle. He was attended by a hundred and fifty-three of his Cattanars, clad in their long white vestments, like cassocks with turn-down collars, the ordinary dress —the officiating vestments being of silk damask, yellow pattern on a scarlet ground. They all wore that peculiar head-dress of red silk, which they retain even during service, and which bears a slight resemblance to the biretta. Six hundred delegates from the various Malabar Churches, besides numerous Shumshanas or Deacons, swelled the body of Syrian representatives to nearly a thousand men.

On that memorable third Sunday after Whitsuntide in the Church of All Saints, in the Bishopric of Augamale of the Christians of St. Thomas, in the Serra of Malabar, the See being vacant by the death of the Archbishop Mar-Abraham, there assembled in a Diocesan Synod, according to the Holy Canons, the most illustrious and Most Reverend Lord Dom Frey Aleixo de Menezes, Archbishop Metropolitan of Goa, Primate of the Indies and the Oriental parts, together with all the priests and curates of the said bishopric, and the procurators of all the towns and corporations in the same, with great numbers of other persons belonging to the said Church, and called to the said Synod by the Most Reverend Metropolitan.[1]

The little Cathedral was crowded to excess, the Archbishop, the Archdeacon and dignitaries of both Churches occupying the sacrarium, the choir and other officials filling the chancel, the ordinary priests, deacons, and laity standing in the nave. The Primate commenced the proceedings with a brief address, in which he urged the duty of thanking God for the extinction of all the commotions by which the evil one had done his best to prevent the assembling of this Synod. He then went on to say that as they were all filled with joy at this splendid and crowded meeting, assembled for the promotion of the glory of God, the purity of the faith, and the good of their own souls, it was incumbent upon them to begin the important business of the day, by the highest act of Christian worship, the celebration of a solemn Mass. Using the form for the removal of schism[2] as given in the Roman missal, he acted as celebrant, without in the slightest degree recognising the claims of the Syrian

[1] Geddes's "Translation of Gouvea." The learned reader who desires more information than our condensed account imparts, is recommended to consult Gouvea's "Jornada" in Portuguese (the true source of all the compilations and paraphrases; Raulin's "Historia Ecc. Mal." in Latin; Du Jarric (Vol. III., p. 622) in French; La Croze, Historie (Liv. III., p. 185) in French, Asia, Portuguesa, Tom. III., part II. cap. III., p. 126, in good Spanish, badly translated by Stevens in "The Portuguese Asia," 1695.

[2] Ad tollendum Schisma.

Archdeacon to participate. He then delivered an energetic discourse on the usual subject—the obedience of Christians throughout the world to the Roman Pontiff. Re-assuming his robes, he read the office for the opening of a Synod,[1] as in the Roman Pontifical, and then, seating himself in his throne,[2] surrounded by all the authorities, ecclesiastic, military, and civil, he declared, in a loud voice, that he celebrated this Holy Synod in virtue of two briefs of 1595 and 1597, from the Holy Father, Pope Clement VIII., in which his Holiness, as Christ's Vicar upon earth, had recommended him, on the death of Archbishop Abraham, to take possession of this Church and Bishopric, so as not to suffer any Bishop or Prelate to come into it from Babylon until this diocese shall be provided by the Holy Roman Church with a proper Pastor; that, moreover, the same belonged now to him as the Metropolitan thereof, and Primate of all India, because the See was vacant, and was without any Dean and Chapter to govern it during the interregnum. All this was in Portuguese, a tongue not understanded of the people, and it was therefore immediately translated into Malabar. This done, the Primate informed the Synod that the next business was the appointment of an interpreter enjoying the confidence of both parties. Whereupon one Jacob,

[1] Ad inchoandam Synodum.

[2] Faldistorium.

Vicar of the little Church at Pallurte, famed for his knowledge of Portuguese and Malabar, was unanimously elected, and sworn upon the Holy Gospels faithfully to discharge the duties of interpreter to the Holy Synod. For greater security, two assistants were appointed, Francisco Roz and Antonio Toscano, Portuguese Jesuits of the College of Vaipacotta, whose long residence and daily intercourse with the students had made them proficient in the native language. Besides these there were many others present, both Portuguese and Indians, who were thoroughly competent to check any attempt at misinterpretation.

These preliminaries being settled, and all placed according to their order, the Archbishop, having solemnly pronounced "In the name of the Father, Son, and Holy Ghost, three persons, and one only true God, Amen," delivered the following address: "My beloved brethren, you, the venerable Priests, and my most dear sons in Christ, you, the representatives and Procurators of the people. Does it please you, that for the praise and glory of the Holy and undivided Trinity, the Father, Son, and Holy Ghost, and for the increase and exaltation of the Catholic faith, and the Christian religion of the inhabitants of this Bishoprick, and for the destruction of the heresies and errors which have been sown therein by several hereticks and schismaticks, and for the purging of books from the false doctrines contained in them, and for the perfect union of this church with the whole church Catholic and Universal, and for the yielding of obedience to the supreme Bishop of Rome, the Universal Pastor of the church, and successor in the chair of St. Peter, and Vicar of Christ upon earth, from whom you have for some time departed, and for the extirpation of simony, which has been much practised in this Bishoprick, and for the regulating of the administration of the Holy Sacraments of the church, and the necessary use of them, and for the reformation of the affairs of the church and the clergy, and the customs of all the Christian people of this diocese; we should begin a Diocesan Synod of this Bishoprick of the Serra."

Pausing here, and looking round upon the assembly, he asked in Portuguese, "Does it please you?" which, being interpreted by Father Jacob, the adherents of the Archbishop shouted with one accord, "It pleaseth us." If there was any dissentient voice, it was drowned in the universal acclaim. Then the most Reverend Metropolitan addressed them thus: "Venerable brethren, and most beloved sons in Christ, since you are pleased to begin a Synod, after having offered prayers to God, from whom all good proceedeth, it will be convenient that the matters to be treated of appertaining to our holy faith, the church, the divine offices, the administration of the Holy Sacraments, and the customs of the whole people, be entertained by you with benignity and charity, and afterwards, by God's assistance, complied with, with much reverence; and that everyone of you should faithfully procure the reformation of such things in this Synod as you know to be amiss, and if any that are present should happen to be dissatisfied with anything that shall be said or done therein, let them without any scruple declare their opinion publickly, that so, by God's grace, it may be examined, and all things may be truly stated as is desired, but let not strife or contention find any room among you to the perverting of justice and reason; neither be ye afraid of searching after and embracing the truth."

The second decree in substance commanded all persons, on pain of excommunication, not to depart from the town of Diamper without express leave from the Metropolitan till the Synod had ended, and the decrees signed by their own hands. The third decree declared that no prejudice should be done to any town, corporation, or village, as to pre-eminence from the holding of this Synod in the town of Diamper; and that, should any doubt arise, the Metropolitan's decision was to be final. The fourth decree admonished all Christians to resort to confession, and to special prayer for the success of the Synod, and that two Masses should be said in the church daily, during the sitting of the Synod, one of the Latins to the Holy Spirit, the other of the Syrians to the Blessed Virgin Mary. The fifth decree was aimed at preventing unnecessary and hurtful debates, and strictly forbade all people discussing in private any of the questions in the programme of the Synod.

The reading of these decrees and their acceptance by the Synod concluded the first day's work. No public disturbance interrupted the harmony of the proceedings; but there was a strong feeling of dissatisfaction amongst all the Cattanars, who still retained attachment to the Church of their fathers. They complained, and justly, that they were being severed in the most unceremonious manner from communion with their Patriarch, and forced into obedience with a branch of the Church in which they had no concern. Still, these feeble murmurings of the struggling captives produced no result. There was no Luther to lead them to battle. "Divide and conquer" had been all along the watchword of Menezes; and if at any time the Syrians had been able to organise effectual resistance, that time was now past, and for ever. Thus closed the fatal Whit-Sunday of 1599.

The sun of the 21st of June had not yet penetrated the deep valleys of the Serra, when the streets of Diamper were filled with the mingled costumes of Roman and Syrian priests, Portuguese officers, and Indian chiefs, hastening to the Cathedral of All

Saints. At seven o'clock precisely the Archbishop, with his usual retinue, entered the church in procession, and was received with all honours. After the customary solemnities, the Antiphony, Psalm, Prayers, and Hymn, as in the Pontifical, he assumed, *as of right*, the chair or throne near the altar, and thus addressed the assembly:—

"Venerable and beloved brethren, the Priests, and you, my dearest sons in Christ, the Procurators and representatives of the people, We having done little more yesterday than celebrate the Divine Offices, and preach to the people, it is fit we should begin to-day to treat of matters appertaining to the Synod; in the first place of those that belong to the integrity and truth of our Holy Catholic Faith, and the profession of the same; which, before we go about, I do again admonish you in our Lord Jesus Christ, that all such things as you do judge to stand in need of reformation in this Bishopric or any part thereof, may be signified to us or to the congregation, that so with the Divine favour and assistance all things by your diligence and charity may be brought into so good estate as is desired for the praise of the name of our Lord Jesus Christ." Then robing himself in his pontificals, but laying aside his mitre, kneeling before the Altar, and placing his hands upon a cross on the Gospels, he recited, in his own name, *and in the name of the Synod*, the following Profession of Faith:—"In the name of the Most Holy and Undivided Trinity, the Father, Son, and Holy Ghost, one only true God, in the year of our Lord 1599, in the seventh year of the Pontificate of our most Holy Lord, Clement VIII., Bishop of Rome, in the town of Diamper, in the kingdom of Malabar in the East Indies, in the Church of All Saints, on the 21st of June, in a Diocesan Synod of the Bishopric of Serra, assembled by the most Illustrious and Reverend Lord Dom Alexio de Menezes, Archbishop Metropolitan of Goa and the Oriental parts, and the See being vacant of the said Bishopric, I (N.) do of my own free will, without any manner of force and constraint, for the salvation of my soul, believing it in my heart, protest that with a firm faith, I do believe and confess all and every one of the Articles contained in the Symbol of Faith which is used in Holy Mother Roman Church."

The Archbishop then recited the Nicene Creed.[1] Next followed a series of declarations, beginning with "I do firmly receive and embrace, I do confess," and such formulæ, admitting all the traditions, observances and constitutions of the Roman Catholic Church ; the seven Sacraments with their accompanying customs, rites and ceremonies, the Mass, "as a true and proper sacrifice for the quick and dead," the

[1] In this we follow Gouvea and all that have written on the subject. We are at a loss to know from what source Hough derives his information when he says in his account of this transaction, "He began by repeating in substance the *Apostles'* Creed," Vol. II., p. 26.

doctrine of transubstantiation, purgatory, the worship of Saints, relics and images, the doctrine of indulgences, the Papal Supremacy, and above all the worship of the Virgin Mary. He concluded by anathematising all who taught anything contrary to the Council of Trent, including, of course, all heretics, especially mentioning Nestorians and the Patriarch of Babylon. These last words of the Prelate were drowned in murmurs of disapprobation. The dissentients loudly declared that a new Confession of Faith was altogether unnecessary, as, of course, it implied that they had never till now been the disciples of Christ. The shrewd Menezes, never off his guard, promptly replied that all good Christians should be ready at any time to make a Profession of their Faith; and that as he, an Archbishop, had done it, they surely had no reason to complain of the hardship. The tumult being thus dexterously quelled, the Archbishop resumed his seat, put on his Mitre, and took the Gospels in his hands. The interpreter Jacob then mounted the pulpit,[1] and read very slowly, in a clear voice, the Profession of Faith which we have just quoted, while the Archdeacon knelt before the Primate's throne and repeated the whole aloud in his own name, and as representative of the Syrian Church, all the assembly joining. And as if this had not been sufficient, the Priests were required, one by one, to

[1] The Preacher's *Chair*, Hough. Vol. II., p. 30.

pass in front of the Primate, kneel down, and swear on Gospels and Crucifix, that they would conform to their lives' end to all that they had promised. The Synod further passed a decree that the same confession should be made by those who were absent, and that none should be admitted to Holy Orders who declined to take these oaths.

These proceedings terminated the second day's work, which has been justly called the life and soul of what followed.[1] For it was really the crowning triumph of the Archbishop's persevering energy in the subjugation of the Syrian Church.

A curious transposition occurred in the order of procedure. The work assigned for the third day's meeting was postponed at the request of the Cattanars and Syrian deputies, who, aware of the disagreeable subjects to be discussed, wished to take advantage of the absence of the Portuguese visitors from the Synod.[2]

The third day's meeting began as usual at seven o'clock, with the same religious solemnities, after which the Synod proceeded, amid some disturbance, easily suppressed, to set forth the doctrines of the Church of Rome as to the seven Sacraments. Twenty decrees passed the house on the subject of baptism;

[1] La Croze, "Hist. du Christianisme," p. 193.

[2] They were about to attend the Festival of St. John the Baptist at a village a few miles off.

the Syrian forms were, of course, abolished, and the Roman introduced ; all baptised by Syrians to be re-baptised by Romans ; holy oils to be used, and many other orders to the same effect. Three decrees settled the doctrine and ceremonies of confirmation.

The fourth session treated of the Eucharist and the Mass, and the Synod passed nine decrees with regard to the first, and fifteen with regard to the second, all tending to the extirpation of Syrian peculiarities, and to the introduction of the Roman doctrine and ritual, without the slighest concession.

The fifth session treated of penance and extreme unction, and at the sixth session the work assigned for the third meeting (but which had been postponed) was completed. *It was a day of utter extinction of the Syrian Church.* The errors in the Syrian scriptures were to be corrected ; heathen superstitions that had mingled with the faith were to be expunged ; and every trace of relation to the Patriarch of Babylon, or to Syrian tenets was entirely condemned. Syriac books were to be delivered up, emended, or destroyed ; and all Syrian Christians were declared by the XXII. decree to be subject to the Inquisition at Goa.

On the seventh day the Synod passed twenty-three decrees on what is called the sacrament of orders, and sixteen on the so-called sacrament of matrimony, prescribing many excellent rules, blended with certain superstitions.

The work of the eighth session referred to a reformation in church affairs, the division of the diocese into parishes, the establishment of fasts and festivals, conveyed in forty-one decrees.

· The ninth, and last, session was devoted to the reformation of manners, and enjoined many admirable regulations against heathenism, fortune-telling, immorality, false weights and measures, slavery, and, strange to say, against the use and sale of spirituous liquors.

These decrees being read and passed, the diocese was divided into seventy-five parishes. Vicars were nominated to each, and severally introduced to kiss the Primate's hand. Then, kneeling in a body before His Grace, they received, in presence of all the people, a solemn charge as to their obligations.[1] The Archbishop next commanded them to sign the Malabar translation of the decrees; after which, taking his seat on the Faldestorium, Mitre on head, he attached his own signature, which was immediately followed by the subscriptions of the eight hundred and thirteen members of the Synod. This important act finished, he rose, took off his Mitre, knelt before the high Altar, and began the Te Deum. A procession was then formed which marched round the church, the choristers chanting the Psalms, "The Latines in Latin, and

[1] This document will be found *in extenso* in Gouvea's "Jornada." La Croze, p. 278. Geddes's "Trans. of Gouvea," p. 415; and in Hough's "Christ.," Vol. II., p. 120.

the native priests in Chaldee, and the people their festivity in Malabar."[1] Returning to the church, the Primate stood at the high Altar, and said the prayer "Exaudi quœsumus Domine"; then re-seating himself, he delivered an able discourse to the people, calling upon them to thank God for the great success which had attended the Synod. Finally, rising from his throne, he advanced with his pastoral staff in hand, "and with abundance of tears," solemnly blessed the people, Archdeacon George adding in a loud voice "Let us depart in peace!" to which the whole Synod responded, "In the name of Christ, Amen!"

Thus terminated the famous Synod of Diamper.[2] Its acts, or sessions, are nine in number, and comprise no fewer than 267 decrees, most of them of considerable length, and, if fairly treated, demanding long and careful discussion. Yet they were so hurried through

[1] Geddes's Hist. p. 243

[2] The opinion entertained by the present generation of the Christians of St. Thomas as to the treatment of their Church by the Portuguese, may be seen in the Rev. G. B. Howard's Translation of the little pamphlet by Philipos. Parker, 1869.—"When the Syrian Church was in this state, the Portuguese not only persecuted and killed all the bishops as they came from Antioch, but their Metran Dom Pre Aleskes de Menesis, residing at Goa, came to the Malayalim country in 1598, and, having visited all the Syrian churches, he bribed the petty princes then ruling the country, and some Syrians, in order to gain them over to his interest. And those Syrians who opposed his designs were persecuted and put to death. So, by main force he assembled all the Syrians in the church at Odyamperoor, and persuaded them to embrace Popery, besides burning all the Syriac bibles and many other Syriac books. Then all the married priests were separated from their wives."

the House, that the business was closed on the sixth day, the 26th of June. This indecent haste clearly proves, if proof were necessary, that this so-called Synod possessed nothing but the outward form of a deliberative assembly, and that its real purpose was to disguise the true nature of the proceeding, to pass without amendment the decrees carefully prepared by the skilful hand of Menezes, and to bind, as he thought, for ever, the afflicted Syrian Church to the throne of the triumphant Pontiff.

CHAPTER VII.

THE TRIUMPH OF ROME.

"Can any read the abstract here given of the proceedings of the Synod, without being convinced that the creed it introduced was a system of darkness? The primary object of these men was to *assert the Pope's supremacy*, and *not* to extend the kingdom of Jesus Christ."
—HOUGH.

BEFORE continuing our narrative of the Primate's visitation of his new conquest, we may present a very brief view of the main points of doctrine in which the Syrian Christians agreed with the Reformed Catholic Church of England, and differed from that of Rome *before* the passing of the decrees of Diamper. In our succeeding chapters we shall have to notice the *numerous changes which took place in consequence of this Papal aggression*; and we shall try to disentangle the threads of conflicting creeds and rituals which distinguish the Churches of Southern India at this moment.

The Church of Malabar held the following doctrines: (1) She condemned the Pope's supremacy; (2) affirmed that the Roman Church had departed from the faith; (3) denied Transubstantiation; (4) condemned the worship of images; (5) made no use of oils; (6) denied purgatory; (7) would not admit of spiritual affinity; (8) knew nothing of auricular confession; (9) never heard of extreme unction; (10) permitted the clergy to marry; (11) denied that matrimony and consecration were sacraments; (12) celebrated with leavened bread, and consecrated with prayer. [1]

Gouvea's account in the XVIII. chapter of the first book of the "Jornada" is, in substance, this: The Church of Malabar is said (1) not to adore images; (2) to hold three Sacraments, Baptism, the Eucharist, and Holy Orders; (3) *to make no use of oils;* [2] (4) to have no knowledge of confirmation or extreme unction; (5) to abhor auricular confession; (6) to hold many erroneous doctrines about the Eucharist, so that the Protestants seem to have borrowed their heresies from them; (7) to approve of the marriage of priests;

[1] Geddes singularly adds as a point of agreement between the Church of England and the Church of Malabar that "She holds but *two* orders, Priesthood and Deaconate," whereas, "It is evident unto all men diligently reading the Holy Scriptures and ancient authors that from the Apostles' time there have been orders of ministers in Christ's Church, *Bishops*, Priests, and Deacons." Preface to Ordination Service. In point of fact, however, the Malabar Church held as we do *three* orders. P. 14 of "The Syrian Christians of Malabar." By Philipos of Cottayam, in Travancore.

[2] Gouvea is incorrect in this statement as the following will show:—QUES. 27: Do they make holy oil, and anoint men with it? ANS.: Three ointments are ordained, two to anoint those who are baptised, and one to anoint the sick.

(8) to abhor the Pope and the Church of Rome as anti-Christian.

Assuming that our readers are fairly acquainted with dogmatic theology and ecclesiastical history, we deem it quite unnecessary to enter into lengthened explanations of the points in dispute, referring the less instructed to the interesting summary in Hough's "Christianity of India." [1]

We may now return to the Archbishop, whom we left dismissing the clergy and others at the close of the Synod. He presented each of the new vicars with a stone Altar, (duly consecrated), a box containing vessels of holy oils, a missal in Chaldee and Syriac, a digest of Christian doctrine for the instruction of children, a surplice, corporals, frontals, caps, and all other ecclesiastical requisites.

These matters being settled, the Archbishop began his visitation, and was everywhere received in the most flattering style. An ode, composed by his sycophants, was chanted in his presence whenever he halted. Music and dancing, flags and cheers, welcomed his arrival. The villages vied with each other in festive decorations, the streets being covered with matting, bright coloured cloths hanging from the windows, and triumphal arches spanning the road. His mode of procedure was nearly everywhere the same. Passing through the kneeling crowds of men

[1] Vol. II., p. 13.

and women, who reverentially kissed his hands, he entered the village church, where, having confessed himself, he said Mass. This ended, Father Francisco Roz and a committee of learned Cattanars assembled in the sacristy to receive the Syrian books belonging to the church, or to private individuals. After a careful scrutiny, some were emended and spared, others that were reputed too hostile to Rome were mercilessly burnt, and thus many invaluable Syrian manuscripts were sacrificed by this Archiepiscopal Vandal. This dark deed accomplished, the Primate assumed his pontificals and preached a sermon of the usual character, and on the usual topics, of course, through the medium of an interpreter. The chief decrees of the Synod were then read aloud, an episode of a procession took place round the church, after which refreshment, the indefatigable Primate gave them a second sermon on the sacrament of confirmation, reducing theory to practice by anointing all *without distinction.* All this pompous display in a quiet little Indian village naturally excited the curiosity of the surrounding heathen, and "such vast multitudes resorted to see the novelty and the pontifical vestments that they filled the churchyard and windows."[1] Not yet exhausted, the zealous Primate delivered a third discourse, this time to the Nairs and other pagans,

[1] Gouvea "Jornada," Geddes's "Acts and Decrees of the Synod of Diamper," p. 429.

who came in crowds to witness the ceremony of baptism. He placed before them in energetic language the leading doctrines of the Christian faith, and denounced with unflinching severity the follies and superstitions of idol-worship. The mountain warriors though fully armed, endured all this denunciation with exemplary patience, but whether their forbearance is to be attributed to Indian apathy, or to their inability to understand the language of the Primate must be left to conjecture. One singular result of this exhortation was, that several of the Nairs, if we may believe Gouvea, desired baptism, and with *no more instruction than what they had thus received, were admitted to the font.* The next part of this busy day's work was a public profession of faith by such of the clergy as had not attended the Synod, followed by a gathering of all the children. These little ones he ordered to kneel down round his chair, and to repeat the Chamaz, a Malabar prayer, then blessing them, he delivered a *fourth* discourse specially to them, thus giving great delight to their parents. He then inducted the vicar in presence of the people solemnly installing him as pastor of the flock. The remainder of the afternoon was spent in marriages, confessions, and other duties. Then followed a few hours' well-earned repose, but the labours of the day did not end till the Primate and his chaplains had examined the Cattanars, requiring license for the Confessional. Now if this account abridged from Gouvea is to be taken as an average specimen of the Primate's work during his visitation, one may cease to wonder at the success which attended his efforts for the subjugation of the Church of St. Thomas to the obedience of St. Peter.

We need not follow the Archbishop from town to town, as his biographer does. There is but little interest in the narrative, the original of which will be found in Gouvea's work, and in the translations or paraphrases of La Croze, Geddes, and Hough. We learn that the Archbishop continued his progrêss, visiting all the towns on the Malabar coast, and destroying every authentic document at Augamale and other places. At Cape Comorin, he found, to his great dismay, that all traces of the Christianity planted by Xavier *had disappeared.* On his return he received at Carturté news of the death of Philip II., which rendered it necessary for him to go back to Goa without delay. The Archdeacon and Cattanars escorted him to his war galley, and farewells, apparently sincere, were exchanged. He touched at the Portuguese "factories" of Mangalore, Barcelore, and Omore, and suppressed a cruel festival, like that of Juggernaut.[1] He landed on the 16th November; and as the Viceroy had just died, he found himself, by Portuguese rule, head of both State and Church in India. Extensive preparations were made to give him a hearty

[1] Buchanan's "Christian Researches," p. 19.

welcome as Viceroy and as a victorious crusader. These intended honours he firmly declined, attributing all the glory to Almighty God.

For some time after his return to Goa, he continued to receive most satisfactory accounts from the scene of his ten months' labours. Small churches had been discovered far up in the ravines of the Ghauts, which had been so long lost sight of that the poor nominal Christians had forgotten almost everything—creeds, sacraments, and prayers. These neglected ones had been sought out by active missionaries, and had been supplied with every essential according to the Roman ritual. Another circumstance occurred at this time which gave unspeakable satisfaction to the Archbishop, as it realised one of the objects which he had most at heart—*the consecration of a Bishop of the Latin church as head of the church of Malabar.* In 1601, Pope Clement VIII. sent Bulls to constitute Francisco Rodriguez (or Roz) first bishop of the Serra, and, four years afterwards, Paul V. transferred the see of Augamale to Cranganor, making the Prelate an Archbishop, but retaining Goa as the Metropolitical See.

We now lose sight of Menezes in his connection with the church of India. We learn that he returned to Europe, filled the exalted positions of Primate of Braga and Viceroy of Portugal under Philip III. His after fate is obscure. He is said to have died in disgrace; but what his faults were are concealed in the darkness of Spanish diplomacy. An analysis of his character is unnecessary; for the intelligent reader cannot fail to glean it even from our imperfect sketch of his marvellous achievements.

BOOK IV.

SUBSEQUENT MISSIONS IN SOUTHERN INDIA, WITH SPECIAL REFERENCE TO THE SYRIAN CHRISTIANS.

CHAPTER I.

RADIATION OF MISSIONS FROM GOA.

"Goa vereis aos Mouros ser tornada
A qual virã despois a ser senhora
De todo o Oriente, e sublimada
Ce'os triumphos da gente vencedora;
Alli suberba, altiva e exalçada,
Ao gentio, que os idolos adora,
Duro freio pora, e a toda a terra,
Que cindar de fazer aos vossos guerra."

CAMŒNS.

A DIFFICULTY here presents itself. If we omit all notice of missionary effort in Southern India during the XVIIth and XVIIIth centuries, we effectually break the chain of events, and render much of the subsequent history unintelligible. If, on the other hand, we enter into minute detail of all the controversies, successes, and defeats, which characterise this period, we should swell our treatise beyond all ordinary bounds, depart from the prescribed limits of the subject, and exhaust the patience of all but the most enthusiastic student. A middle course seems, therefore, the only one left to us. Proceeding, then, with a still more rigorous plan of condensation, we shall give only such salient points in the history of the Malabar church and the influence of the Portuguese missions as will serve to connect the causes in the XVIth Century with the effects in the XIXth.

At the close of the fifty years in which the Portuguese missions had been operating, from Xavier to Menezes, we find the condition of Roman Catholic Christianity in Southern India thus stated by one of the Jesuit writers :—"Catholic and Christian India is divided into four great Bishoprics—Goa, Cranganor, Cochin, and St. Thomé. The Archbishop of Goa is Primate of India. The primatial chapter is composed of European canons and of Indians of various shades of complexion, a combination which produces a singular effect when they are seen in the choir, or officiating together in religious ceremonies." The Portuguese Government, which felt the necessity of forming a body of native clergy, had recommended the missionaries to give every encouragement to the Indians to take Holy Orders, and to become members of the religious communities. It was also the desire of the Central Council of the Society of Jesus, as it has been part of the policy of the propaganda, and every subsequent missionary society. The project had been tried again and again, but as often abandoned from the fear that the Indian priests, retaining the national character, and slaves to their customs, would not dedicate themselves to that purity of life which true religion demands. We shall see in the sequel, not only amongst the Roman Catholics, but in our own missionary colleges at home and in the colonies, that this difficulty has been overcome.

Goa was not only the metropolis of Portuguese India, the seat of its Government, and the centre of its trade, but the *source whence flowed the streams of missionary influence over all the Peninsula of Hindostan.* The College of St. Paul, to which we have already alluded possessed at this time a thorough organisation, including professors of the native languages for training candidates, not simply for ordinary parish work, but for the spread of Christianity. Nor was this all. The power of the Jesuits at home had increased to an amazing extent; the little company of ten had, in fifty years, grown to ten thousand, and their emissaries not only filled all the countries of Europe, but penetrated into the most distant regions of the globe. Portuguese Asia had its full share; for the brethren of the order felt that Xavier had been a noble pioneer amongst the Mohammedans and idolaters, that Menezes had opened a *splendid field for their efforts amongst the Syrian Christians*, and that the powerful and wealthy city of Goa was a fortress from which their forces might issue to subdue the surrounding nations, and to which they might retreat in the event of disaster.

At the time of which we write there was but one

Goa,[1] situated on an island[2] and separated from the mainland by marshy grounds frequently covered by the sea. The city is first mentioned in the ancient history of the Deccan, in speaking of the reign of Mujahid Schah in 1347. According to the tradition communicated to the first Portuguese settlers, Brahminism was the only religion professed in Tissuary, the original name of this island. In 1479, the Mohammedans erected the first buildings about the centre of the island, and, at the time of Vasco da Gama's arrival, a Mussulman vassal of the Emperor of the Deccan resided here. Albuquerque took possession of the city in 1510; and soon afterwards the island was covered with magnificent public edifices, splendid churches, palatial residences of the Vice-Regal Court, while towards the sea, there were extensive docks, enormous warehouses, and rich arsenals of naval and military stores. In 1567 Antonio De Moronha surrounded it with a vast wall so that in 1571, two years after the poet Camœns had left it, Goa had reached the highest degree of its splendour. The city of this period had completely replaced a

[1] "There are now two, the old and the new, the former being about eight miles up the river, abandoned to the priests by the viceroy and chief inhabitants, who reside at New Goa."—Buchanan's "Researches," p. 129.

[2] "Situated 15° 27′ N. and 73° 53′ E. two leagues in length and above six leagues in circuit, connected with the mainland by the Isthmus of Ballagate. The island is well watered, and filled with numerous gardens and orchards."—Barreti De Resende.

town already important by the magnificence of its edifices. In the time of John III. about 1530, the beautiful Indian Pagodas and the elegant Moslem minarets had entirely disappeared. All the splendour of the the capital of India was due to the souvenirs of Italy. It wore the aspect of a glorious city of the renaissance, transplanted to the shores of Hindostan. We borrow a condensed account from the Prior of one of the monasteries of this opulent city, a writer whose work is almost forgotten. After a minute description of the town, he speaks of the Governor's palace as "très vaste et très haut," elevated above the river, and having before it an extensive square surrounded by beautiful private residences. The Vice-regal mansion contains a splendid hall and suites of magnificent apartments, decorated with portraits of the discoverers of India and the successive Viceroys, with pictures representing the early scenes of the conquest. Not far from the palace is the Cathedral Church of the Archbishopric, dedicated to St. Catherine, because the town was taken on the day of her festival. It is a large and beautiful edifice with an altar piece of the Saint's martyrdom and with an interior combining all that is gorgeous in European art and Oriental splendour. The other Churches of Goa are also richly decorated, and on feast days they are resplendent with gold and silver, with taffetas of divers colours, and with the richest carpets of India. But the Church of Jesus surpasses all others. The chapel, in which reposes the body of St. Francis Xavier, is a remarkable specimen of architecture; the door is made of valuable wood, and covered with plates of gold. In the middle of the chapel rises a pyramid of different marbles elaborately ornamented, and sculptured with the principal actions of the great Apostle, whose body, with the exception of the right arm (sent to Rome) is enclosed in a shrine so magnificient, that diamonds and rubies sparkle without number in pure gold, most exquisitely chased. The statue of St. Francis, in massive silver, ornaments the high altar of the Church, and, what is still more precious, a picture represents the Saint a few hours after death. The upper town is formed of the Convents of the Dominicans, Franciscans, Augustines, and Jesuits, of the Archbishop's palace, the Viceroy's, and the mansions of the officials and merchant princes. We have no space to speak of the great street of shops full of gold, silver, and precious stones, nor to do more than allude to the immense building yards from which issued the vast teak-built galleons, which bore the riches of India to the quays of Lisbon—the enormous magazines destined to provision the Portuguese Navy, the cannon foundry, which furnished an incessant supply of guns for field, fortress, and fleet, and the extensive stables in which were kept, not merely the cavalry horses, but the war-elephants, so essential a part of Oriental pageantry. Well might such a city be called "Goa the Golden," and well might the Jesuits value it as the grand centre of all their missionary movements in the east.

Our picture of Goa, at the close of the XVIth century, would not be complete if we omitted all mention of the Inquisition. This terrible institution founded by the Friar Dominic in the XIIth Century was introduced by John III. in 1557 into the kingdom of Portugal, and three years afterwards it was established with a complete staff of officers and the amplest powers of jurisdiction in the capital of Portuguese India. There can be no doubt that this horrid tribunal formed a most powerful instrument in the hands of the Portuguese missionaries, which they knew well how to use, not simply in its terrible reality of imprisonment, torture, and public execution by fire, but also in the terror which it inspired amongst men of all ranks, ages, and creeds. *To its influence, therefore, may be fai.ly attributed no small portion of the rapid success attending on the Crusade of Menezes amongst the churches of the Serra*; for the Syrian Christians well knew, that, had they offered any decided resistance, the arm of the Inquisition was long enough to reach them even in the fastnesses of their mountain homes.[1]

[1] Limborch's "History of the Inquisition." "Dellons Relation de L'Inquisition de Goa." Geddes's "View of the Inquisition in Portugal." Buchanan's "Christian Researches."—Ed. 1811, p. 129.

The statistics of the Roman Catholic Church in Portuguese India about this period may be summed up in a few words; our authorities, however, being the Jesuits themselves. The Archbishopric is said to have had 400,000 souls under its jurisdiction, but what was the precise religious condition of this population is not stated. The Archbishopric of Cranganor (that is the Bishopric of the Serra) removed from Augamale is affirmed to have included an equal number, though the Madura mission (of which more presently) had not attained its full growth. The See of Cochin which comprehended Travancore and the fishery coast, contained 50,000 Christians; while the diocese of St. Thomé embracing an immense territory, from Cape Comorin to the north of the Ganges, and thence to Pegu, numbered as many Catholics as all the rest of India.

The Jesuits, at first Portuguese, but afterwards including French, Italian and Spanish brethren, divided the theatre of their zealous operations into several great missions, of which each was sub-divided into minor ones, recognising for their chief the superior of the principal mission. The first great mission is that of Madura which extends from Cape Comorin as far as Pondicherry; the second is that of Maissour (Mysore), a large kingdom whose monarch is a tributary of the Great Mogul; the third is that of the Carnatic which commences at Pondicherry, and stretches to the north as far as the boundaries of the Mogul empire.

CHAPTER II.

THE MADURA MISSION.

"The Christianity of Madura under the Jesuits was indeed undisguised idolatry."—KAYE.

" Every Protestant writer, with two or three exceptions, has ascribed the success of the mission of Madura to a guilty connivance with Pagan superstitions."—J. W. M. MARSHALL.

THE kingdom of Madura is bounded on the east by Tanjore and the Palk Straits, on the south by Tinnevelly, on the west by Travancore, and on the north by Coimbatore and Trichinopoly. It is about the size of Portugal; and, at the time of which we write it was governed by seventy Palléacarens, or petty princes, the vassals of the Rajah. This Sovereign could bring into the field 25,000 men and a hundred elephants. The capital of the State is a city of the same name, defended by a fortress, and famed amongst the surrounding idolaters for the possession of three enormous triumphal cars. One of these can only be drawn by a thousand persons, and, when it is adorned by silks of various colours, flags, and festoons of flowers, and dragged during the night, amid the blaze of torches, the roll of drums, the clang of cymbals and the blast of trumpets, "it cannot be denied the spectacle is extremely interesting."[1] On the northern side of the town were the churches of the Christians, one founded by Dei Nobili, and the other, more ancient, dedicated to Nôtre Dame and served by the Jesuits. These Churches were utterly destroyed when the town was sacked by the Rajah of Mysore, but since then, a new one has been erected in the suburbs.[2] After this irruption the King transferred his Court to Trichinopoly, a hundred miles north of the former capital. Here the Jesuits founded several churches, though at a later period of the mission.

There are few questions that have given rise to more controversy between Roman Catholics and Protestants, and amongst Romanists themselves than the Jesuit missions in Madura;[3] and although the date (17th century) taken strictly, places it beyond the boundary line of our subject, yet the mission is so *essential an off-shoot from the Portuguese centre* that

[1] At least in the opinion of the Jesuit writer, whose precise words are "on ne peut nier que le spectacle n'en soit agréable."—"Lettres Edifiantes," Tom. IV., p. 19.

[2] "Madura was the capital of the Hindoo kingdom of Madura, and the seat of learning in Southern India. It is of great antiquity and contains many remarkable pagodas. The province contains 13,000 square miles and 2,000,000 of inhabitants."—Duncan's Geog., p. 25.

[3] Du Jarric Hist., Tom. III., p. 750.

we cannot, with safety, omit this link. The conflicting testimony is so extensive that we can only afford the barest outline.

Beginning, as is just, with the Roman Catholic version of the history, we may say that it is founded on the letters of Perè Robert and his fellow-labourers, on the compilation of Du Jarric, from whom we have so largely quoted, on the "Relation Derinerè de ce qui s'est passé dans Maduré, par le Perè Hyacinthe de Magistris, Paris 1633," and on "La Mission du Maduré par le Perè Bertrand," one of the recent missionaries. The chief Romanist writers on whose testimony the general opinion is founded are Norbert, and Dubois, both hostile. Marshall, in his compilation, "Christian Missions" writes with all the bitterness of a neophyte, to prove that Romanist missions have always been successes, and Protestant ones always failures. He defends the conduct of Perè Robert as not only expedient but lawful, fully justified by the example of St. Paul. Speaking of Nobile's falsehoods to the Brahmins, he says, "he had as good a right to make them as St. Paul to declare at one time that he was a Hebrew, and at another that he was a Roman citizen."[1] Marshall is very severe on La Croze, Hough and Kaye, denouncing them as slanderers of a holy man whose virtues were too sublime for their appreciation; and he indulges in a

[1] Marshall's "Christian Missions," p. 219.

sneer at their credulity in accepting "the mendacious narrative of the renegade Norbert."[1] With every desire to be strictly impartial, we think that the weight of testimony is decidedly against Dei Nobili, even if we were to decide solely from his own account of his proceedings.[2]

A certain Father Fernandez had gone to Madura about 1592, and had laboured long without making a single convert. Robert dei Nobili, hearing of this, determined, in 1806, to devote himself to the work on new principles: "I will make myself an Indian, in order to save the Indians," was the watchword of his plan. Discerning the cause of Xavier's failure or partial success even with the lowest Castes, he resolved to disguise himself as a Brahmin and to aim at converting the highest.[3] For this purpose he devoted himself to years of study in order to acquire not merely the vernacular, but the ancient Sanscrit and the Vedas. In this arduous task he succeeded

1 "Memoires Historiques," par R. P. Norbert.

2 Du Jarric, Tom. III, p. 71.—In "Catholic Missions" in South India by Father Strickland, the disguises and forgeries perpetrated by the Jesuits are defended on the ground that "*ordinary* methods had failed and that the imposture was sactioned by the Pope!" p. 48. Ranke's "History of the Popes," Vol. II., p. 231. Nicolini's "History of the Jesuits," p. 108. Juvenciu's "Hist. Soc. Jesu.," Tom. II., Lib. XVIII.

3 "That Jesuit being arrived in the East Indies, said he was a Brahmin, which was no lie (!) After the death of that Father the true method of keeping and increasing the number of the new converts fell to the ground."—Urbano Cerri.

so thoroughly that he deceived even the Brahmins themselves.

Avoiding a long digression for the purpose of explaining the Brahmin's influence over the other Hindoos, we may briefly say that this sacerdotal Caste claimed direct descent from the God Brahma, and are therefore held so sacred, that the natives fall prostrate at their feet. Their source of power is an ascetic life, while their scientific attainments, though unequal to ours, are by no means despicable, especially in astrology and metaphysics.[1]

To imitate these men, to secure the love of the people, and thereby effect the conversion, first of the nobility, and then of the masses, formed the arduous task on which Perè Robert now entered. "I am neither a Prangui nor a Portuguese, but a Roman Rajah. I am also a Saniassi, that is a penitent." His apologists defend these assertions as strictly true; for, say they, as an Italian noble he was a Rajah, and as a Jesuit he was, of course, a penitent. But Paley argues that "it is the wilful deceit that makes the lie"; and as the statements of Perè Robert were not

[1] For further accounts, see the Letters of the Abbé Dubois, p. 88, and Choix des "Lettres Edifiantes," Tom. IV., pp. 150, 197, and 272. "The Brahmins are often erroneously regarded as constituting the Hindu priesthood, but the priestly office was so far from being esteemed their first and most distinctive privilege, that to the present day it is accounted one of the least honourable which a Brahmin can discharge."—Trevor's "India," p. 40.

literally true, and as they practised what is admittedly a "pious fraud," the defence falls to the ground. For, by their own confession, they wore the Cavy, or distinctive yellow cloth, they bore on their foreheads the sandal-wood powder; they fed on rice and bitter herbs, and drank only water; they lived in the most wretched huts; and won a reputation for sanctity by their silence and solitude. They even went so far as to assume heathen names; and, to answer objectors, Perè Robert applied his great skill to the production of a forgery in Sanscrit on an old bit of parchment. When questioned as to the genuineness of this certificate he solemnly swore before the council of Brahmins at Madura that the document was authentic and that he, like all Jesuits, was directly descended from their Indian Divinity! Nor was this all. He forged a new Veda which was so well executed that, for nearly two centuries, it imposed upon the natives themselves. The trick was at last discovered; and it has recently been thoroughly exposed by Mr. Ellis of Madras, who declares that the Ezour-Vêdam was a "literary forgery," or rather "of religious imposition without parallel."[1]

By these and similar frauds[2] the new Brahmins

[1] See Mr. Ellis's disquisition in "Asiatic Researches," Vol. XIV., p. 35. Hough's, "Christianity in India," Vol. II., p. 239.

[2] "De la se recontrans les uns les autres à la presence des gentils pour se mieux déguiser, ils ne se parloient que par Truchement."—Hyacinthe de Magistris, p. 407.

secured the protection of the Rajah and permission to preach throughout Madura. The Franciscans, whose feeble efforts had been so unproductive, were now fairly driven from the field by their daring and unscrupulous rivals. The Jesuits, finding the coast clear, pushed concession to idolatry to its utmost limit. Observing the love of display in the Hindoo character, they resolved to add the frivolous and disgusting rites of India to the superstitious pageantry of Rome. This, of course, Marshall denies,[1] but there is abundant proof from the letters of the Jesuits (authority which he surely cannot dispute) that images and pictures, music, fireworks, flags, flowers, and theatrical exhibitions were all employed as *means of conciliation and conversion.* Having secured the co-operation of some real Brahmins, the Jesuits made rapid strides. Thousands were added to the Roman Church, upon the easy conditions to which we have more than once referred. Even one of their own missioners has acknowledged that they were justly chargeable with the most culpable indulgence in winking at all kinds of idolatrous superstitions among their proselytes; and with having themselves rather become converts to the idolatrous worship of the Hindoos, than converters of the Hindoos to the Christian religion.[2]

Such proceedings roused the indignation of all the

[1] "Christian Missions," p. 226.
[2] Abbè Dubois, p. 7.

other religious orders. When the intelligence reached Goa, the greatest excitement prevailed; and a strong remonstrance was immediately sent to Rome. In 1620, Paul V. ordered the Archbishop to investigate the case. All the charges were fully substantiated; and when the report was laid before the Pontiff and Cardinals, Bellarmine, though Uncle of Dei Nobili, condemned him in the strongest terms. This well-merited rebuke has, with singular audacity, been represented by the apologists from Du Jarric to Marshall as "the persecution of innocent men."[1] Unterrified by the thunders of the Vatican, the Madura missioners continued their career; and, without denying the truth of the accusations, they offered such ingenious explanations, that the succeeding Pontiff, Gregory XV., somewhat modified the terms of censure. Yet he distinctly stated in a dispatch (1623) that if they continued in the slightest degree any practices of an idolatrous character, they were to give them up or take the consequences. This document is said to have been suppressed till 1680, during which time the Jesuits persevered in their old courses utterly regardless of Papal disapprobation. But we need not pursue the matter further at present.

The principal points in the early history of this famous mission are the labours of Fernandez from 1592 till 1606—Perè Robert's conversion of the

[1] Du Jarric, Tom. III., p. 770. Marshall, Vol. I., pp. 227-229.

Brahmins from 1606 till 1610—"the persecution from 1611 to 1622 and the death of Perè Robert at Meliapour in 1656." The influence of this mission would have been felt directly or indirectly in Southern India to the present hour, even if it had not been revived with extraordinary vigour in our own day. We may anticipate certain portions of our history by mentioning that during the XVIIth Century, the famous Portuguese missionary, John de Britto,[1] made numerous proselytes between 1673 and his martyrdom in 1693; and that he was assisted in these labours by his countrymen Morato, Martins, Daresi and others.[2] From causes which we cannot here discuss, the mission of Madura died out last century. In 1837 it was revived, being restored to the Jesuits by Gregory XVI.; and, in 1846, a bishopric was erected, including Madura, Marara and Tanjore.[3] "There is no more pregnant chapter in the whole history of human imposture, than that which embraces the astonishing *narrative of the Jesuits' Missions in Southern India.* For a time the Order 'stooped into a dark tremendous sea of cloud,' and the Jesuits, under the ban in Europe, disappeared from the Indian coasts. But they are *now again overrunning India*, and working mightily as of old: Great as is their apparent activity,

[1] "Histoire du Jean de Britto," par. Prab. 1853.

[2] "Hyacinthe de Magistris," p. 427.

[3] "Les Jesuits dans l'Inde," par. Louis St. Cyr, 1863.

perhaps the full extent of their efforts is hardly known, for, although they may not now simulate Brahmins, it is more than suspected that they have not yet abandoned their old love of disguise."[1]

[1] Kayes, "Christ. in India," pp. 36-7. "Jesuit Missions," by the Rev. W. S. Mackay, in "Calcutta Review," Vol. II. Nicolini's "History of the Jesuits," p. 113.

CHAPTER III.

PORTUGUESE MISSIONS IN THE CARNATIC.

"Toutes les Missions de l'Inde étaient des Missions Portugaises ; il est vrai qu'on y admettait des sujets des autres nations ; mais ces sujets devaient par la même perdre pour ainsi dire leur nationalité."—BERTRAND, Vol. I., p. 323.

"ALL the missions of India were Portuguese missions," says the Jesuit Father from whom we have just quoted, and though this chapter will carry us to the Eastern side of the great peninsula of India, and away from our Syrian friends, yet, "Portuguese Missions in Southern India," as a whole, would be incomplete without some reference to their operations on the coast of Coromandel.

This well-known coast extends from Cape Comorin to the Northern Circars, or from lat. 8 to lat. 16. It is otherwise called the Carnatic, and is distinguished by the possession of Madras, Pondicherry, and many important towns. The Eastern Ghauts rise behind the coast, spread into numerous branches, and leave a broad plain between their feet and the sea. Into this rich and fertile district the Portuguese Missionaries penetrated from Madura, and established what was technically called the Mission of the Carnatic, including not merely the kingdom of that name, but stretching over a vast district, nine hundred miles from north to south, and one hundred and thirty-four from east to west. The principal states which formed the fields of their operations were the Carnatic, Visapour, Bijanacaron, Ikkeri, Golconda, besides many other petty principalities chiefly subject to the Great Mogul.

According to histories, which some call traditions, the first Christian missionary in this region was the Apostle St. Thomas. It is confidently stated that after planting the churches on the Malabar coast, he continued his journey eastward to Meliapour,[1] then the chief city of the Carnatic. Thence he went to China, and returned to Meliapour; and at a place now called St. Thomas's Mount, about eight miles from Madras, suffered martyrdom at the hands of the Brahmins. There is a tradition that the Apostle erected a pillar here with an inscription to the effect

[1] Meliapour or Mailapoor, is now one of the suburbs of Madras.

"Aqui a cidade foi, que se chamava
Meliapor, fermosa, grande e rica:
Os idolos antiguos adorava,
Como inda agora faz a gente inica.
Louge do mar n'aquelle tempo estava,
Quando a fe, que no numdo se publica,
Thormé vintra prégando, e ja passara
Provincias mil do mundo, que en sinare."—CAMŒNS.

that the religion which he had planted would be revived by a race of strangers when the waves should wash the base of the column, at that time forty miles from the sea. Vasco da Gama, it is said, saw, in 1502, this very column close to the coast, with the prophecy literally fulfilled.[1] In 1522, the Portuguese, when exploring the Carnatic, are said to have found a cross at Meliapour with this remarkable inscription :—"At the time when Thomas founded this temple the King of Meliapour made him a grant of the customs of all the merchandises that were brought into that port, which duty was the tenth part of the goods." According to the Portuguese tradition, the bones of St. Thomas were also found, though Geddes dryly suggests that "they were reckoned by all the world before to have been lodged at Edessa."[2] An ancient record was discovered at the same time, stating that St. Thomas had converted the Rajah by a miracle. We next find a tradition that another cross and relics were dug out in 1544 by some Portuguese who were pulling down an old chapel, and who add the wonderful statement that they saw all the earth deeply stained with newly-shed blood, and much more to the same effect.[3] These dates are quoted to show that even before the time of St. Francis Xavier, Portuguese

1 Bruce's "Scenes and Lights in the East," p. 75. Howard's "Christians of S. Thomas," p. 10.

2 Geddes's "Hist. Ch. Mal.," p. 7.

3 Geddes's "Hist. Ch. Mal.," p. 6.

adventurers, including missionaries, were exploring the coast of the Carnatic. And, as we have already seen, that Xavier effected many conversions amongst the natives of the extreme south, and that, at an early period, he made Tutucurin his headquarters, the probability is that he travelled to the north, or appointed some of his converts to carry the Gospel along the coast to the ancient settlements of Indian Christianity. During the fifty years which succeeded the establishment of the Missionary College at Goa, while the Portuguese military and mercantile powers were approaching their climax, many enthusiastic followers in the footsteps of St. Francis were carrying the cross into Madura, the Carnatic, and the distant regions of Bengal. To enter into any minute detail of these transactions would be to repeat much of what has been stated in previous chapters, and we may, therefore, pass over the operations of the Portuguese missionaries on the east coast, and allude briefly to the work performed by the emissaries of another nation.

We must take it for granted that our readers are already acquainted with the events which took place in India shortly after the Synod of Diamper, the establishment of the East India Company, the wars between French and English in India, the attacks of the Dutch on the Portuguese settlements, and the rapid decline of an empire which had so rapidly risen.

About the year 1660, the French were making great efforts to obtain a share in the commerce of the East; and, in 1664, two years after the Portuguese cession of Bombay to the English,[1] they took Pondicherry, and made it the centre of their possessions in the Carnatic. No sooner had they secured a firm footing than various orders of monks commenced their labours amongst the heathen. They were not long permitted to conduct this enterprise alone. Irrespective of earlier plantings of the Cross by explorers from the Central Station at Madura, the successors of Perè Robert resolved to thrust themselves into the field which was now certainly the province of the French Capuchins. The Portuguese Jesuits and the Pondicherry Monks, though aiming at the same end, ***pursued it by means entirely different;*** the former, as we have seen, bending Christianity to the idolatry of Brahma, the latter protesting against such wicked degradation, and preaching, in comparative purity, the faith of Christ on its own merits. The followers of Loyola had secured the "Constitution" mentioned in our last chapter, but they concealed it for sixty years; and, assuring the Pope that the objectionable rites were merely civil forms without any religious reference, they contrived to evade all obedience to the Papal injunction, to hoodwink the

[1] Bombay, Algiers, and £500,000 formed the dowry of Catherine of Portugal on her marriage with Charles II.

Roman Court by skilfully-contrived and specious reports, and thus to pursue their arrogant course almost unchecked.[1] What we have already described at Madura was repeated at Pondicherry. The image of the Virgin was borne aloft in precisely the same way in which the Pagans carry their idols. Bands of heathen musicians were engaged from the Pagodas; and their rude drums, gongs, and hautboys mingled in discord with the cries and shouts which accompany a Hindoo procession.

The chief of the French Mission, feeling that the Jesuits, by this miserable pandering to Pagan folly, were deeply injuring the cause of true religion that they might promote the interests of their Order, protested most strongly against these profane exhibitions, and wrote to the Pontiff to invoke his interference. But not only did the arrogant ambition of the Jesuits embroil them with their co-religionists, but it involved them also in serious disputes with the Brahmins, which, early in the XVIIIth Century, had reached such a height that Pondicherry itself was in danger. Their infatuation was conspicuously displayed in their destruction of the images of Brahma, Vishnu, and other idols,[2] an extraordinary deviation from their

[1] "The Jesuits stirred themselves up in their own defence and represented to Gregory XIII., Paul's successor, that those rites were merely civic ceremonies and not at all religious ones."—Nicolini, p. 113. See also "Cretinean," Vol. V., p. 47.

[2] A parallel case occurs in the case of Willehad. His discourses here

general subserviency. The natives who witnessed this insult, thus publicly offered to their divinities, resolved to avenge the wrong, and they immediately sent a message to their brethren at Tanjore to aid them in their purpose. The Rajah eagerly and instantly responded, the Christians were everywhere openly beaten, and starved to death in prison. Many fled to the Christians of the coast, many more renounced their faith, and a few submitted to martyrdom. One Jesuit died in prison, another was banished; all the churches were demolished, and Christianity for years extinguished.[1] Such was the result of Jesuit zeal, and such will ever be the effect of the lack of common sense in dealing with the prejudices of the heathen.

In 1702, the Pope resolved to send a special legate to French India to check the unruly proceedings of the Jesuits. When Cardinal Tournon landed in November, 1703, he was kindly received by the Brethren, who succeeded in making him suspend his Edict for three years. At last, those very men who, as the successors of Loyolo, had, of course, taken an oath of implicit obedience to the Pope, positively re-

had begun to meet with much acceptance, when some of his scholars suffered themselves to be led away by intemperate zeal, and hastened to destroy the idolatrous temples, instead of first banishing, by the power of Christ, the idols from the heart of their worshippers.—Neander's "Memorials of Christian Life," p. 480.

[1] Condensed from Norbert's "Memoires Historiques."

belled and refused to admit the legate's right to control their foreign missions. They even went so far as to declare that their Bishop at St. Thomé had a jurisdiction in India equal to that of the Pope elsewhere.[1] The Cardinal, finding no good was at present to be done, sailed for China in 1704, and, in 1706, the Council of Pondicherry solemnly protested against his jurisdiction in the East. His tragical death at Macao, in 1710, is attributed to the intrigues of the Jesuits.[2]

In 1714, we find that a Monsieur de Visdelon, a Jesuit, was appointed Bishop of Clandiopolis, and Vicar Apostolic of India *with full power from the Pope to purify the Church from the idolatrous rites by which her services had been polluted.* Hence another contest arose between the Pope's Vicar and the Bishop of St. Thomé, soon after which the Jesuits obtained powers from the King of France for the suspension of the Vicar and two Superiors of the Capuchins. It is quite impossible, however, to describe the perpetual conflicts which disgrace the Roman Church at Pondicherry, in consequence of the rebellious spirit of the Jesuits. In conclusion, we may briefly mention that, in 1742, Benedict XIV. issued a bull demanding implicit obedience; and, at last, after forty years' contumacious resistance, the refractory Fathers were

[1] Hough's "Christianity," Vol. II., p. 442.

[2] "Memoires Historiques," par Norbert, Vol. III., pp. 97, 149.

obliged to yield. From that time their hitherto prosperous missions in South India began to decline. The arrogance of the missionaries had rendered the very name of Christianity odious, the detection of cunningly devised imposture had shaken all faith in the Jesuits, and the suppression of their Order in Europe had been severely felt in India, especially by drying up the fountain which had furnished a regular supply of educated clergy. Add to these causes the commencement of modern missionary efforts by men whose lives were the best comments on their doctrines, and whose method of teaching was the strongest possible contrast to that of the Jesuits, and one is not at all at a loss to account *for the failure of the Romish Missions in Southern India, and for the odium which they brought on the Christian name.*

CHAPTER IV.

SYRIAN CHRISTIANS IN THE XVIIth CENTURY.

"If any man teach otherwise, and consent not to wholesome words, even the words of our Lord Jesus Christ, and to the doctrine which is according to godliness; he is proud, knowing nothing, but doting about questions and strifes of words, whereof cometh envy, strife, railings, evil surmisings, perverse disputings of men of corrupt minds and destitute of the truth, supposing that gain is godliness: from such withdraw thyself."—1 Tim. vi.

DURING the last three chapters we have attempted to give some idea of the Portuguese missions in the XVIth Century, with brief notices of important matters during the XVIIth and XVIIIth Centuries. It is true that some of the events therein narrated do not directly bear on the Malabar Church; yet it is unquestionable that in all history one event leans upon another, and small causes frequently produce great results. The present case forms no exception. The spirit by which the Portuguese missionaries were actuated did not fail to excite a universal feeling of resentment; and though no electric spark conveyed the message from the Carnatic to Malabar, yet every-one familiar with India well knows the mysterious rapidity with which reports are transmitted to the most distant regions. Thus the whole South of India was filled with opposition to the Portuguese missionary efforts and to the Christianity which they attempted to propagate.

The standard authorities for this portion of our essay are Raulinus, Urbano Cerri, La Croze, Barreto, and Vincent Maria.[1] The English reader will find the substance of these narratives in Hough's "History of Christianity in India," Book VI., and, in a briefer form, in Day's "Land of the Permauls."

After the signal triumph of Rome at Diamper, accomplished by the skill, courage, and perseverance of Menezes, the history of the Syrian Christians seems to lose much of its interest. Reduced to abject submission, the followers of St. Thomas appear to have had no heart left for literary work, or possibly they were only too glad to let silence cover their defeat. On the other hand, the Jesuits, though victorious, exhibited no anxiety to proclaim to the world the misconduct of their leaders, which, more than anything else, contributed to their ruin in the East. Hence the obscurity which prevails at this period of our history, and hence, too, the conflicting statements of the chroniclers as to dates and names which render it next to impossible for the compiler to construct a

[1] Barreto, Relat. Status Christ. Malabar Romœ, 1645. Vincent Marie, Il viaggio all'Indie Orientali Fol. Romœ.

consistent narrative. This being premised, we must make the best of the material at our command.

The first Romish Bishop, Francisco Rodriguez (Roz), was succeeded by another Xavier, who, in turn, was followed by Stephen de Britto. In 1634, a Jesuit prelate, named Garcia, ruled the poor Syrian Christians with a rod of iron. He attempted to abolish the Syriac language and to introduce Latin in the Church Service, and he persecuted every Syrian who differed in the minutest trifle from the ritual of Rome. He enjoyed a "bad eminence" amongst his fellow-Churchmen, avaricious, as nearly all of them were, for his intense love of money, and his unscrupulous extortion. Such oppression, continuing for fifty years, gradually roused the patient spirit of the Syrians into violent action, and completely undid all the work of Diamper. They complained especially of the enforced celibacy of their own clergy, of the seizure of their churches, of the introduction of images, of the bribed silence of the Cattanars, and of the tyranny exercised by the Romish priests over both clergy and laity of the Malabar Church. Their numerous overtures to the Roman Pontiff were treated with contemptuous neglect, for the Pope could not afford to quarrel with the Jesuits. The exasperated Syrians at last revolted, threw off the Roman yoke, and resolved to elect a bishop of their own. The Portuguese missionaries, terribly alarmed, applied at once to

Alexander VII., who, well aware of the true cause of this rebellion, instantly dispatched four Carmelites to still the tempest. But, while these events were going on in Malabar, an unexpected ally was contributing the means of breaking the chains which Portuguese tyranny had forged. The Dutch, who had for half a century been gradually gaining power in the East, in 1656, drove the Portuguese out of Ceylon, and, encouraged by success, soon afterwards attacked the settlements on the Malabar coast.

Once fairly roused to action, the Malabar Christians took the decided step of writing to the three Patriarchs—the Nestorian at Mosul, the Coptic at Cairo, and the Jacobite in Syria, imploring each to send them a Bishop without delay. The first to reply was the Primate of the Copts, who immediately dispatched Attala (Theodore)[1] to Mosul, that he might receive his commission from the Nestorian Patriarch. But this account is doubted;[2] and it seems impossible to determine whether he was a Nestorian from Mosul or a Jacobite from Antioch.[3] Be that as it may, on his arrival at Surat, he incautiously took some Capuchins into his confidence, who immediately betrayed him to the Inquisition. On his journey toward the south he was seized, and, notwithstanding the attempt at a

[1] Raulin, "Diss V. De Ind. Orient Diocesi," p. 441. Day's "Land of the Permauls," p. 234.

[2] La Croze, p. 358.

[3] Vincent Maria, L. II., p. 163. La Croze, p. 359.

rescue by 25,000 armed men, who marched upon Cochin, he was detained a prisoner. The defeated Syrians held a meeting at Alangat, and swore a solemn oath to drive out the Jesuits; and a second at Mangate, where they took the extraordinary step of requesting twelve Cattanars to consecrate Archdeacon Thomas, of Palokamatta, as their Bishop,[1] imploring him to repent of his mock consecration, but in vain. Fifty years of suffering had forced him and his followers into a position which they would not lightly abandon.

Meantime, the captured Attala was sent from Cochin to Goa, where he suffered a cruel death in the dungeons of the Inquisition.[2] It is but fair to say that the Jesuit missionaries, ashamed of this murder, have tried to prove that the unhappy Prelate was drowned, by the orders of the Governor, in the harbour of Cochin, when the Syrian army invested the place.[3]

We left the Carmelites on their way from Rome to India. On their arrival at Surat, they were placed in a most embarrassing position, for they not only encountered the resistance of the civil power, but the hostility of the Jesuits; the former pleading their possession of the sovereignty of India, the latter

[1] See an admirable discussion of this irregularity in Hough's History, p. 306-7-8.

[2] Raulin, "Hist. Ecc. Mal.," p. 442.

[3] La Croze, p. 362.

jealous of any interference with the interests of their Order. The Carmelites, thus checked, applied to the Dutch commander, by whose intervention they succeeded in reaching Cananore, early in 1657. Thence they were obliged to go by water, in order to avoid their own countrymen and co-religionists. They found their mission hedged about with difficulties. The Archdeacon naturally received them with distrust; and the Jesuits exhausted every expedient to obstruct their course. The Papal commissioners, in several conferences, attempted to influence the Archdeacon to deny his consecration and resign his office, but failing in this, they determined to apply for aid to Francis de Mello, at Goa. The Governor, fully alive to the importance of conciliating the Syrian Christians, that their co-operation might be secured in defending Cochin and other towns against the Dutch, resolved to receive the Carmelites as the ambassadors of peace. The Jesuits, perceiving that their influence was verging to its close, made the most desperate efforts, including the use of a forged letter, to excite the suspicion of the Governor of Goa against the Carmelites. But in vain. Father Vincent, thus protected, waited on the Jesuit Bishop at Cranganor, who received him kindly, admitted his credentials, and implored the Christians of St. Thomas to submit to his authority. Proceeding on his mission, he found Carturte, and one or two other places, essentially Roman Catholic ; but even they hated the Jesuit yoke. This complication was increased by the fact that the Syrian Christians were divided into two parties, even before the arrival of the Romanists, and that since that time there had been an augmented feeling of rivalry in consequence of the adherence of the Southern division to the Roman Communion. With the latter section of the Syrians the Carmelites succeeded, and the Portuguese authorities were so delighted with the prospect thus afforded of securing the alliance of 40,000 well-armed mountaineers, that, in their gratitude, they gave a splendid public reception to the Carmelites at Corolongate. The Northern division of the Malabar Church still held out under Archdeacon Thomas. Success began to dawn upon their efforts at Mangate, but Jesuit influence again interfered, and was potent enough to extort from Goa a letter, ordering the Carmelites to quit the country. The Governor of Cochin, dreading the approach of the Dutch, and desirous of retaining the affection of the Syrians, resolved to support the Carmelites in their mission at all hazards. And so for years this singularly intricate series of intrigues went on, the chief agencies being, as we have already seen, the Portuguese and the Dutch, the Romish Syrians and the Christians of St. Thomas, the rival Orders of Jesuits and Carmelites, and the Inquisition ever watchful and ready to interpose. We fear that few of our readers would have any curiosity to know how Bishop Garcia tried to ruin the Carmelites, how the latter began to despair of their mission, and how they were encouraged by the dreaded tribunal at Goa to persevere, how four different assemblies met and discussed the question of the Archdeacon's consecration, the propriety of submitting to Rome, and many other matters deeply interesting to them, but not directly affecting the question now before us. One circumstance only is perhaps important. In an assembly in the Church of St. Thomas, near Cochin, Joseph,[1] one of the Carmelites, was elected Bishop of Malabar, and his appointment confirmed by the Pope. The Southern Churches were then united; Garcia in vain tried to recover his diocese, and two of the Carmelites returned to Rome to give an account of their operations.

On the 10th of March, 1658, Father Hyacinthe once more appeared in Malabar, and, finding persuasion ineffectual, he subdued the refractory by means of fines and imprisonment, which he caused the Rajahs to inflict on his fellow Christians. But as the agency was limited, so was the success. The northern portion of the Syrian Christians supported their Archdeacon as firmly as ever, and, to add to the perplexity of the case, Bishop Garcia nominated a new Archdeacon. A change, however, soon came o'er the scene. Garcia

[1] Day's "Land of the Permauls," p. 237.

died in 1659, and, the year after, his rival Father Hyacinthe expired at Cochin.

Meantime, the Carmelite Joseph, who had been consecrated at Rome as Bishop of Hierapolis, reached India in April, 1661, and was welcomed at Cochin by all parties of his countrymen, except the Jesuits. The Syrian Archdeacon, of course, endeavoured to prejudice the people against the new Bishop, and did not hesitate to follow the example so frequently set by the Jesuits, of circulating false reports. Bishop Joseph, meantime, disregarding these calumnies, took possession of the cathedral at Cranganor, and, on the 22nd of August, commenced the visitation of his diocese with a grand display of ecclesiastical magnificence. Then followed the old story of endless conferences between the Bishop and the Archdeacon, who was at last obliged, dreading the fate of Attala, to escape to the mountains. This flight left the Syrian Christians at the mercy of the new Bishop, who, like a second Menezes, forced them to bend to his authority on the battle-ground of Diamper. This effected, Bishop Joseph ordered a large fire to be kindled before the church, in which he burnt the Archdeacon's palanquin, his books and garments, and regretted that his body was not there also.[1]

The unholy alliance between the heathen Prince Codormo and the Romish Bishop had enabled the

[1] La Croze, p. 409.

latter to promote his mission by force of arms. But the time of retribution was at hand. The Eastern Empire of the Portuguese was now rapidly crumbling before the advancing power of the Dutch. In 1660 they captured Negapatam, and thus secured the Coromandel coast. Advancing to Malabar, they took Coulan in 1661, and Cranganor, the cathedral city of the Jesuits, in 1662. Cochin fell before the arms of the invader in 1663; the Portuguese power received its death blow, and the Christians of St. Thomas once more began to breathe the air of civil and religious freedom. The conquerors, whose experience in their native land had taught them to dread the presence of the Romish priests, insisted on the immediate departure of all the Jesuits and Carmelites from Malabar. Bishop Joseph, thus compelled to depart, consecrated a Cattanar, named Alexander, to act as Vicar-Apostolic during his absence. The new Prelate (the first native Indian Bishop) was protected by the Dutch commander, whose mind was strongly prejudiced against the Archdeacon. Bishop Alexander, who persuaded forty-five of the Syrian Churches to return to the Communion of Rome, ruled the diocese till 1676 when he was succeeded, according to one report, by a Raphael Figuredo; according to another by Dom Diego, as Archbishop of Cranganor.

Our readers must not forget, amid this confusion and strife, the existence of that body of Syrian

Christians who were struggling to consolidate their newly-won freedom under Archdeacon, or, as we perhaps should call him, Mar-Thomas. We learn that about the year 1665, Gregorius, Bishop of Jerusalem, arrived at Malabar, and consecrated Archdeacon Thomas to be the Metropolitan of what remained of the Syrian Church. And, it is stated, that this was the occasion on which the Jacobite liturgies and ritual were adopted, instead of the Nestorian in use before the Synod of Diamper. From this date the Syrian Christians have been a sadly divided Church, some following Rome, acknowledging one of three prelates at Cranganor, Verapole, or Quilon, but all called by the common term Romo-Syrians. The remainder, that is, those that preserved their ecclesiastical independence, are, of course, stigmatised by their foes as schismatics, heretics, Jacobites, or Nestorians, but are generally known as the Christians of St. Thomas, the Church of Malabar, or simply as the Syrian Christians. On the death of Mar-Thomas, in 1678, Mar-Andrew succeeded, and governed the diocese till 1685. From that period till the close of the century, there is a dreary record of petty strife and competition for the bishopric, with all the painful discussions which invariably accompany such unseemly struggles. As we have already observed, there is nothing in the history of the Church of the Serra in the least calculated to interest the general reader.

Still, for the sake of continuity, we shall be obliged to give a brief summary of the Church's vicissitudes during the XVIIIth Century.

CHAPTER V.

SYRIAN CHRISTIANS IN THE XVIIIth CENTURY.

"We are already debtors to that ancient people, the Syrian Christians. By their long and energetic defence of pure doctrine against anti-Christian error, they are entitled to the gratitude and thanks of the rest of the Christian world. Their Scriptures, their doctrine, their language, in short their very existence, all add something to the evidence of the truth of Christianity."—BUCHANAN.

DURING the century which we have just sketched in relation to the small but interesting Church of the Serra, great events had been taking place all over India. The East India Company had secured their first and second charters and laid the foundation-stone of their colossal empire. The Dutch,[1] entering the Indian Ocean as modest traders, had succeeded in dispossessing the Portuguese of their richest settlements, leaving them but a shadow of their once splendid dominions. The French, eager to share the glories which the "wealth of Ormuz and of Ind" promised to the adventurer of every grade had secured the Carnatic. These three powers were

1 "Niehoff's Voyages," Valentyn's "History," Baldaens's "Description of Malabar," Hough, p. 52.

engaged, as every student of history knows, in perpetual intrigues, diplomatic contests, and open war with each other, and with the native princes. There was, therefore, but little time or thought to spend on missionary enterprise, and but little taste or talent in soldiers, merchants, or buccaneers, to record conversions among the heathen, even had such existed.[1] Nay, more, there is but too much proof that the lives which Europeans led, when freed from the restraints of Rome, were calculated rather to impede than to promote the spread of Christianity and civilisation amongst the surrounding tribes of Hindostan.[2]

These great events, occurring in the immediate vicinity of the Malabar Church, affected its fate indirectly, and often directly; and we shall frequently have to show in our chronological summary, for it can be little else, how the *Portuguese influence still continued to operate*, modified as it often was by the interference of its European rivals. At the beginning of the XVIIIth Century we find one Didacus abdicating the

1 "They had no grand thoughts of the diffusion of civilisation and the propagation of Christianity. The conversion of the Moors or the Gentoos was assuredly no part of their design."—Kaye's "Christianity," p. 38.

2 "His doings on those far off shores were unknown to his countrymen in England; perchance there may have been a parent or a brother, or a friend in whose eyes the adventurer might desire to wear a fair aspect; but in India he was far beyond observation as though he welt in another planet."—Kaye's "Christianity," p. 45.

Romish Bishopric of the native Christians in favour of John Ribeiro, a Jesuit. This gleam of triumph for the Order would have been still more evanescent than it was, but for the fact that the talents of the Prelate were of use to the Rajah of Calicut, and a few other neighbouring chiefs. Between 1707 and 1715 the Christians of St. Thomas seemed to have been governed by two Bishops—Mar-Thomas, a Monophysite, ruling over the southern portion of the diocese, with but twenty-two churches; the other, Mar-Gabriel, a Nestorian, presiding over the north. These two were rivals in doctrine and office, and, of course, at open war. Into all the petty details we dare not enter, but refer our reader to authorities that will give ample scope to his investigations.[1]

The line of Romish Prelates seems to have terminated about the year 1721, when Ribeiro, Bishop of Cranganor died.[2] Still, the Bishops of Cochin and Verapoli exercised their functions, though in utter estrangement from each other. The Syrian Christians, about the year 1720, were equally divided, 50,000 acknowledging Rome, and as many adhering faithfully to their native pastors. In 1727 an important event occurred in the history of their Church, produced by the following causes:—As far back as 1705

[1] "Lettres Edifiantes" (Dowzième Recueil), p. 383. La Croze, p. 420. Mosheim. "Eccl. Hist." Cent. VI., Part II., Chap. V. Day's "Land of the Permauls," p. 246. Asseman, Tom. III., Part II., p. 464.

[2] Raulin, "De Ind. Orient. Dio. Dissert," V., p. 449.

the Danes had formed a mission at Tranquebar,[1] on the Eastern coast, under the sanction of Frederick IV.,[2] and in 1709 the S.P.G. (established eight years before) sent its first pecuniary contribution of twenty pounds towards the support of missionary efforts in the East. Soon afterwards, this English Society suggested to the Danish Mission the possibility of effecting a union with the independent portion of the Syrian Church, with the hope of being able to make it a nursery of missionaries for the conversion of India. The Danes immediately wrote to the Dutch Chaplain at Cochin, who, however, gave no encouragement to the project, declaring that the education and habits of the Cattanars wholly unfitted them for missionary life. Undeterred by this repulse, the zealous Danes wrote, in 1727, a friendly letter to Mar-Thomas, expressing their desire to co-operate with the Syrian Churches, and begging him to state, without reserve, his opinion as to the best method of improving and strengthening his own Church, so as to make it a centre from which the Gospel might be spread amongst the surrounding nations. The Prelate's answer came next year, and afforded no satisfactory solution of the question; but, on the contrary, seemed to consider the Romish usurpation in Malabar

[1] In the North of Tanjore.

[2] Hough's "Christianity," Vol. II., p. 390. Kaye's "Christianity India," p. 66.

and the unhappy divisions amongst the Syrians themselves as sufficient excuses for taking no action in the matter. On the death of this Prelate, in 1729, his nephew, of the same name, succeeded; and we read that he almost immediately charged the other Syrian Bishop (Mar-Gabriel) with heresy, and appealed to the Dutch Governor of Cochin, requesting his interposition. The Dutch Chaplain wrote to both the Prelates offering to act as mediator; but as each believed himself right, the intercession failed. In 1730, Mar-Gabriel died, after a residence of more than twenty years in Malabar; but though a stranger (from Jerusalem), he appears to have so identified himself with every petty dispute, and to have so completely yielded to Roman influence, as to have done no permanent good during this long episcopate to the churches under his care. A new Syrian Bishop was immediately sent from Babylon, and succeeded in reaching Surat, but the rival Jesuit and Carmelite Prelates, forgetting their animosities for a time, combined to intercept this dangerous opponent; and they appear to have succeeded, but by what means there is no evidence to show. Their reciprocal anathemas were then resumed with as much heartiness as ever.

The Christian Knowledge Society's reports state that, in 1732, Cattanars from the Serra of Malabar were in the habit of performing a journey of six hundred miles across the peninsula to attend as pilgrims at the great festivals held at St. Thomé,[1] near Madras. This celebrated shrine has been already noticed as the residence of the Roman Catholic Bishop, and as attracting annually crowds of devotees from all parts of India. There are several churches, of which the most remarkable are Nôtre Dame Dumont and the Resurrection. The former is held in such esteem that, when the Portuguese ships first perceive it on approaching land, they fire a salute in its honour. Above the grand altar there is a Cross, traditionally reported to be the work of St. Thomas, and which possesses miraculous powers, especially in healing diseases. Eight days before Christmas, the Portuguese celebrate with much solemnity the feast which they call the expectation of the Blessed Virgin. During this festival, the grey Cross changes colour, becoming red, brown, and, at last, a dazzling white, distilling water so abundantly that it flows over the altar. This prodigy is said to have been witnessed by four hundred persons, who felt constrained to avow that it bore unmistakable impress of supernatural power.[2] Such being the objects

[1] "On l'appelle aussi Meliapour, ou, pour parler les Indiens, Maila bouram, c'est à dire la ville des paons."—"Choix des Lettres Edifiantes," Tom. IV., pp. 6, 68.

[2] "Ce prodige, rapporté par des missionaires qui en ont été deux fois témoins. est d' ailleurs constaté par le témoignage de plus de quatre cents personnes, de tout âge et de tout état, parmi lesquelles on compte des Anglais Protestans qui, apres avoir examiné, avec la plus sévère attention, si ce n'était point là quelque prestige employé pour surpendre

which annually attracted Syrian pilgrims to St. Thomé, no doubt can exist as to the faith which these men professed. Indians by birth, they were Romanists by creed; and though they employed Syriac in the service of the Church, they hardly possessed sufficient knowledge of the language to read the public prayers, and frequently were unable to explain what they had recited.

Between the years 1730 and 1750, the Danish Mission at Tranquebar was frequently visited by Cattanars of all creeds from Cochin and Travancore. The impression which these priests made upon the Danes was far from favourable. They seemed to possess little or no theological knowledge; their literary attainments were of the slenderest character; their whole attention seemed to be devoted to controversies of a ritualistic character; and their prejudices of caste were so strong that they would not eat even with the Christian converts at Tranquebar. One of them said, that though he admired the Danish missionaries as good men, he objected to their religion because it was deficient in three things, viz.: Fasting days, the sacrifice of the mass, and the adoration of the Virgin. Nevertheless, the good missionaries tried to take the most charitable views of their fellow-

la crédulité des peuples, ont été constraints d'avouer que ce prodige ne pouvait être opéré par aucun moyen naturel, et que, dans toutes ses circonstances, il portait les caractères d'un effet surnaturel et divin."—"Choix des Lettres Edifiantes," Tom IV., pp. 89 90.

Christians; they dwelt upon the numerous points of agreement between the Syrians and themselves, and they softened as much as possible the asperities produced by ritual or doctrinal differences. But all in vain. Their experience agreed with that of Chaplain Nicolai at Cochin. They concluded that the minds of these Syrians were too bigoted to admit of any reformation, that they were obstinately attached to their ancient traditions, and to the recently introduced Romish superstitions.

After this failure, no further attempt seems to have been made for many years; and meantime the history of the Syrian Church is shrouded in obscurity. In 1747, a Bishop is said to have arrived from Babylon, and three years later several Jacobites came from Antioch. The Maphrian Basilius, commissioned by the Patriarch of Antioch, in the year 1750, entered Travancore. Furnished with crozier, crucifix, and ring, he intended to consecrate Thomas to be Metropolitan; but a dispute arose; the commissioner therefore selecting one Cyril, whose learning and general religious character pointed him out as the more suitable person for this dignity. Nineteen years of incessant dissension followed this decision; and at last order was restored by the award of the Rajah in favour of the native Bishop, Mar-Thomas, who succeeded to the primacy under the name of Mar-Dionysius.

In 1772, new discussions arose, in which Gregorius, Cyril, and others, play conspicuous parts. Cyril soon afterwards retired; the two foreign prelates died; and Mar-Dionysius once more governed in peace. He seems to have been in every respect an admirable man, and true Christian. His government was firm, yet gentle; he did his utmost to promote practical religion amongst the poor Syrians; and he made every effort to allay the ferment of theological strife. He lived to a great age, and was visited, in 1806, by Dr. Claudius Buchanan, who has left us an interesting account of the interview. "He was dressed," he says, "in a vestment of dark red silk; a golden cross hung from his neck, and his venerable beard reached below his girdle. Such, thought I, was the appearance of Chrysostom in the fourth century." "I found him," he adds, "to be far superior in general learning to any of his clergy whom I had seen. . . . He descanted with great satisfaction on the hope of seeing printed Syriac Bibles from England, and said they would be a treasure to his Church."[1]

Here we must end our brief résumé of the Syrian Church in the eighteenth century, leaving for discussion, in the concluding part of our essay, those portions of its history which fill above sixty-five years of the present century.

[1] "Christian Researches," p. 105.

BOOK V.

THE PORTUGUESE MISSIONS, WITH SPECIAL REFERENCE TO MODERN MISSIONARY EFFORTS IN SOUTH INDIA.

CHAPTER I.

THE FIRST PROTESTANT MISSIONS IN SOUTH INDIA.

"The experiment has been made now for upwards of a century by Protestant missionaries in India, and with a measure of success that warrants the inference that God has not shut against His people the door of hope."—HOUGH.

WE propose in this, the concluding book of our Essay, to lay before our readers a brief, but, we hope, a distinct outline of *Modern Missionary Efforts in Southern India.* We shall attempt to show how the reformed churches inaugurated their missions to the nations of Hindostan; how the Syrian Christians were affected by the various societies; how the Romish Missions gradually died out, and how they have been revived. And we shall finish our work by submitting the most recent accounts of the actual condition of the Malabar Church, with a few suggestions as to the most promising means of purifying its doctrine and ritual, contaminated by the Portuguese, and receiving it into union with the Reformed Catholic Church of England.

It would, of course, be foreign to our purpose to enter upon any historical sketch, however condensed, of the early English settlements in India. The achievements of Drake and Cavendish, the voyages of Lancaster and Middleton, the conquests and annexations under Clive, Hastings, Cornwallis, Wellesley, and their successors, and all matters of ordinary history must be studied in the numerous volumes which record the origin and progress of our Eastern Empire. Our business is to treat of a nobler theme though with an humbler pen. We must, therefore, assume that the reader is already in possession of a sufficient knowledge of the history of India, and especially of the South, to be able to follow our narrative without our entering into such explanations as would form too extensive digressions from our main subject.

In the last chapter, reference was made to the Tranquebar [1] Mission, founded by the Danes in the year 1705. The two pioneers were Ziegenbalg and Plutscho,[2] educated at Halle, under Professor Frank, whose greatest pleasure was to train young men, as Dr. Vaughan does in our own day, for the work of the ministry. *Their theory was essentially different from that of the Portuguese missionaries.* The

[1] Tranquebar, between two arms of the Caveng in the District of Tanjore, Diocese of Madras, 140 miles S.S.W. of Madras. Pop. 20,000. This town was Danish from 1621 to 1846, when it was ceded to the English. The Portuguese Missions had a church there from a very early period.

[2] Dean Pearson's "Memoirs of Schwartz," Vol. I., p. 14. Niécamp's "Histoire de Missions Danoises," Tom. I. p. 4

young Danes had sworn no allegiance to the Pontiff, but had solemnly dedicated themselves to God. They were destitute of Papal bulls and briefs, but they carried the Bible in their hands, their heads, and their hearts. They put no faith in external baptism as a mere *opus operatum*, but they believed in it as one of the sacraments. Firmly resolved, in the fervour of youthful enthusiasm, to do and suffer all things for the cause of Christ, they were yet entirely free from any morbid love of ostentatious mortification; and, while ready to die, if necessary, in the propagation of the faith, they felt it no part of their duty to seek death for the glory of a martyr's crown. In one respect they pre-eminently differed from some, at least, of the Roman "Missioners," for they were thoroughly conscientious men, acting in the most straightforward manner, and, therefore, holding in abhorrence the policy of Dei Nobili and his followers, who unscrupulously employed disguises and forgeries as instrumentalities for converting the heathen. Landing at Tranquebar, they met with a cool reception from their cautious and phlegmatic countrymen, who, looking on the enterprise from a commercial platform, ridiculed the young men as visionaries, or pitied them as victims. Unshaken in their resolve by this welcome, they determined to trust in God and use means to ensure success. They saw at once that nothing could be done without a thorough knowledge of Tamil (the language of the country), and, therefore, without dictionary, grammar, or Monshee, they sat down on the sand with the Hindoo children and mastered the subject. This gained, they had still to face the apathy of the Indian character, the bigotry of the Brahmins, the hostility of the Romish priests, and, above all, the prejudice against Christianity, produced by the scandalous lives of the European residents.[1] In spite of all these obstacles, they made way. In 1707 they baptised their first convert, and built their first church. Between 1708 and 1711 the New Testament was translated into Tamil,[2] and, at a later period, the Hebrew Bible, as far as Ruth. How different is this from the methods of conversion pursued by the Portuguese missionaries, who relied on preaching in a language which the natives utterly failed to understand, and on the repetition of creeds and paternosters which the superstitious heathen were apt to regard as incantations like their own. The Portuguese never dreamt of doing more than correcting certain alleged errors in the Syrian manuscripts of the Cattanars; but it was *no part of their plan to diffuse the Scriptures amongst the people.*[3] The Danes, on the contrary, looked upon

[1] Niécamp's "Histoire des Missions Danoises," Tom. I., p. 206. Kaye's "History of Christianity," p. 41.

[2] The New Testament was also printed in Portuguese by the S.P.C.K., and sent out to Tranquebar for the use of the Mission—a proof of the extent of the *Portuguese* population in this district. Pearson's "Memoirs of Schwartz," p. 19.

[3] "Niécamp's Hist.," Tom. I., p. 214.

the Church and the Bible as the two great pillars of God's truth; and while not neglecting the doctrines and ceremonies of the former, they felt it their duty to translate the Word of God into the vulgar tongue, to employ the printing press as a means of cheap and rapid reproduction, and to educate the young in a knowledge of the sacred volume. The experience of more than a hundred and fifty years has confirmed, in a remarkable degree, the sagacity of the two students of Halle, in devising the only effectual method of converting the heathen.

Ziegenbalg's death, in 1719, left the Tranquebar Missions to the charge of Gründler, who survived him but a year. Some pleasant intercourse had taken place between the Danes and Mr. Lewis, the English chaplain at Madras,[1] who wrote, in 1712, to the Christian Knowledge Society in the following terms: "The Tranquebar Mission must be encouraged. It is the first attempt the Protestants ever made in that kind. We must not put out the smoking flax. It would give our adversaries the Papists, who boast so much of their congregations De Propagandâ Fide, too much cause to triumph over us."[2] The next chaplain at Madras (Sterenson) took the deepest interest in the Danish efforts, assisted them with money, and wrote an interesting account of a visit to Tranquebar

[1] See an interesting account in Pearson's "Memoirs," p. 18.
[2] Hough, Vol. III. Kaye's "Christianity, p. 75.

in 1716. Passing over several eventful years, we find the Danish Mission, under English auspices, extending itself throughout the Presidency of Madras. At first success was small, owing to their cautious and conscientions system of conversion; for, as we have already shown, their theory did not contemplate the possibility of baptising the battalions of nominal proselytes. Still, at the close of 1756 (the jubilee of the mission) they numbered nearly three thousand disciples, and they had established stations at Madras, Tanjore,[1] Trichinopoly, Negapatam, and other towns.

Nearly half a century of this mission (1750 to 1798) is covered by the life of Frederick Schwartz,[2] one of the greatest heroes of the missionary cause in the East. Like Ziegenbalg, he was a graduate of Halle; but, taught by his predecessor's experience, he had devoted himself to the study of Tamil before leaving home. He was, therefore, able to preach to the natives within a few months of his landing. The name of Schwartz is always associated with Tanjore, which he first visited in 1759, and where his interviews with the Rajah[3] read almost like a romance, and, as has been suggested, would afford fine scope for the

[1] Tanjore Lat. 10° 47', Long. 79° 127; 170 miles S.E. of Madras. Pop. 40,000. For a full account see Niécamp's "Histoire des Mission Danoises," Vol. I., p. 19, and McCulloch's "Geog. Dict."

[2] Pearson's "Life of Schwartz." "Life of Schwartz," published by Religious Tract Society. The real name is Schwartz, but he allowed it to be spelt and pronounced Swartz, as it was found to be easier.

[3] Pearson's "Memoirs," Vol. I, p. 179.

genius of an artist great in the expression of human character.[1] In 1777, while Hyder Ali was devastating the Carnatic, Schwartz became a permanent resident at Tanjore;[2] and so widely diffused was the fame of his virtue, that the fierce Rajah of Mysore selected Scwhartz as the only one with whom he would treat as representative of England. Though his mediation was unsuccessful, his influence was not diminished. Hyder[3] issued orders that the Christian missionary should be respected; and, after the peace of 1784, he was no less conspicuous for his administrative ability than for his devotion to the great duty of preaching the Gospel. His friend, the Rajah of Tanjore, was so devoted to Schwartz, that he appointed him the guardian of his heir; and though there is no proof that Swajee ever openly professed Christianity, it is evident that the lessons of his guardian had sunk deep into his heart, and had produced, not only a purity of life, rare in Eastern potentates, but that still rarer virtue, toleration for other forms of faith. And not only had the German missionary succeeded in winning the heart of the enthusiastic Rajah, but he had accomplished the far more difficult task of rooting out the prejudices of East India directors, and enlisting them on the side of religion. When he died[4]

[1] Kaye's "Christianity," p. 79.

[2] Pearson's "Memoirs," Vol. I., p. 289.

[3] *Ib.*, Vol. I., p. 318.

[4] Pearson's "Memoirs," Vol. II., p. 310. Kaye's "Christ.," p. 83.

these merchant princes, who, a few years before, would have sneered at him as a visionary, now ordered Bacon and Flaxman to sculpture two marble statues, one for the great church at Madras, the other for the Mission Church at Tanjore. Sermons were preached in his honour, and great companies and religious societies vied with each other in efforts to perpetuate the memory of such transcendent worth, and to express their sense of the benefit which Christianity and civilisation had derived from his exertions.

Though our attention has been fixed on the grand central figure of Frederick Schwartz, it must not be supposed that he was the only one in the missionary picture Tanjore, no doubt, was the focus during the latter half of the century, as Tranquebar had been during the former. From these points, lines of light were continually penetrating the surrounding gloom. Gerické, Kohloff, and many others[1] advanced into Trichinopoly to the north, into Madura, Tinnevelly,[2] and even as far as Travancore, each mission becoming in turn the centre of others. In fact, the progress of the first Protestant Missions finds a fitting illustration in that magnificent Indian tree which, beginning

[1] Schultz, Dahl, Keistenmacher, Bosse, Pressier, Walther, Kiernander, Fabricius, Zegler, were the chief missionaries from Halle and Copenhagen. See Pearson's "Memoirs," pp. 25, 27, 29, and 39; also Niécamp's "Hist.," *passim*.

[2] Tinnevelly, to the S.W. of Madura and E. of Travancore. Area 5590 square miles, pop. 900,000. Tinnevelly is the chief town.

from a single insignificant stem, throws out its wide-spreading branches ; and as each droops to the earth it strikes into the soil, and repeats the example of its parent till the plain is arched with its glorious foliage, and nations seek shelter beneath its shade. "Quot rami tot, arbores."

CHAPTER II.

ENGLISH MISSIONS TO THE SYRIANS.
1806-1816.

"To unite them to the Church of England would be, in my opinion, a most noble work; and it is most devoutly to be wished that those who have been driven into the Roman pale, might be recalled to their ancient Church."—R. H. KERR.

WE are not writing the history of all missionary efforts to convert the heathen of India; nor are we directing our attention to the operations of the various societies throughout India. Our subject, though extensive enough for an Essay such as this, is limited to a narrower field; and we must, therefore, pass over the new era of Protestant Missions with which the XIXth Century opened. The labours of Carey, Ward, and Marshman, at Serampore, in translating the Scriptures;[1] the efforts of the London Missionary Society, beginning in 1798 at Chinsurah, on the Hooghly, and the extensive organisations of the great

[1] "From the year 1800 to the present date, the Bible has been translated into forty-seven dialects of India, Ceylon, Malacca Burmah, Java, and China; while above a million of copies have issued from the press at Calcutta in the principal languages of Northern India."—Trevor's "India," p. 316.

Missionary Societies of England, America, and the Continent, will only incidentally be noticed as they bear upon our subject. For the same reason the honoured names of Brown, Martyn, Corrie, Thomason, Duff, Middleton, Heber, Wilson, Hough, and many others must be passed over.

Returning to the Malabar coast, we find that after the failure of the Danish missionaries, nothing was done in relation to the Syrian Churches till the year 1806. In point of fact, the various agencies for the conversion of the natives were so intent upon their new and interesting work, that they seemed to forget the existence of the ancient Church of India, and to feel it no affair of theirs to purify her from the errors which she had been forced to adopt by her Portuguese oppressors. And, if this apathy influenced men who were devoting their lives to the spread of Christianity, one need not feel surprised at the slight interest which the existence of this early Church excited in the minds of the politicians and merchants of our Indian Empire. Still, there were some distinguished exceptions, and one of these, Lord William Bentinck, Governor of Madras, addressed a letter to Dr. R. H. Kerr, then Senior Chaplain of Fort St. George, to make enquiries as to the state of the native Christians in Cochin and Travancore. Dr. Kerr's official report[1]

[1] This document will be found at the end of Buchanan's "Christian Researches." Ed., 1812.

is dated 3rd November, 1806; and although it must be admitted that it is hardly minute enough to give us an exact idea of the position of the Syrian Christians at that date, as to churches, divisions, ritual, doctrine, members, &c., still it possesses a certain interest as showing that the Church of England was desirous of effecting a union with a body of Christians whose creed was, in all essentials, nearly identical with her own. His testimony, moreover, is important as to the religious and moral character of these mountaineers, of which his acquaintance with the ordinary Indian type would make him a competent judge. He says: "The character of these people is marked by striking superiority over the heathens in every moral excellence, and they are remarkable for their veracity and plain dealing. They are extremely attentive to their religious duties, and abide by the decision of their Metropolitan in all cases, whether in temporal or spiritual affairs." He expresses his conviction as to the truth of the tradition that their first head was the Apostle St. Thomas, and adds, "There can be no doubt whatever that the St. Thomé Christians settled on the Malabar coast at a very early period, whence they spread to St. Thomas's Mount, near Madras." The divisions of the Malabar Church at this period are thus reported.[1] First the *St. Thomé* or *Jacobite Christians*, preserving their

[1] Dr. Kerr's Report in "Christian Researches," p. 147.

original independence, in consequence of the revolt of 1663, and enjoying the use of the Syriac language in the Church Service. They do not permit the use of images as objects of adoration, but every Church contains a statue of the Virgin Mary with the Infant Jesus in her arms. The Metropolitan at this time was Mar-Dionysius, of whom we have already spoken, and who will again be introduced. This division contained, in 1806, fifty-five churches, and 23,000 people, but so imperfect were the statistics that another report raises the number to 70,000.[1] The second division Dr. Kerr calls the *Syrian Roman Catholics*, who were forced to join Rome at Diamper. They are distinguished from their Syrian brethren by being under Papal government, and from the Latin Roman Catholics by employing the Syriac language in Divine Service, in virtue of a dispensation from the Pope. They are ecclesiastically subject to the Archbishop of Cranganor and the Bishop of Verapoli. They wear white dresses, while the Latin priests have black. This body was said to possess 86 parishes, 400 priests, and 90,000 people. And if Dr. Kerr's information, gleaned on the spot, can be trusted, these so-called Christians were still groaning under the weight of the burden, to which we have already referred, of combined Roman and Pagan superstitions, using a "swamy" coach or car, like the heathens, on their

[1] Niécamp's "Hist.," Vol. I., p. 64.

grand festivals. This is a striking illustration of the influence which the Portuguese Missions of the XVIth Century still continue to exercise over the Syrian Christians in the XIXth. The third body is the Latin Roman Catholics, then under the jurisdiction of the local Archbishops of Cranganor and Cochin, but under the Primacy of the Archbishop of Goa. These Prelates were nominated by the Sovereign of Portugal, and sanctioned by the Pope. There were only seven or eight European priests, but a great number of natives, whose education appeared extremely imperfect, many of them, indeed, being hardly able to read the Service. The total population of Latin Roman Catholic Christians, Portuguese and natives, using the Latin language, was estimated at 35,000. These dry statistics contain the essence of Dr. Kerr's report, and we shall now turn to one of a more interesting character.

Dr. Claudius Buchanan[1] says, in his interesting "Christian Researches," that "Two centuries had elapsed without any particular information concerning the Syrian Christians in the interior of India. It was

[1] Dr. Buchanan, the son of a Scottish schoolmaster, was born at Cambuslang, near Glasgow, in 1766, educated first at the University of Glasgow, and sent by Henry Thornton to Cambridge, in 1791. Under the influence of Simeon his mind was directed to Indian labours, and in 1797 he landed at Calcutta. In 1806 he visited the Malabar coast, made many interesting discoveries, obtained valuable Syriac MSS., and, returning to England, printed the first version of the Scriptures in that language. He died at Broxbourne in 1815.

doubted by many whether they existed at all; but if they did exist, it was thought probable that they must possess some valuable monuments of Christian antiquity. The author conceived the design of visiting them in his tour through Hindostan. He presented a short memoir on the subject, in 1805, to Marquis Wellesley, then Governor-General of India, who was pleased to give orders that every facility should be afforded to him in the prosecution of his enquiries."[1] The principal objects of his tour were to investigate the literature and history of this ancient Church, and to collect MSS.; also to employ the most intelligent of their priests as translators of the Bible into the languages of Southern India, and as missionaries to preach to their fellow-countrymen, both Christians and pagans. In May, 1806, he started for the south, but it was October before he reached Travancore,[2] where he was kindly received at the Palace of Trevandrum. Col. Macaulay obtained an audience from the Rajah, who was very anxious to know the precise purpose of his visit. "When I told the Rajah that the Syrian Christians were supposed to be of the same religion with the English, he said he thought that could not be the case, else he must have heard of it before; if, however, it was so, he considered my desire to visit them as being very reasonable. He said he would

[1] "Christian Researches," Cambridge, 1811, p. 91.

[2] Pearson's "Memoirs," Philad., 1817, p. 313.

afford me every facility for my journey, and he directed his Dewan to furnish me with guides."[1] From Travancore he proceeded, early in November, to Mavelycar,[2] and was much struck by the grandeur of the mountain scenery in this sequestered region of India, by the simple beauty of the churches, surrounded by woods, and by one circumstance, which we quote in his own words: "In approaching a town in the evening I once heard the sound of the bells among the hills; a circumstance which made me forget for a moment that I was in Hindostan, and reminded me of another country."

The first Syrian church Dr. Buchanan saw was at Mavelycar, but the Syrians here are close to the Romish Christians, and had been often visited by Portuguese and other Romish emissaries. The Cattanars had heard of the English, but so little did they know of the outer world, that they thought the English Church was under the Pope. They naturally looked on their new clerical visitor with suspicion, especially when he entered on a discussion as to the original language of the four Gospels, which they, of course, maintained to be Syriac. After a time their suspicions subsided, they received him as a friend, and appointed one of their number to accompany him to the

[1] Letter dated "Palace of Travancore, 9th Oct. 1806."—"Christian Researches," p. 93.

[2] Pearson's "Memoirs," p. 319.

churches of the interior. At Chinganoor[1] he met one of the Cattanars, or genuine Syrian clergy, dressed in a white loose vestment, a little like a surplice, with a cap of red silk. The Englishman saluted him, to his great surprise, in Syriac, "Peace be unto you," and he answered, "The God of peace be with you." Turning to the guides, the Syrian asked them, in Malayalim, who the stranger was, and then accompanied him to the door of the church, where he was received by three Casheeshas, similarly vested. The eldest was a very intelligent man, with a long white beard, reverend and courteous in his demeanour. The people of the neighbouring villages flocked around, men and women, the presence of the latter proving that the country was a Christian one. Still, though the whole bearing of the villagers indicated intelligence and a certain amount of moral culture, there were symptoms of poverty, depression, and fallen greatness. Dr. Buchanan said to the senior priest, "You appear to me like a people who have known better days." "It is even so," said he. "We are in a degenerate state, compared with our forefathers. About three hundred years ago an enemy came from the west bearing the name of Christ, but armed with the Inquisition, and compelled us to seek the protection of the native princes. And the native princes have kept us in a state of depression

[1] Pearson's "Memoirs," p. 322.

ever since. They, indeed, recognise our ancient personal privileges, for we rank in general next to the Nairs, the nobility of the country; but they have encroached by degrees on our property, till we have been reduced to the humble state in which you find us. The glory of our Church has passed away; but we hope your nation will revive it again." Then followed an interesting conversation, during which the Syrian said that they had preserved the Bible, that the Hindoo princes had never touched their liberty of conscience, that they had occasionally made converts, but that it was not now creditable to become a Christian. He lamented that their knowledge of the Bible was very limited, that they had few copies, and that, as none were printed, the writing out was enormous work, with little or no profit. On this Dr. Buchanan produced a printed copy of the Syriac New Testament. Nothing could exceed their astonishment. Each eagerly seized it in turn, and began to read with great fluency. They all professed an earnest desire to have the *whole* Bible printed in Syriac, for, added the principal speaker, "Our Church languishes for want of the Scriptures." They then discussed the practicability of preparing a translation in the Malayalim, or Malabar, the language of the people, and a most interesting conversation closed by the Englishman's giving, at their request an account of the Reformation while they in return narrated the recent history of their own Church.[1]

Dr. Buchanan attended Divine Service, and found the liturgy nearly the same as that formerly used at Antioch. During the prayers, there were intervals of silence for private devotion. Incense was employed, and several ceremonies were noticed closely resembling those of the Greek Church. There was little or no preaching; but the spirit of the Church had been preserved by the Bible, and by a Scriptural liturgy.[2] Still, there was too much formality and coldness in the service; and the whole tone of the Syrian worship indicated a want of spiritual life.

On the 24th of November, the English missionary had a kind reception from the Indian Bishop at his residence of Candenad—the Mar-Dionysius, of whom we have already spoken.[3] Between fifty and sixty priests had been assembled to meet the stranger at the humble episcopal palace. "You have come," said the prelate, "to visit a declining Church. I am now an old man, but the hopes of its seeing better days cheer my old age, though I may not live to see them." In reply to Dr. Buchanan's proposal to trans-

[1] For a full account of this interview, see Dr. Buchanan's letter of 10th November, 1806.

[2] This was Dr. Buchanan's impression, but, as the reader will observe later, there are expressions which seem scarcely "Scriptural" in several of the liturgies. See "Asseman. Bil. Orient.," Hough's "Hist.," Vol. V., and Howard's "Syrian Christians."

[3] Pearson's "Memoirs," p. 328.

late and print the Bible, Dionysius said: "I have already fully considered the subject, and have determined to superintend the work myself, and to call the most learned clergy to my aid. It is a work which will illuminate these dark regions, and God will give it His blessing." The Englishman was delighted with this declaration, for he had ascertained that there were upwards of 200,000 Christians in the south of India, besides the Syrians who speak Malabar.

Next day there was another important conversation on the possibility of union with the Church of England. *The influence of the original Portuguese Missions, supported by constant accessions from France and Italy, was still so powerfully felt by the promoters of modern efforts* that it seemed almost impossible to arrest the march of the Church of Rome. It was, therefore, an object of the greatest consequence to secure the hearty co-operation of the Syrian Christians, not merely on account of the prestige afforded by antiquity, but because of the peculiar fitness of the Cattanars for preaching a pure Gospel in a pure language. Still, it was a delicate and difficult subject, and there was evidently much reserve on both sides. The Syrian clergy had been designedly led to doubt the validity of English Orders. They could not understand the controversy; and Dr. Buchanan had to enter into full details, with which the Bishop and his clergy appeared to be satisfied. He said, "I would sacrifice much for such a union; only let me not be called to compromise anything of the dignity and purity of our Church." Assured on this point, he conferred with his Cattanars, and sent an answer: "That a union with the English Church, or, at least, such a connection as should appear to both Churches practicable and expedient, would be a happy event, and favourable to the progress of religion in India." This important document was signed "Mar-Dionysius, Metropolitan of Malabar."

From Candenad, Dr. Buchanan went to visit Col. Macaulay (the British resident), in whose company he made a short excursion to the interior, spending a few hours at the too famous Diamper.[1] He then paid a second visit to Dionysius, who, though seventy-eight years of age, had actually begun the translation of the Bible. On the 9th of December we find the traveller at the ruined tower and fortress of Cranganor, where St. Thomas landed from Aden, and where the Portuguese once possessed a splendid emporium. One relic still exists. The descendants of the Portuguese merchants have passed away, but the successors of the Portuguese missionaries hold their ground, represented by the Archbishop of Cranganor at the head of forty-five churches.

Dr. Buchanan resolved to secure as much information as possible from both sides, called on Bishop

[1] Pearson's "Memoirs," p. 239.

Raymondo, the Pope's Apostolic Vicar over the churches of Malabar. This prelate was warden of the Theological College at Verapoli, where about twenty students were instructed in Latin and Syriac; while at Pulingalla there was another college, in which Syriac alone was taught to twelve students. The Papal Bishop superintended sixty-four churches in his own diocese, and many others in the dioceses of Cranganor, Quilon, and Cochin. "The view of this assemblage of Christian congregations," says the traveller, "excited in my mind mingled sensations of pleasure and regret; of pleasure, to think that so many of the Hindoos had been rescued from the idolatry of Brahma and its criminal worship; and of regret, when I reflected that there was not to be found among the whole body one copy of the Holy Bible." [1] The Apostolic Vicar, an Italian, and one of the Society De Propagandâ Fide, gave his visitor free access to the college archives, in which were volumes marked "Liber hereticus prohibitus." Here again was an instance of *Portuguese influence still at work.* "Every step I take in Christian India I meet with a memento of the Inquisition," is the testimony of Dr. Buchanan on this point. The Italian prelate, too, confirmed the impression, for, alluding to his visitor's intention of translating the Scriptures into Malabar, he said, "I have been thinking of the good gift you are meditat-

[1] "Christian Researches,' Ed. 1811, p. 114.

ing for the native Christians, but, believe me, the Inquisition will endeavour to counteract your purposes by every means in their power." When these words were spoken, the Inquisition still held sway at Goa, where it was visited by Dr. Buchanan in January, 1808, and though it is now suppressed, moral influence continues to operate, even where physical force is no longer feared.

Early in January, 1807, Dr. Buchanan penetrated once more inland, and visited the ancient Church of Angamale,[1] once the residence of the Syrian Bishop, where he found many valuable MSS. Amongst these was discovered a splendid folio, containing the Old and New Testaments, beautifully engrossed on strong vellum, in Estrangelo Syriac. The Bishop presented this precious MS. to the Englishman, saying, "It will be safer in your hands than in our own, and yet we have kept it for near a thousand years."[2] How wonderful to reflect that during the dark ages of European history, the Bible should have been preserved in the mountains of Malabar, where it was *then* freely read in a hundred churches.[3] After

[1] Pearson's "Memoirs," p. 333.

[2] "Christian Researches," Ed. 1811, p. 118. Howard's "Christians of St. Thomas," p. 59. Bagster's "Bible of every Land," p. 44.

[3] Most of the MSS. which I collected among the Syrian Christians, I have presented to the University of Cambridge; and they are now deposited in the Public Library of that University, together with the copper-plate fac-similes of the Christian and Jewish tablets. — Buchanan's "Christ. Res.," Ed. 1811, p. 121.

Dr. Buchanan left Travancore, the aged Bishop persevered in his translation of the Scriptures, till he had completed the New Testament; and next year, the first edition was beautifully printed at Bombay and circulated through the whole of the churches of the Seira. In order to conclude this notice we may anticipate part of our narrative by stating that Dr. Buchanan returned to England in 1808; but, owing to various delays, it was not till 1815 that the first sheets of the Syriac New Testament issued from the press at Broxbourne. On the good doctor's death, soon afterwards, Dr. Lee, of Cambridge, continued the work; the New Testament complete was published in 1816, and in 1826 the whole Syriac Bible was circulated in Malabar.

One portion of Dr. Buchanan's experience amongst the Syrian Christians must not pass unnoticed, as it bears directly on the subject of this paper, and proves that the Portuguese Missions of the XVIth century continued to exert *the most baneful influence on the Churches of Malabar.* He says that though he had heard much of Papal corruption, he certainly did not expect to see Christianity in the degraded state in which he found it. The priests were, in general, better acquainted with the Vedas than with the Gospel! At Aughoor, the Tower of Juggernaut solemnised a Christian festival; and the old priest of the Syrian Church described the idolatrous car, the painted figures, and the heathen rites, as if *himself unconscious of any wrong!* "Thus by the intervention of the Papal power are the ceremonies of Moloch consecrated in a manner by the sacred Syriac language. What a heavy responsibility lies on *Rome for having thus corrupted and degraded that pure and ancient Church.* While the author viewed these Christian corruptions in different places, and in different forms, he was always referred to the Inquisition at Goa as the fountain head."[1]

An incidental proof may be added of the extent to which the *original Portuguese element continues to* influence this part of India, for our author says "that the *Portuguese language prevails* wherever there are, or have been, settlements of that nation. Their *descendants people the coasts* from the vicinity of the Cape of Good Hope to the Sea of China"; and in a long list of places he mentions *Calicut, Cochin, Tranquebar, Tanjore,* &c. He founds on this fact an argument for the circulation of the Scriptures in a language so generally known in the European settlements, adding, '*the Portuguese language is certainly a most favourable medium for diffusing* the true religion in the maritime provinces of the East." In another part of his interesting work he throws out the important suggestion that as Goa is, and probably will long be, the centre from which Portuguese Missions will radiate

[1] "Christian Researches," p. 126. Ed. 1811.

through Southern India, every effort should be made to *purify the fountain head.* And he has reason to believe that the three thousand priests connected with Goa would gladly receive copies of the Latin and Portuguese versions of their authorised Bible, that is the Vulgate.

We have thus given an account, necessarily imperfect, of the condition of the Syrians in 1806, and we strongly advise our readers to peruse the whole of the Doctor's work if they desire further information. Great as was his success in securing a complete version of the Bible in Syriac for the use of churches, and in Malabar for general circulation, this was not the only result. His interesting description of the Syrian Christians excited much sympathy in England, and the *Church Missionary Society* organised a mission to Travancore for *the purpose of teaching the clergy and people*, *counteracting the influence of the Romish Missionaries,* and restoring the Church to its original purity. This mission will form the subject of our next chapter.

CHAPTER III.

THE ENGLISH MISSIONS AND THE SYRIAN CHRISTIANS.

1816-1838.

"I hasten to remark generally what charity and tender sympathy we should cultivate towards these and similar relics of Apostolical Churches. How readily should we acknowledge what is good in them; *without requiring of them conformity to our Protestant models of liturgical worship* or our Western notions."—BISHOP WILSON (of Calcutta).

IT is scarcely possible to over-estimate the continuation of an influence, however trifling or remote, in the production of a long series of results. All the great events of history may be traced to comparatively insignificant causes. A word, a gesture, a phrase misunderstood, a hasty despatch, an intercepted letter, may be, without exaggeration, considered the immediate cause of some event, which in turn produces another, and that a third, till it becomes quite impossible to say when or where the action ceases. So it is in the history before us. *The Portuguese Missions of the XVI*th *Century*, not only in their *direct* bearing on the *Syrian Church in* 1599, but also by their *fomenting unhappy divisions during the last two hundred years*—divisions still in activity—may be fairly held *responsible for the difficulties* which have since arisen, and which have hitherto frustrated the well-meant efforts of the English Church to restore peace to this afflicted portion of Christ's vineyard.[1]

We have just seen how Dr. Buchanan's narrative had the effect of exciting a warm interest amongst English Churchmen in favour of the Syrian Christians. But, meanwhile, the old difficulty had arisen in the Church of the Serra. The aged Dionysius had, some nine years before Dr. Buchanan's visit, consecrated Mar-Thomas as coadjutor and successor, while he nominated his own nephew to be *his* successor. Great dissatisfaction prevailed. But, at last, a sort of consecration was performed at the bedside of the expiring Metropolitan, and Mar-Thomas succeeded. The irregularity of the proceeding strengthened the hands of the discontented faction, who appealed to the British resident, and wrote to Antioch for a regularly consecrated Bishop. The death of the quiet and

[1] "These people were also fearfully persecuted some three hundred years ago by the crafty and bloodthirsty Popish agent, Menezes, who by the power of the Portuguese, not only stole some of their churches and persecuted numbers to death, but succeeded also in corrupting the whole Syrian Church with their own abominable doctrines and idolatrous practices. So that if you wish to know what practically the Syrian Church is now, I have but to refer you to Indianised Popery."—Paper by the Rev. J. Peet, of Marelikara, Travancore. Read at the South India Miss. Conf. at Ostacamund, April 28th, 1858.

inoffensive Mar-Thomas terminated the dispute, and the Ramban Joseph, a man of decided piety, succeeded for a time in restoring tranquillity.

At this favourable juncture, Colonel Macaulay, resident at the Court of Trevandrum, took a deep interest in the resuscitation of the Syrian Church, in which he was followed by his successor, Colonel Munro. The result of their interposition, and of the friendliness manifested by the Queen or Ráni, was a decided amelioration in the political condition of the oppressed Syrians. But though Colonel Munro did his utmost to restore peace, his mediation was fruitless till the period of which we are now speaking. Undeterred by previous failure, the Colonel took the decided step of making an application to the Church Missionary Society to send out clergy for the purpose of instructing these Christians whom he had found in a sadly debased condition.[1] The expression is not too strong, for as we have already seen, the word of God, though nominally possessed by the people, was in Syriac, while the vernacular was Malayalim; the prayers of the Church were chiefly in what was, practically, an unknown tongue; the priests were almost entirely uneducated, and there was little or no vital

[1] Ch. Miss. Rep. 1815-16., South Indian Miss. Conf. Mullens's "South Indian Missions," p. 127. Captain Swanston's "Rep." Vol. II., p. 66. "Royal Asiatic Journal." Day's "Land of the Permauls." Howard's "Christians of S. Thomas."

religion in this fallen Church. The problem, therefore, now to be solved was how the *Church of England missionaries might, with God's blessing, impart spiritual life to this decaying branch.* The application to the parent society was favourably entertained, and in 1816[1] Messrs. Bailey, Baker, and Fenn were sent out to the Syrians in Travancore, while Mr. Norton was settled at Allepie among the Romanists and a large heathen population. In 1817 Mr. Bailey opened a mission at Cottayam, where the Ráni of Travancore had largely endowed a college, built in 1815 by a rich Syrian noble, for the residence of the Bishop, and for the education of the clergy. Colonel Munro, in order to effect a permanent union on the most friendly basis, formed a committee of management of the Metran and the three missionaries, while the English resident at Travancore, and the Dewan, or Prime Minister, were to form a tribunal of appeal in all civil matters. The collegiate staff included the Metropolitan as principal, two English clergymen, two Malpans (Syrian doctors), a teacher of Hebrew, and two teachers of Sanskrit. Nearly fifty students soon joined the new institution, and according to good authority "their ability seemed high, their spirit and conduct excellent, and their desire for learning not inferior to what is found in English lads of the same age." The missionaries appear to have proceeded

[1] "Madras Ch. Miss. Rec.," Nov., 1837.

upon a *thoroughly matured plan*, for we find the principle of graded schools simultaneously introduced. Three free grammar schools were opened, one in each division of the diocese, not only for the purpose of affording a higher education, but for preparing youths to enter at Cottayam, while no fewer than thirty-seven parish schools were established throughout the mountains, glens, paddy-grounds, and coast of this hitherto uneducated land. Another important duty was undertaken by the indefatigable Mr. Bailey and his zealous coadjutors. The existing translations of the Scriptures were so defective that it was necessary to prepare a new version, and, therefore, Messrs. Bailey and Thompson, taking the Tamil of Fabricius as the basis, completed a new rendering more agreeable to the idiom of the country. This done, types were founded, a press constructed with the aid of a native blacksmith, and in a short time there issued from it the Scriptures, the Common Prayer, two complete dictionaries, and many religious books.[1] The missionaries felt the importance of the maxim, "Divide and conquer," for while Mr. Bailey was engaged in the literary work, Mr. Baker's sphere was the constant visitation of seventy-two Syrian churches, which had

[1] See a most interesting description of "Mr Bailey's labours in South India Missions" by Dr. Mullens, p. 128. The printing-office at Cottayam flourishes still. Howard's "Christians of S. Thomas," p. 89, and "Madras Ch. Miss. Rec.," Sep., 1834.

either not been subdued by the Portuguese in 1599, or had thrown off the yoke in 1663. To Mr. Fenn was assigned the chief direction of the educational department at Cottayam, wherein he was assisted by a European layman and a staff of native teachers as already stated. The public worship was generally conducted in the grammar school of the college, or in the house of one of the missionaries. "On Sunday morning I collect all the boys from the grammar school, at ten, into the college, where we are going through the Bible in the presence of all the teachers and boys of the college and grammar school. At these lectures I speak the pure truth in love, and often when they have closed, have taken the Malpan and other Cattanar teachers aside to ascertain whether they have comprehended all that has been said, and what has been their opinion about it. On Sunday afternoon we have full service in Malayalim in the grammar school. I, or a deacon, read the morning prayers, as I am so partial to the Litany, and a Cattanar preaches, as it was not till last month that I was enabled to perform full service, on which occasion, after reading, I commenced my preaching course, by addressing them from the words 'Behold, the Lamb of God.' After this service is concluded, I have been in the habit, for the last six months, of collecting the teachers, boys, *i.e.*, those who know anything of English, and preaching to them in English in a familiar style. The whole number at this service does not exceed nine."[1] Some of the missionaries seem also to have preached in Malayalim in the Syrian churches, but their course must have been rather difficult, for though the Cattanars were liberal, or indifferent enough to allow the Englishmen to officiate, the latter could not conscientiously take part in the Corbano (Eucharist), as it too nearly resembled the Mass.[2]

For a time everything worked smoothly. The missionaries took the deepest interest in their new duties; and we have several independent testimonies as to their zeal, prudence, tact, and courteous treatment of the Bishop and clergy of the Syrian Church. Thus Principal Mills says:—"The persons to whom I was chiefly indebted for my intercourse, both with the priests and laity of this extraordinary people (of whose Indian language I was wholly ignorant), were three clergymen of the Church of England, resident at Cotym, in Travancore, and actively employed in superintending the college of the parochial schools; the former of which by the grant of the heathen government of that country, the latter, by the desire and contribution of these Christians themselves, have been recently established in their community. Singular as

[1] "Madras Ch. Miss. Rec.," 1834.

[2] The missionaries seem generally to have acted with great tact and delicacy, but yet it was hardly prudent of one of them to speak of this part of the Syrian Service as "a most wretched piece of buffoonery."—Howard, p. 92.

such superintendence may appear, and almost unprecedented, there is nothing in it, as exercised by these clergymen, which they visit, or as far as I am capable of judging of that to which they themselves belong." And again: "They do nothing but by the express sanction of the Metropolitan consulting and employing them; their use of the Anglican Service for themselves and families at one of his chapels is agreeable to the catholic practice of these Christians (who allowed the same 250 years ago to the Portuguese priests, as to persons rightly and canonically ordained, even while they were resisting their usurpations) and is totally unconnected with any purpose of obtruding even that Liturgy upon the Syrian Church; while their conduct with respect to those parts of the Syrian ritual and practice which all Protestants must condemn, is that of silence; which, without the appearance of approval, leaves it to the gradual influence of the knowledge now disseminating itself to undermine, and at length by regular authority to remove them."[1]

Similar testimony may be found in the interesting diary of Major Mackworth. "After five hours' sail and row we came in sight of the several houses of the missionaries at Cottayam, erected on some rising grounds, at no great distance from each other; and soon after

[1] Professor Mills' Letter of 29th July, 1821, quoted in "Missionary Register" for 1823.

we discovered an ancient church on our right hand in a romantic situation amongst the trees, and slightly elevated above the valley through which flows the stream that we were ascending. A little further to the left, and in the valley, was the Syrian College. I landed about half-a-mile from Mr. Fenn's house, and proceeded towards it on foot; but, before I entered his ground, he came himself to meet me, and gave me a Christian welcome." . . . "All the missionaries and their wives dined this evening with Mr. and Mrs. Fenn, and I was a delighted spectator of their mutual cordiality and Christian friendship. It seems, indeed, a peculiar blessing from the Almighty to this fallen Church, that those whom, I hope without being presumptuous, we may venture to regard as *sent to be His honoured instruments in restoring her to her pristine faith, should be all unquestionably pious men;* surely it is an earnest that His blessing will attend their labours." In another passage he says, speaking of the Metropolitan, "Whenever the missionaries express a wish he gladly accedes to it, as far as he is able; but this they seldom do, in a direct manner, as their object is rather to let improvements spring from their suggestions, acting on the gradually-increasing light of his own mind." . . . Major Mackworth describes his interview with the Metropolitan in a most interesting passage too long to quote, and he adds, "When he, at length, retired, the three missionaries accompanied him to his palanquin, *with the greatest respect and deference;* by which, and similar means, they render him venerable in the eyes of his people, from the honour which the notice of Europeans in this country always confers."[1] We may add one brief quotation from Captain Swanston who, five years after Major Mackworth's visit, speaks of the satisfactory working of the College: "The missionaries conducting themselves with *great prudence, and being respected and beloved by the people.*"[2] We consider it no digression to have cited these authorities in favour of the English missionaries, because, at the time of the disruption in 1838, they were severely blamed by many of their fellow-countrymen as having caused the separation by their own officious zeal.

From the missionaries we may turn to the Syrian Church. There can be no doubt that at first all was *couleur de rose.* They could not fail to see the deep interest taken in their welfare by their English fellow-Christians. They were delighted to observe the kind and conciliatory spirit of the missionaries who were *more anxious to infuse the real principles of religion into the people than to dictate any alterations in the ritual or doctrine of the Church.* The Metropolitan

[1] Diary of a Tour through Southern India in 1821-22, by a Field Officer of Cavalry.

[2] Captain Swanston's Memoir in Vol. II. of the Royal Asiatic Soc. Journal.

and his clergy being, on the whole, interested in the promotion of the Gospel, felt, at first, no jealousy of the plans which the English clergymen suggested; and, as the head of their Church (a religious and amiable man), was fully recognised in his official capacity, and duly consulted on every important occasion, they were not apprehensive of any aggression on their rights and privileges, or of any attempt to destroy their independent existence. Many years passed in this state of harmony. The College and the schools did the work of education effectively; the press continued to pour forth numerous contributions to the nascent literature of Malayala; the pioneers of peace went from church to church preaching the Gospel message; and, as new missionaries joined, fresh stations were opened at Cochin, Trichur, and Mavelicary. After a time, however, all these bright prospects were clouded over, and symptoms of disturbance began to appear; but whether this interruption of amicable relations must be attributed to the Syrians or to the Englishmen, it is difficult, perhaps impossible, clearly to determine. Those who lean to the former say that "the missionaries, beginning to gain a clearer estimate of their true position, saw that in relation to the Syrian Church they were absolutely without authority; they were mere volunteers in the attempt to get rid of existing evils; they were physicians ready to assist the cure of a disease of which *they* had clear perceptions, but which the patient scarcely felt, and in regard to which he might at any time decline their services *in toto.* They found that when the novelty of the thing had worn off the old Adam in the people had greatly revived. They saw that the spiritual worth of the Church, and the task of raising it up, had been much overrated. They found the people careless about real religion; they found the priesthood unconverted, looking after their fees, formal in their service; the whole body lifeless and cold."[1] On the other hand it is confidently affirmed that the missionaries had never entered heartily into the feelings of the people or even of the clergy; they believed them sunk in ignorance and superstition, and directed their efforts, not so much to restore that which might be wanting, as to persuade them to abolish, *en masse*, all that was offensive to their own prejudices—and this comprehended apparently the entire Syrian ritual—and to substitute what are technically called Evangelical principles both in doctrine and in worship, in place of the ancient usages and doctrines of the Church.[2]

Of course different views will be taken of these

[1] Mullens's "Missions in South India," pp. 129-130.

[2] Howard's "Christians of S. Thomas," p. 94. The curious reader desirous of further information as to the progress of this lamentable quarrel is referred to the "Madras Church Missionary Record" for 1836-7-8, to Hough's "Christianity in India," Vol. V., p. 386, and to the "Missionary Register" for 1838.

transactions according to the ecclesiastical bias of the reader. Some will look upon the rudeness of a young missionary fresh from Islington[1] to the Metropolitan of the Syrian Church as an outpouring of that righteous indignation which should characterise a true reformer, while others will be ready to condemn such intemperate zeal as calculated to hinder, rather than to help, the purification of the Syrian ritual and the promotion of true religion. Our space will not permit us to discuss this painful question, or to adjust with perfect precision the amount of right and wrong on each side; but we hasten to say that matters had gone so far in 1835 that it was necessary for Bishop Wilson to visit the mission stations, for the purpose, if possible, of pouring oil upon the waters. At the conference which took place at Cottayam[2] six points were submitted by the English prelate for the consideration of his Syrian brother. The discussions which followed were conducted with Christian courtesy; the English Bishop, at the Metran's request, preached to 2,000 persons for an hour, and received the thanks of the Syrian prelate. In a charge which Bishop Wilson shortly afterwards delivered at Bombay, he called attention to the distinctive peculiarities of the Syrian Church, and he urged, in the spirit of the extract at the head of this chapter, that all English clergymen should deal charitably and

[1] Howard's "Christians of S. Thomas," p. 99.

[2] See the 2nd Vol. of Bateman's "Life of Bishop Wilson."

tenderly with these ancient usages. The advice, unfortunately, was not taken, and it soon became apparent that the reformers were determined to rest satisfied with nothing *less than a complete change in the Communion Office, in order to assimilate the Syrian Liturgy to that of the Church of England.* The most painful scenes occurred between 1833 and 1838, and the opposition to the missionaries grew stronger every day.[1] At length the breach, which had long been imminent, began in 1836, and was consummated by a complete separation in 1838. This must, however, be discussed in a separate chapter.

[1] "Madras Church Missionary Record," Vol III., pp. 35-6-7.

CHAPTER IV.

THE DISRUPTION AND ITS RESULTS.—1838-1858.

"Now, I beseech you, brethren, by the name of our Lord Jesus Christ, that ye all speak the same thing and that there be no divisions among you; but that ye be perfectly joined together in the same mind and in the same judgment."—S. PAUL.

BEFORE resuming the narrative in our last chapter, it will be necessary to refer to an almost forgotten consecration in 1772, in order to trace the causes of a dissension which tended still further to complicate the condition of the Syrian Church. We allude to Cyril, created Metropolitan by Mar-Gregorius. In 1805, Cyril had consecrated a successor, who in turn appointed *his* successor, named Philoxenus, in 1812. All these Bishops had lived amongst the mountains at Agugnur, and had rarely been heard of on the Malabar coast. When, however, Mar-Joseph died, and the direct line became extinct, the Prelate of the Serra was called to preside over the whole Church. Again the most violent controversy raged amongst this excitable race, the whole question turning, as usual, on the validity of the consecration. After much discussion his rights were confirmed, and after appointing a coadjutor and successor, he retired from the stormy scenes of the coast to the quiet of his mountain home. The defeated party at length succeeded in inducing the Patriarch of Antioch to send two Syrians, named Athanasius and Abraham, to take full charge of the Malabar Church. On their road they were kindly received by Bishop Heber at Bombay, who implored the new Metropolitan to use all moderation, and enjoined the missionaries to keep as free as possible from the coming strife.[1] Athanasius arrived at Malabar in 1825, and, so far from using the moderation which Bishop Heber had desired, he acted in the most arbitrary manner, summoned the native Metropolitan to appear before him, declared all ordinations, since 1810 null and void, threatened all opponents with excommunication, and obstinately refused to listen to any advice. In the midst of this general confusion, Bishop Heber was appealed to as a mediator; and he was actually at Trichinopoly on his way to the south when he entered the fatal bath. Several interesting letters from Bishop Heber and Archdeacon Robinson, too long for quotation here, will be found in the third volume of the "Journal."[2] The dissensions at last reached so violent a pitch that the English Government was obliged to interfere. Athanasius was ex-

[1] Heber's "Journal," Vol. III., pp. 448-9. Howard's "Christians of S. Thomas," p. 68.

[2] Also in Howard's "Christians of S. Thomas," pp. 71-86.

pelled, several of the ringleaders were fined, the native Metropolitan reinstated, and peace restored. This occurred in 1826.

We have already seen that the union, cordial at first, but gradually cooling, between the Church of England missionaries and the Syrian Christians, continued from 1816 to 1838. The kind-hearted Metran, Dionysius, who lived on such friendly terms with his English visitors, and who really desired to resuscitate his Church, had been succeeded by one whose character was not so good, and whose views of Church questions were decidedly opposed to any approach to union. Colonel Munro had left Malabar, and the fickle natives, keenly alive to the influence of political power, no longer respected the missionaries as they had previously done. Superstitions which had been shaken, if not abolished, began to reassert their ascendency. Prayers for the dead afforded a handsome revenue to the priests, and the doctrines of the missionaries on this point, of course, made them feel that their craft was in danger. The avarice of the new Bishop exhibited itself not only in his ordination of uninstructed lads, but in his letting the College lands for his own benefit. "On more than one occasion a missionary in charge of the College, returning suddenly to his class-room after going homeward, caught the Metran, or one of the native professors, in the act of teaching some doctrine the very opposite of that which he had just laid down, and purposely undoing all the good which the missionary had just endeavoured to do."[1] As the doctrine in dispute is not mentioned, it is quite impossible for an impartial historian to determine which was right, the Metran or the missionary; but the very manner in which this characteristic anecdote is related, proves most clearly that suspicion and subterfuge had reached such a pitch that longer co-operation was impossible. Before, however, taking the decided step of abandoning the Syrian Church, the missionaries prevailed upon the Bishop of Calcutta to expostulate with the Metran and clergy. Dr. Wilson accordingly proposed that the Church should, by its own act, purify itself of all errors that had been derived from Nestorian sources, and, at a later period, from the Portuguese missionaries, beginning with Menezes.

The Syrian Metropolitan, acting on this suggestion, convened a Synod, ostensibly for the purpose of discussing the points at issue; but if the missionary version is a correct one, "he succeeded by bribes and intimidation in preventing the reforming party from being heard; and then, by means of a majority of his own followers, dissolved all connection with the Church Mission, their Church, and objects. The engagements made between the Syrians and the Church Mission by Colonel Munro were thus broken

[1] Mullen's "Missions in South India," p. 130.

by the Syrians. I would particularly notice that *we* did not leave the Syrians to their own blindness, nor did Bishop Wilson wish to force them to adopt our creed or forms; but, on the contrary, *they refused our help*, and determined not to return to their own rules, tenets, and doctrines of centuries gone by." [1] On the other hand it is alleged that attempts were made in 1820,[2] and again in 1836,[3] to introduce the English Communion Service, or an office much modified from their own; and one of the missionaries, in the report for 1838, says "it was hoped that the people would be willing, ere long, to substitute our English Sacrament Service in its stead." [4] Now, if these statements are correct, with every desire to do justice to the good intentions of the zealous missionaries, one cannot help feeling that these attempts to tamper with the liturgy of an independent Church are quite indefensible. Granting that there are expressions in the Syrian liturgy which demand reform, and which no sound Churchman would desire to retain, it by no means follows that three or four private clergymen of another Communion were in a right position when venturing to alter, without due authorisation, the service of a Church into which they had been admitted by courtesy. Make the case our own, and we shall see the question

[1] Rev. Henry Baker in "South India Miss. Conf.," 1858, p. 67.
[2] Hough's "Christ, in India," Vol. V., p. 386.
[3] Madras "Ch. Miss. Rec.," Vol. IV., p. 60, and Vol. V., p. 39.
[4] "Madras Ch. Miss. Rec.," Vol., VI., p. 45.

in its true light. The conduct of these missionaries, admirable in every other respect, seems, so far as we can judge even from their own testimony, to have been an illustration of the difficulty of doing the right thing in the right way.

The rupture, so long imminent, became a reality in 1838; but the account given by Dr. Mullens does not perfectly agree with that just quoted from Mr. Baker's paper. "After submitting to this opposition for a long time, and seeing the labours of the missionaries set at nought, the Bishop of Calcutta, a few years ago, resolved to disconnect the Church Missionary Society from the Syrian Church altogether. The missionaries left the College, their assistants left the Syrian body; their converts did the same; and the whole drew off from the decayed Church, exactly as converts in Bengal or Tinnevelly separate themselves from the heathen."[1] The union being thus dissolved, an arbitration was appointed by the Travancore Government, and the endowment of the Syrian College was equitably divided; half being assigned to the Metran for educational purposes, and half to the C.M.S. for training native Christians. With the English share, new college buildings were erected at Cottayam; and the most recent information is, that the new institution flourishes under a Cambridge graduate and assistant tutors, with above sixty pupils. The Syrian portion

[1] Mullens's "South India," pp. 130-1.

seems as yet unemployed owing to the distracted condition of the Church and the conflicting claims of rival Metropolitans.

The Travancore Church Mission was distinctly authorised by the London Committee of the C.M.S. to commence direct mission work under the Bishop of Calcutta, but independent of the Syrian Metropolitan, in whose diocese they were labouring. A few of the Syrian clergy and a small body of the laity seceded with the English party; and an entirely new system of operation commenced. The field was by no means solely or chiefly the heathen population. On the contrary, the English clergymen built churches close to those of the Syrians at Cottayam, Trichoor, Pallam, and many other places, and began a course of proselytising amongst the members of the Syrian Church in spite of the sentences of excommunication pronounced by the Metropolitan. "A new method of proceeding was adopted. From 1838 to the present time, the Gospel has been preached to all alike, Syrians and heathens, and all have been exhorted to come out and separate themselves from false Communions and join themselves with a pure Scriptural Communion. The blessing of God seems to have followed the new plan. Since 1838 twelve thousand persons have come out and joined the Protestant Church of England."[1]

[1] "Ch. Miss. Intelligencer," Oct., 1868, p. 314.

Space forbids our tracing the progress of this Mission, for the details of which we must refer to the annual reports of the Church Missionary Society. Dr. Mullens also says: " These converts, and the Missions founded for their benefit, have since greatly prospered; large congregations exist at every station, including no fewer than 4,000 persons, young and old, of whom 1,000 are communicants. Fifty day-schools exist for boys, and 150 girls are instructed in the boarding-schools. The chief stations are six in number, of which five are in most important localities among the Syrian Christians. Trichoor contains 12,000 Syrians. Cottayam, Márelikáre, Tirmvella, and Pallam are in the very heart of the churches, and are advancing in usefulness every year. Their handsome Gothic churches, their school and mission houses bear testimony to a purer faith and purer missionary zeal for the true Head of the redeemed Church, than their dull neighbours, the venerable buildings of former times."[1]

This was written in 1858. Since that time the Travancore and Cochin Mission has been thoroughly worked by the Church Missionary Society with constantly-increasing success. The field is divided into nine districts, viz., Allepie, Cottayam, Cochin, Márelikáre, Trichur, Pallam, Tirmvella, Hunnankullam, and Mundakayam, to which, in 1869, was added the

[1] Mullens's " South India," pp. 130-1.

new district of Candanade. The most recent information speaks of the Cambridge Nicholson Institution, under the Rev. J. M. Speechly, as having been designed for the preparation of an Evangelistic and educational agency. It now contains thirty-one students, who seem to be educated chiefly as schoolmasters, catechists, and itinerants. The Cottayam College, under the Rev. J. Bishop, contains nearly 150 pupils, in the two departments, the college proper (in affiliation with the University of Madras), and the grammar-school, consisting entirely of day scholars, fifty Syrians and eight heathens. Eight deacons of the Syrian Church form a class in this College. We may quote one fact in illustration of the hopes of a reform in the native Church. The Rev. G. Matthan (native) states that a neighbouring minister of the Syrian Church, "having had his education in our College at Cottayam, is prepared to support the reformation of this Church to the fullest extent consistent with its distinct existence. He has discontinued the Invocation of Saints, Prayers for the Dead, and Auricular Confession. He uses the vulgar tongue in the Church services, solemnises matrimony on week-days, and administers the elements in both kinds. Some of our people observed to me, with regret, that the better portion of the Syrians in this neighbourhood would ere this have come over to us had it not been for the faithful ministry of this man among them; but

I told them that we should rather rejoice in the success of all Christian ministers if they did indeed preach Christ and Him crucified, as this man did, for the *object of our Mission was not so much to gain proselytes to our Church* as to win souls to Christ."[1] Yet, in spite of this disclaimer, we find, scattered throughout the recent reports of the Society, constant allusions to the "conversion" of the Syrian Christians from their own Church to ours. For instance: "Twelve thousand persons of all classes have been brought out of religious error, and united in a profession of Scriptural Christianity. To this body of *converts* the *Syrians*, Chogans, and slaves have contributed most numerously."[2] And again: "The Churches of Kollatta and Erecalta now consist of *Syrian* Christian and slave converts, and that of Thottakalta is composed of Syrian and Chogan Christians."[3] Further: "At Thalawadi people are *converts from Syrians*, Roman Catholics, and Chogans. At Neranum all are *converts from Syrians.* The remaining four congregations are entirely composed of Pulayan slaves. Of 852 professing Christians of the district, 200 are *Syrians* by birth, forty-seven are converts from Chogans, and 605 are converts from Pulayan slaves."[4] Nay, more, the Rev. G. Matthan,

[1] Reports of Ch. Missionary Society, 1868-1869, pp. 153-4.

[2] "Church Missionary Record," Oct., 1868, p. 291.

[3] "Church Missionary Record," Oct., 1869, p. 305.

[4] "Ch. Miss. Rec.," Oct., 1868, p. 298.

already quoted, says in his reports of November 25th, 1868, that "the members of the congregation here and of the one at Niranem are composed of *seceders from the Syrian Church*, and a few converts from the Izhamas."[1]

Such statements as these will be approved or condemned, as the reader may belong to one or other of the great parties into which the Church of England is divided. Most High Churchmen[2] will consider that the missionaries, in converting so few of the heathen and so many of the Syrian Christians, are departing from the purpose for which they were sent out, and that in doing this in the diocese of a Christian Bishop, in the face of his distinct prohibition, they are guilty of encouraging secession and schism, especially when they do not deny that saving Christianity is to be found in the Syrian Church of Travancore.[3] Low Churchmen, on the other hand, maintain that they have abundant justification for the course which they

[1] "Ch. Miss. Rec.," Oct., 1869, p. 306.

[2] "The church was closed, and I could see little of the internal arrangements, but my interest in it, and in the Mission generally, was much diminished when I learned that converts were invited, not only from among the heathen, but from *the Christian population around*, and that the Holy Communion was celebrated only once in three months."—Howard's "Christians of S. Thomas," p. 115.

[3] "Her errors are grievous, but she is not an apostate Church, and we doubt not but that she has in her a 'seed which shall be counted unto the Lord for a generation.'"—Madras "Ch. Miss. Rec.," Vol. IV, p. 1.

have pursued in the errors which still exist in the Syrian Church, of Nestorian or of Romish origin, and they enumerate Transubstantiation, the Sacrifice of the Mass, Prayers for the Dead, Purgatory, the Worship of the Virgin and of Saints, Prayers in an Unknown Tongue, Extreme Unction, &c., and certain observances, such as the Elevation of the Host, burning incense, ringing of bells at the Elevation, &c.[1] The great problem, then, is to accomplish the reformation of the Syrian Church *from within;* and though Bishop Gell says that "for many years nothing has occurred to revive those bright anticipations of reformation which Bishop Wilson and many others for a time entertained,"[2] there are, according to last year's Reports, decided indications of approaching change. For example, Mr. Maddox reports: "The Syrians do not join our Church in such large numbers as they did; and there is a reason here also which will account for the fact. The Syrian Church itself has undergone a wonderful change during the last ten or fifteen years. In the south of Travancore, and especially in the eastern part of my district, and I believe the neighbouring district of Tiruwella, reform has been carried out to a considerable extent. Those things which

[1] "Madras Ch. Miss. Rec.," November, 1835. The *original* Syrian Church held none of these errors.—See Geddes's "Hist. Mal. Ch."—See quotation from Philipos, p. 17.

[2] Charge of the Bishop of Madras, 1863.

once shocked men of religious principle and enlightenment have been entirely removed in many churches. If it be asked, What, under God, has brought about so great a change? we answer, *The wholesome influence of our own Church in its midst, with its printing press, institutions, educated clergy, and European management.*"[1] To the same purpose we may cite, "Among the Syrians in the neighbourhood, the effect of our work becomes more and more apparent. The reforming party among them is become so strong that the superstitious party is contemplating to separate and build another church for themselves, where they can have their own ways without molestation. The chief stumbling-block with them is communion in both kinds, which the reforming party has strenuously adhered to as being Scriptural, and which the superstitious party greatly oppose, as being an innovation adopted from the Protestant mode of administering the Lord's Supper. The reforming party has, in addition to the force of truth on their side, the support and patronage of the Syrian Metropolitan, who advocates their cause. These circumstances contribute to their winning the day."[2]

When the English missionaries thus speak of a reformation in the Syrian Church, we presume that they allude to the *original* Church of the Serra,

[1] "Ch. Miss. Rec.," 1868 (Oct.), p. 301.

[2] "Ch. Miss. Rec.," Oct., 1868, p. 298.

though it is evident that some of their remarks refer to the *Romo*-Syrians. Even of them, however, there seems some hope, despite their numerical superiority (119,000), for Bishop Gell says: "Amongst those who have been subject to the Latin Bishop, *i.e.*, in the Syro-*Roman* Church, there is a dissatisfaction with Romish rule. They have very recently received a new Bishop, a native of Travancore, consecrated by the Syrian Patriarch of the East, and are desirous of being allowed to read the Scriptures." [1]

We have endeavoured, in treating of this difficult part of our subject, to discuss the question with the strictest impartiality. Still, we have viewed it from the English platform; and it is quite possible that with all our efforts, we may not have done complete justice to the native Church. We shall therefore, in our next chapter, allow *one of her clergy* to give a *Syrian's* view of her history, doctrines, ritual, and present condition.

[1] "Charge of the Bishop of Madras, 1863," p. 6.

CHAPTER V.

PRESENT STATE OF THE SYRIAN CHRISTIANS.

"It is not necessary that Traditions and Ceremonies be in all places one, and utterly like; for at all times they have been divers, and may be changed according to the diversities of countries, times, and men's manners, so that nothing be ordained against God's Word."—ARTICLE XXXIV.

WE are fortunately in the possession of a treatise, written two years ago, by the Rev. Edavalikel Philipos, Chorepiscopus, Cathanar of the Great Church of Cottayam, in Travancore, translated from his Malayalim by himself, and edited by the Rev. G. B. Howard, late Assistant Chaplain in the Diocese of Madras. This curious document is in the form of a catechism, and explains *from an Eastern Jacobite's point of view* the first four general Councils, with much information as to the ecclesiastical observance, and doctrines of his co-religionists. It is simply impossible, with due regard to the main object of our own Essay, to enter with anything like a discussion of the points of agreement and disagreement between the Church of England and the Church of Malabar, especially as the chief doctrine involved, is one of such deep mystery as to demand a volume rather than a chapter for its investigation. As the Editor justly observes, "the contention between the orthodox and the Jacobites, so far as my weakness is able to apprehend its nature, is one that none but the most profound theologians could enter into. Surely this consideration should make us cautious as to the language we use in reference to these separated Churches, even while, following the guidance of the Holy Fathers, we ourselves adhere rigidly to the teaching of the Catholic Church." The reader is referred to the treatise itself for full satisfaction; it must be our province to give such an outline as will convey to his mind a Syrian's view of the Syrian Church.

First, then, as to its history. "In A.D. 52, the Apostle Mar-Thomas came to Malabar in the reign of Choshea. He was so successful in his preaching that seven Christian Churches were founded by him there.[1] But for a long time after his death Christianity was in a declining state in Malabar. But as India and the countries in the East fell to the share of the Patriarch of Antioch in the Nicene Synod, he appointed a maphriana, at Tigris, in Bagdad, to conduct all the religious affairs of the Eastern Churches under the care of the Patriarch. This maphriana, coming to know from Thoma, a

[1] The Roman coins of Augustus, Tiberias, and others, found on the Malabar coast are a strong corroboration of the general tradition. —"Madras Journal of Literature and Sc.," Vol. iv., p. 212.

prince of Canan, of the decline of the Churches in Malabar, informed the Patriarch of the same; when, in pursuance to (of) the orders of the Patriarch, he sent the above-mentioned prince Thoma, and Joseph the Bishop, a native of Orfa, and other bishops, priests, and deacons, and a colony of Syrians with their families. They landed at Kodingaloor in the reign of Chernan (Cheruman) Perumal, A.D. 345, when the king received them gladly, and gave them certain privileges and names of honour as accounted by the natives, and a place to live in. By them and their successors to the office of Bishop who came from Antioch were the Syrian Churches founded (? firmly settled) and governed.

"When the Syrian Church was in this state, the Portuguese not only persecuted and killed all the Bishops as they came from Antioch, but their Metran. Dom Pre Alleskes de Menesis (Alexius de Menezes), residing at Goa, came to the Malayalim country in 1598, and having visited all the Syrian Churches (he) bribed the petty princes then ruling the country, and some Syrians, in order to gain them over to his interest. And those Syrians who opposed his designs were persecuted and put to death. So by main force he assembled all the Syrians in the church at Odyamperoor and persuaded them to embrace Popery, besides burning all the Syriac Bibles, and many other Syriac books. Then all the married priests were separated from their wives. (Menezes) also drew up a book regulating their future mode of living, and enjoined a strict obedience to these laws on the part of the Syrians. And anyone may know the great enmity and wickedness which this Alleskes practised towards the Syrian Church, if he thoughtfully reads that book containing his visit news (? visit news) of the different Churches, printed in Portuguese, in 1606, in the office of Deogoo Gomis Low Tire, printer, of a place called Vui Wersi Dadi,[1] in the country Coempra, in Goa. After this, in 1685, Mar-Evanious, the Bishop, came from Antioch, and with much difficulty redeemed the now existing Syrian Churches from the Portuguese; and those Churches which could not be reclaimed by Mar-Evanious still continue Romish; yet their liturgy is to this day in the Syriac."[2] Nothing can show more clearly than this quotation the opinions which the Syrians still entertain of the conduct of the Portuguese missionaries. Philipos goes on to say that the Malabar Christians rose against the Portuguese, and threw off their yoke, after eighty-six years' slavery; but that a large party still

[1] We have given the English of the worthy Cattanar exactly as it stands in his own translation (Mr. Howard being only the *Editor*), and we must, therefore, explain the mysterious account of the book which he calls the "visit news." What he means to say is this that Gouvea's Jornada was printed at a place called the University of Coimbra, which he innocently supposes to be in *Goa*, instead of *Portugal*.

[2] Syrian Christians of Malabar, pp. 22-24.

clung to Romanism. He divides the whole Syrian Church into six parts: 1st, the Jacobite Syrians; 2ndly, the Maronites, once Jacobites, but now Romanists; 3rdly, the small Church at Bagdad, also converted to Rome; 4thly, the old Chaldees of Nestorian views; 5thly, the new Chaldees, or Poothenkoorkar, who had re-adopted Syrianism, and 6thly, the Palayakoorkar, that is, old partisans who have adhered to Romanism.

The present Bishop of the Syrian Church in Malabar is Mar-Coorilos Joyakim, but as he is unwell, another named Mar-Devanasious has recently arrived from the Patriarch of Antioch. There is, however, as has been already stated, a rival in the person of Athanasius Matthew, of whom an unfavourable account is given by Philipos, and who was deposed by the Patriarch from all his offices. Into these particulars we need not enter.

Secondly, as to the doctrines of the Church. The Syrians "believe in the Holy Trinity, which is the Father, the Son, and the Holy Ghost, the only and true God." They have only one creed, the Nicene, though not verbatim the same as ours. The Syrians assert of the union of Christ's Divinity with His humanity. "Not like oil and water, but like wine and water they are joined together and are become One; and they believe in Him as perfect God and perfect Man both at His conception and birth, His sufferings, death and resurrection, and at His coming at the last Day; and that He did not destroy His humanity by His divinity, nor His divinity by His humanity."[1] The Cattanar next gives an account of what he calls the Synods (that is the Councils), of which he admits three, viz.: Nice, Constantinople, and Ephesus, but rejects Chalcedon, in this respect differing essentially from the Church of England, which recognises the four first General Councils.[2] The rejection of the Council of Chalcedon, which expressly condemned Eutyches, and declared the Catholic doctrine to be that "in Christ two distinct natures are united in one person without any change, mixture or confusion," seems to identify the present Syrian Church with the Eutychian or Monophosite Doctrine, if we assume that the Cattanar's statements are authoritative. In reply to the question, "Why are the Syrians called Jacobites?" he gives a somewhat confused answer to the effect that Jacob Boordana (Baradœus) opposed Nestorius, but he does not seem to be aware that the Jacobites, in escaping from Nestorianism, were led into the other extreme, maintaining that "the Divine and human natures of Christ were originally distinct, but after their union they became but one nature, the human nature being transubstantiated into the Divine."[3]

[1] "Philipos," p. 2.
[2] "Theophilus Anglicanus," pp., 19, 39, 40, 73, 326, 343.
[3] Harold Browne on the Thirty-nine Articles, p. 63. Mosheim

With regard to the Eucharist, "they believe the offering of the Kooroobana to be a holy sacrifice, and the bread and wine in it to be the real body and blood of Christ."[1] Of course, in so brief a definition as this, it is impossible to conjecture the *exact* sense in which the words are to be taken. There are those in the Church of England that would consider them perfectly correct, and even others of different Protestant communions have declared that Christ's "body and blood are verily and indeed taken."[2] On the other hand, these words might be interpreted to mean the Sacrifice in the Mass, and Transubstantiation. If this is really the doctrine of the Syrian Church, there must have been a strong infusion of Romanism by the Portuguese missionaries, for, before 1599, she distinctly denied Transubstantiation and all the concomitant errors. This is clearly proved by Action V. of the Synod of Diamper.[3]

They honour and worship the Virgin Mary and the Saints, but they do not give them that praise and worship which are due to God alone. They pray to the Saints, and they also pray for the dead (Questions 22-23). The 26th Question is, "Do they confess their

Cent. v. Pt. ii., Ch. v. Neander, Vol. IV. pp. 203-231. "Theophilus Anglicanus," p. 201.

[1] "Philipos," p. 11.

[2] Harold Browne on the Articles, p. 680. Bishop Taylor on the Real Presence, Section i., p. 9.

[3] Geddes's "Hist. Ch. Malabar," p. 217.

sins before the priest?" And the answer is, "It is commanded that all persons, above seven years of age should confess their sins." This again must be an instance of Portuguese influence, for Geddes states, speaking of the *original* Syrian Church, "She denies the necessity of Auricular Confession." A further difference between the ancient and modern usages is found in the employment of oil. *Before* the Synod of Diamper we read the Church of Malabar "makes no use of oils in the administration of baptism," and "She knows nothing of Extreme Unction";[1] whereas the *present* Church employs two anointings of the baptised, and one of the sick with holy oil.[2] In the account given of the doctrines of the Church of Malabar in the XVIIIth Chapter of the 1st Book of the Visitation,[3] it is made matter of complaint that "she ordains such as have been married several times, and that she allows her priests to marry as often as they please; but the present Syrian Church does not allow an unmarried deacon to be married *after* his ordination to the priesthood; and, if a priest marries a *second* time, he is considered to have fallen from his office." Further, "they consecrate those who keep the vow of celibacy, and those who keep that vow on the

[1] Geddes's "Hist. Ch. Malabar," p. 117
[2] "Philipos," p. 13.
[3] Gouvea's "Jornada," Coimbra, 1606.

death of their first wives, to the office of bishops, but only those who keep the vow of perpetual celibacy to the office of patriarchs."[1]

The Syrian Church recognises the usual three orders of bishops, priests, and deacons, but has three degrees in each of these offices. First, the Episcopal Order is subdivided thus: the patriarch, who is the "over-ruler and lord of everything connected with the Syrian Church"; secondly, the mapriana, a sort of suffragan, deputy, and heir of the patriarch; thirdly, the metropolitan, corresponding to our bishop, who governs the different parishes entrusted to his care, and ordains both priests and deacons. The three kinds of priests are, first, prampan living in convents under a vow of celibacy; second, chor-episcopa, a sort of inspector, or examining chaplain; thirdly, kashisha, a married priest, vicar of a parish. Of deacons there are: first, the archdeacon, whose business it is to examine the deacons, and to assist the bishops; secondly, meshamshana; thirdly, hypodiaconon, who assist the priest in divine service and read the Old Testament and Epistles, but not the Gospels. The Syrian priests are not, however, generally called by these titles, but by the word Cattanar, as the bishops are more frequently called Metrans.

[1] "Philipos," p. 14

The allegation made in the "Madras Church Missionary Record," that the Syrians believed in the existence of Purgatory, is positively denied by Philipos, who also repudiates the charge that they make images and worship them. The only way of reconciling these discrepancies is to suppose either that the accuser has not carefully distinguished between the Syrian and the *Romo*-Syrian Churches; or that in some special instances the Portuguese missionaries may have left their mark.

Thirdly, as to rites and ceremonies, the Cattanar gives us but a meagre account, taking it for granted, probably, that the forms familiar to him are equally so to us. He merely says: "Every morning and evening all the priests assemble in the church, when they pray and read portions of the Bible, as regulated in their office-book, and offer incense. But on certain festivals, and during Lent, and on other fast days, they pray thrice a day, and perform the other rites as explained above."[1] We must, therefore, avail ourselves of the narrative by Mr. Howard, and endeavour to condense a few of its interesting statements. The description of a Syrian church will be found at pp. 123 and 125 of "The Christians of S. Thomas." The author describes the dress of the Cattanar as consisting of (1) a pair of shoes, contrary

[1] "Philipos," p. 17.

to Oriental custom; (2) a robe of black serge, or coarse calico, worn in compliance with the former custom of the Syrian priests, whereas the common dress of the Malabar Christian is white; (3) the *cuthino*, like a surplice; (4) the *orro* or stole; (5) the *zunro*, a girdle or cord; (6) the *zando*, sleeves or maniples; (7) the *phaino*, chasuble, or probably cope, made of handsome silk damask, sometimes of velvet, nearly square, fastened over the shoulders by a button in front; (8) the cap. Describing a visit to one of their churches, Mr. Howard informs us that the congregation consisted of men and women, on different sides, of dusky complexion of course, but robed in dazzling white dresses; and while waiting for the commencement of the service, gratifying their curiosity at the expense of their visitor, many never having seen a white man. The service followed this order: The Cattanar, standing before the step of the throne or altar, repeated the Gloria, the prayer "Make us worthy," and the "Sedra" (*order* or *series*), then putting on his black dress, recited the 51st Psalm. Kneeling before the altar, he kissed it, repeating appropriate ejaculations, chiefly from the Psalms, and, assisted by his deacon, lighted the candles on the altar. The Trisagium and the Lord's Prayer followed, and thus ended the first service. The second service, that of "the Corban" (*oblation*), or what we shall call the Communion Service, began by the priest vesting and washing his hands, after which the bread and wine (the latter *mixed*) were brought from the prothesis, or credence table, and placed on the altar. After the oblation each vessel was veiled, and a large veil thrown over all. The Cattanar next prostrates himself, prays silently, rises from his knees, removes the veils, and, crossing his right hand over his left, elevates the paten and cup, with the accompanying prayers. The commemoration ended, the deacon begins the exhortation, "Στῶμευκαδῶς,"—*i.e.*, "*Let us stand in seemly order*," etc., the people immediately answering with a loud voice, "*Kurielison! Kurielison! Kurielison!*"—I give *their* pronunciation of the well-known words—drawling out the last syllable with a peculiar and most disagreeable flattening of the voice."[1] The officiating priest, placing the cup and paten on the altar, covers them with a light veil, and then, after the recitation of the general "Sedra," censes the altar, and proceeds to recite the Nicene Creed, and several short prayers. The large bell is then rung, and the people sing the hymn Kadisha Aloha, accompanied by the clash of cymbals. This ended, the curtain was drawn across the chancel arch, and two assistants placed a small table, covered with red cloth, in the middle below the steps; and on this they put a small cross, a bookstand, and two lighted tapers.

[1] Howard's "Syrians of S. Thomas," p. 137.

This being prepared, the curtain was drawn aside, and the Cattanar read the Epistle and Gospel for the day, after which the Cattanar returned to the altar, the bells and cymbals were again sounded, and a short prayer was uttered by the people.[1]

We have thus given a specimen of one portion of the service, referring our readers to the volume from which we have condensed this account, and to the authorities cited below.[2] Our object has been to state facts, rather than opinions, so that all may be able to judge whether it is probable that the Syrians can be forced into uniformity with the Church of England in matters of ritual. And yet, are there not those in our own Church whose ritualistic practices differ but little from those which we have attempted to describe? Nay, more, do we not retain in our ordinary service many significant ceremonies which, to the Nonconformist, appear as unnecessary as those of the Syrians do to us? The hope that must be cherished is that the authorities of the Syrian Church may be prevailed upon in Synod to purify their ceremonial from merely superstitious observances, retaining such

[1] Howard's "Christians of S. Thomas," pp. 139-147.

[2] Madras "Ch. Miss. Rec.," Vol. IV., p. 134. Asseman, "Bibliotheca Orientalis," Vol. II., p. 25. Renandot "Lit. Orient. Col.," Vol. II., pp. 12-21. An analysis of the Ordo-Communis, and a conspectus of the six Anaphoræ will be found at the end of Mr. Howard's volume, translated from Syriac MSS. obtained in Travancore. See also appendix to Vol. V. of Hough's "Christ. in Ind."

rites and ceremonies as are fairly representative of Christian truth.

The difference in ritual, however, between the two Churches is by no means the obstacle in the way of communion. If the present Malabar Church determines to use theological language which asserts Jacobite error, and expressly rejects the Council of Chalcedon, union with the Church of England is simply impossible. "Even if the Jacobite heresy were healed by explanations, the Filioque clause would still remain between ourselves and the Syrians of Malabar, as, unhappily, it does between ourselves and all other Easterns. We do not say that this, too, could not be explained. But it would need explanation. However, we can still deal with them in charity and brotherly love, remembering our own shortcomings, not to add their weak and depressed state, and the worldly prosperity, comparatively speaking, of our own. It is to be feared that we have not always done so."[1]

From a careful examination of the whole question, of which this chapter is an imperfect summary, there can be no reasonable doubt that the errors which at present afflict this unhappy Church are due in doctrine, if not in ritual, to the instruction of Nestorian, or rather of Jacobite teachers, quite as much as to the

[1] Review of the Syrian Christians of Malabar in "Guardian" of Wednesday, 13th April, 1870.

influence of the Portuguese missionaries in the XVIth Century." As they retain all their ancient dislike of the Church of Rome, it is little probable that these corruptions have been imported from that quarter ; it would rather appear that there is a natural tendency in the human heart to engraft them on the Christian system, when not continually irradiated with the light of God's Word. It may still be not impossible, if the Syrian clergy could be raised from their depressed condition, and persuaded to embrace the means of education, that their teaching should be reduced to a more scriptural standard, without any disturbance of their ecclesiastical system. The moral character of their people is still admitted to present many points of superiority over other natives. A simplicity of manner, accompanied by no small degree of honesty and plain dealing, distinguishes their intercourse with others, and renders it the more to be regretted that designs undertaken for their spiritual improvement should for the present be so unhappily interrupted.[1]

[1] Trevor's "India," pp. 287-8.

CHAPTER VI.

THE REVIVAL OF THE ROMISH MISSIONS IN INDIA.

"We must also remember that some of the Hindostan Missions are of recent foundation, and others *date from the Sixteenth Century*. Through many vicissitudes, *these last have preserved Christian traditions, which rendered the apostleship of our Missionaries more easy.*"[1]

Our readers will recollect that the Jesuits, by their disobedience and general misconduct, provoked Pope Clement XIVth so far, that in 1773, he suppressed their Order. A general restoration took place under Pius VIIth in 1814, and, from that time to the present, they have gradually increased until they are said to number in 1834, 2,684 members; and, in 1867, they had reached the extraordinary number of 7,956.

Many years previously, however, to the abolition of their Order, Pope Benedict XIVth had put an end to their refractory policy in India by the Bull of 1741, in which he calls the Jesuit Fathers "incbedientes, contumaces, captiosi, et perditi homines,"[2] and in

[1] "Annals of the Propagation of the Faith," Vol. XXVI., No. 161, p. 104.

[2] Nicolini's "History of the Jesuits," Edin., 1853, p. 128.

which he laid down such clear and stringent regulations that the prevaricating sophistry of the Jesuits could find no plausible means of evasion. From that moment the influence of the Portuguese missionaries and their followers began to decline. The supplies from Europe were stopped, and, so far were the million of converts which the Roman Catholic missionaries had made from showing any gratitude to their instructors that, according to Romish evidence, the Archbishop of Cranganor and the Bishop of Cochin were reduced to such poverty that they had to live upon alms.[1] The Portuguese Government, in 1755, under Pombal, seemed impressed with the necessity of extinguishing this obnoxious Order, for we learn that a hundred and forty-seven Jesuits were seized at Goa and sent to Lisbon, where they languished in prison for sixteen years. According to the authority which we have cited, "forty-five Fathers survived, sole remnant of all the missionaries of India, China, and America, amounting to many thousands. About the time when this suppression took place, the success of their efforts in India had been so great that the total number of Christians in the Madura Mission must have amounted to more than a million.[2] Yet, no sooner had the Jesuits been forcibly carried off than their sheep, left without

[1] Marshall's "Catholic Missions," Vol. I., p. 244.
[2] "Lettres Edifiantes," Tom. X., p. 54 and p. 285.

shepherds, vanished as snow before the sun; for we read that in 1776, Fra Paolim found but 18,000 in Madura, and 10,000 in Tanjore.[1] For nearly sixty years (1760-1820) scarcely any care was taken of the Catholic Missions and of their numerous converts. The older missionaries gradually died out, while none arrived from Europe to fill their place.[2]

But after 1822, there were unmistakable signs of revival. The torpor that had existed for more than half-a-century gave way to sudden activity. The few quiet, inoffensive priests who ministered to some respectable families of middle rank and a numerous body of Indo-Portuguese were gradually supplanted by men whose energy and learning contrasted strongly with the feeble powers of their predecessors. Colleges and schools, nunneries and other institutions sprang up on all sides. The Roman Catholic clergy during the last fifty years have so rapidly increased that *they far outnumber those of any other persuasion.* There can be no doubt that this wonderful revival is mainly owing to the re-establishment of the far-famed Society of Jesus; and here, as elsewhere, we find these "vigorous and experienced rowers," as Pope Pius VII. happily terms them, once more at the oar.[3] The glory

[1] Bartolomeo's "Voyage to the East Indies," Lond., 1800, p 65. "Calcutta Review," Vol. II., p. 95.

[2] Mullens, p. 135.

[3] "Calcutta Review," Vol. II., p. 74.

of the Jesuits was unquestionably their missionary spirit, and the glory of their missions was that of Southern India. Cardinal Wiseman says, "Although there may have been among them defects, and numbers of them unworthy of their character (for it would not be a human institution if it was not imperfect), it must be admitted that there has been maintained among them a degree of fervour and purest zeal for the conversion of heathens which no other body has ever shown."[1]

We shall attempt to exhibit in the few pages which we can devote to this subject the condition of the Roman Catholic Church in Southern India, first as to its statistics, and secondly, as to the state, intellectual, moral, and religious, of its converts, deriving our information chiefly, though not exclusively, from Romanist sources.

In a previous chapter it was stated that the Archbishopric of Goa was the metropolitical See of India, but a question, too long for discussion here, arose as to the rights of patronage enjoyed by the Crown of Portugal. The Archbishop determined to adhere to his Portuguese allegiance, while the Pope was as determined not to tolerate State interference with his prerogative. He, therefore, sent out a number of vicars-apostolic, who were regarded as intruders by

[1] "Lectures on Catholic Church." London, 1842, Vol. I., p. 218.

the Indian Roman Catholic clergy. The representatives of his Holiness, on the other hand, regarded with European contempt the claims of the Archbishop of Goa and his subordinate bishops. A schism was the result, which continues to the present hour, for we find that while fourteen bishops, seven hundred and seventy-four priests, and nine hundred and eight thousand laity, acknowledge the Papal authority in India, one archbishop, three bishops, a hundred and forty-one priests. and a hundred and twenty-nine thousand laity continue to yield obedience to the Indian primacy.[1] "In 1837 a furious war was waged between the vicar-apostolic (an Irish monk) and the Bishop-elect of the see of Meliapore. The former having received consecration as a bishop in *partibus infidelium*, pressed the Portuguese hard with his episcopal and apostolical powers; while the latter, though rightfully elected by the chapter of Goa, and in possession of the temporalities, remained without Papal confirmation, and was consequently unable to obtain episcopal consecration. The dispute came at last into the British courts, which, strangely enough, were employed in adjudicating on the rival pretensions of two foreign potentates to exercise jurisdiction within the dominions of the English crown."[2] Setting aside, then, the Archbishop of Goa and his adherents,

[1] "Summary of Catholic Statistics of India," &c., 1866, quoted in "Catholic Directory" for 1867. "Christian Year Book," 1867, p. 322.
[2] Trevor's "India," p. 296.

we observe that the Catholic missions in India are divided into twenty apostolic vicariates, each under its vicar or bishop, of which a complete list will be found in the authorised directories.[1] Of these vicariates, Verapoli or Malabar dates as far back as 1659; and Northern Bombay, 1669; Ava and Pegu, 1721; Pondicherry, 1776; Agra, 1820; Western Madras, 1132; Bengal, 1834; Eastern Bengal, Canara, Coimbatore, Hyderabad, Mysore, Patna, Quilon, and the Malay Peninsula, all in 1845; Madura, 1846; Jaffna in 1847; Vizagapatam in 1849; Poonah in 1854; so that the reader will be able to see at a glance, by a comparison of dates, how rapid has been the progress of revival. Roman Catholic writers see in this resuscitation a convincing proof "that the permanence which so wonderfully distinguishes these missions is not the privilege of one or two places only, but is equally conspicuous in every part of the country. It will be observed that the Mission of Madura, founded by de'Nobili, still counts one hundred and fifty thousand Catholics; while that of Verapoli, the field in which so many of the Jesuit missionaries laboured, numbers nearly two hundred and thirty thousand."[2] Verapoli, it will be remembered, is in the heart of the Malabar Christians, to the east of Cochin, and, of course, these

[1] "Catholic Directory" for 1870. London, p. 67, and in *Ibid* for 1867, p. 15.

[2] Marshall's "Christian Missions," Vol. I., p. 247.

figures bear directly on our subject. Another Roman Catholic authority gives the number in Malabar at 228,000, and in Quilon, 56,000;[1] but in 1866 we find it thus given, 230,000 under the Pope, and 40,000 subject to the Portuguese Archbishop of Goa. On the other hand, the Protestants affirm that these numbers are grossly exaggerated, and that the total Romanist population of the district of Travancore and Cochin amounts to about 140,000, including not merely the converts from heathenism, but those who have been proselytised from Syrianism to Romanism.[2] The total Roman Catholic population is asserted by Marshall to be 1,200,000 in 1857; but if we compare his statement with that of the "Annales de la Propagation de la Foi" (800,000), we are forced to one of two conclusions, either that Marshall, with the characteristic zeal of a pervert, has added one third to the actual number, or that between 1857 and 1866 the numbers must have fallen to that amount.[3] Still there can be no doubt that, after every deduction from party exaggerations, the Roman Catholic population is very much greater than Protestant missionaries seem dis-

[1] "Madras Directory" for 1857.

[2] "Ch. Missionary Intelligencer," Oct. 1868, p. 313.

[3] A total of 1,200,000, the living witnesses of the labours and triumphs of the Missionaries of the Catholic Church. Marshall, Vol. I., p. 248. "The total number of Catholics in Hindostan rises to about 800,000; but this, when divided into the several vicariates, presents very considerable variations." "Annals," March 1866, p. 103.

posed to acknowledge, and that if any reliance can be placed in official documents, in the year 1859 the converts of Madura were 2,614, while in the diocese of Verapoli "more than a thousand heathens are baptised yearly, besides many Nestorians and some native Protestants."[1]

Though our enquiry refers more immediately to the Syrian Christians, it unquestionably embraces missionary efforts in South India generally, and we therefore do not hesitate to refer to the accounts of Madura by Father Saint-Cyr, in 1859. In this interesting volume he records the conversion of 5,000 schismatics, 500 idolaters, and 400 Protestants, the result of the efforts of forty-three Jesuit Fathers.[2] This is, however, not quite confirmed by the list of conversions in 1864, when Coimbatore furnished 100; Mangalore, 174; Mysore, 200; Vizagapatam, 300; and Madura, 1400.[3] A similar discrepancy as to the number of converts appears in the letter of Monsignor Dufal, vicar-apostolic of Eastern Bengal, dated 21st February, 1865:—"Notwithstanding our constant efforts, the number of conversions is very small, almost insignificant, when we compare them with the population of this vast country. *Seventy-six*

[1] "Madras Catholic Directory" for 1860, p. 154.

[2] "La Mission de Maduré," par Louis Saint-Cyr, S. J. Paris, 1859, p. 5.

[3] "Annals," March, 1866, p. 96.

during the year 1864! Alas! it is indeed so difficult to make any one amongst the Hindoos, that the catechists are very few."[1] To the same effect the vicar-apostolic of Patna writes on 20th November, 1864: "To preserve the faith in the hearts of our Christian flock seems to be the only thing we can hope to realise at present, until it pleases Almighty God to render this arid and immense country fruitful."[2] How is this inequality of results to be accounted for, notwithstanding the equally devoted zeal of the missioners in each of those districts. The answer is to be found, according to Roman Catholic writers, in the motto at the head of this chapter, and, if so, we may consider this admission as direct testimony to the influence which the Portuguese missions of the XVIth Century are still exerting in Southern India.

The condition of the Roman Catholic Christians must next be considered, and it is but just that the missioners themselves should be first heard. These, of course, coming fresh from Europe, had no knowledge whatever, except from books, of the Indian converts, amongst whom they were to labour; and they therefore may be supposed to give their opinions without any bias. One of these missioners describes his first impression in the simple but significant

[1] "Annals," March, 1866, p. 89.
[2] "Annals," March, 1866, p. 89.

phrase, "I am astonished at the faith of these Christians."[1] In 1829, M. Bonnand rejoices that half-a-century of trial had failed to destroy the faith; and ten years later, Father Garnier writes that "the Christians of these countries are in general well-disposed and strongly attached to the faith. *The usages introduced amongst them by the Jesuits still subsist.* But we shall have a good deal to do to form them into a people of true Christians." Father Louis de Saint-Cyr, in 1842, observes, "Within a certain radius around the centre of the mission, *all the villages*, with rare exceptions, *are Christian;* beyond this circle you enter the region of Paganism. This fact proves how valuable was the presence of the evangelical labourers in this country, and what a vivifying influence has been diffused by the exercise of the holy ministry."[2] These testimonies are sufficient to prove our point, that the revivalists found the *influence of previous labourers by no means extinct;* whether for good or evil, is another question.

Many Protestant writers have also borne testimony to the zeal and influence of the Roman missioners, as well as to the faithfulness and good conduct of their flocks. Henry Martyn says: "Certainly, there is infinitely better discipline in the Romish Church than in ours, and if ever I am to be the pastor of

[1] "Annales," Tom. IV., p. 152.
[2] "Annales," Vol. IV., p. 70.

native Christians, I should endeavour to govern with equal strictness."[1] Dr. Claudius Buchanan declares that "there are at this day in India members of the Church of Rome who deserve the respect and affection of all good men," and throughout his travels in Southern India there are numerous expressions such as these: "From Cape Comorin to Cochin there are about one hundred churches on the sea-shore alone. Of these, the chief part are the Syrian-Latin, or, more properly, the Syrian-Romish Churches;" and again, "at Manaar they were all Romish Christians;" and "I visited Mahé and Calicut; the Romish Christians are numerous."[2] Dr. Kerr, chaplain at Calcutta, confirms this account, stating that "the Roman Catholic Syrians are much more numerous than the members of the original Church."[3] Dr. Middleton, first Bishop of Calcutta, remarks that, "Protestants as we are, it were bigotry to deny that the Church of Rome, notwithstanding that she may have exaggerated her successes, has done wonders in the East."[4] Hough, whom we have so often quoted, is candid enough to admit that "there are native Christians of the Roman Church in India, whose character is unexceptionable, and who occupy stations of respon-

[1] Martyn's "Memoirs," IXth Ed., p. 288.
[2] "Christian Researches," p. 75, et passim.
[3] Dr. Kerr's "Reports," p. 10.
[4] Webb Le Bas' "Life of Middleton," Vol. II., p. 96.

sibility in the public service. Some have given satisfactory reasons to believe them to be sincere Christians."[1]

While searching for authorities in illustration of this part of our subject, we have met with many striking proofs—all the more valuable because "undesigned coincidences"—of the *depth and permanency produced by the labours of the early Portuguese Missions.* Mr. Thornton, estimating the population of Goa at 313,000, considers that two-thirds are Roman Catholics.[2] An officer, generally hostile to the Romanists, concedes that "in *their whole course in India, the Portuguese have left the traces of conversion;* and around the coast, from the Cape of Good Hope to Canton, the Portuguese language is spoken, and the Cross of Christ adored."[3] General Parlby writes: "Amidst the ruins into which their temporal possessions have fallen, the *vestiges which they have left of their faith* seem destined to survive the *débris* of their earthly grandeur, and to be *so firmly rooted* that they will never be wholly effaced."[4]

Witnesses on the other side must now be called into court. Of course there can be no question that very large numbers of so-called converts have been admitted into the Romish communion, and that, even

[1] Hough's "Hist. of Christ.," Vol. II., p. 491.
[2] Thornton's "Gazetteer of India," vol. ii., "Goa."
[3] "Fifteen Years in India," p. 360.
[4] "The Establishment of the Anglican Church in India," 1851, p. 19.

supposing the probability of occasional exaggeration, accessions are continually made. But the doubt which we have expressed in previous chapters, on the conversions effected by Xavier, and in Madura by de Nobili and his successors, recurs at the present hour. What is the difference of the word "*conversion*" as used by a Roman Catholic and a Reformed Catholic? *On that definition the whole question seems to hang.* Nothing can be easier than to enrol whole battalions of nominal converts if due care is taken to make the change from one faith to another as slight as possible. "The rules of caste," says Mr. Trevor, "were retained so vigorously that churches are still found in the south of India divided into compartments, and provided with separate entrances, for the respective orders of worshippers. The feasts and ceremonies of the new religion were purposely assimilated to the old one, so that while acquiring many substantial advantages of a temporal character, the neophytes should be scarcely conscious of parting with a single rite of superstition."[1] Dr. Allen, an American missionary by no means opposed to the Romanists, thus writes: "In other matters, also, they

[1] "Trevor's India," p. 290. We cannot ascertain if this division of churches into compartments still continues, for the most recent information merely says; "One of our chief obstacles in establishing the Christian religion amongst the Hindoos is their social system of castes. The missioners are endeavouring to put an end to this exclusiveness by means of orphanages and schools.—"Annals," March, 1866, p. 91.

retain much of their former heathen customs. The Hindus are very fond of show and noise in their religion; and it is a frequent custom, in some districts, to put the idols of their gods on a car or carriage of some kind, on festival days, and then draw it about in procession. This *usage has been retained by the Roman Catholics*, only substituting the images of their saints for the idols of the gods. In some places the same car is used on Hindu festival days for the idols of the gods, and on Romish festivals for the images of the saints." Similar evidence is given by Dr. Middleton, Bishop of Calcutta, perfectly applicable to the system, though in a different part of India. In the Island of Salsette, there were about 8,000 Romanists, who, though enrolled as Christians, and attending divine worship at the Portuguese churches, were yet wedded to all the absurd ceremonies of the Hindoo mythology, of which they were particularly observant, on births, deaths, and marriages. "At the very time that they were in the habit of attending a Christian sanctuary, and professedly acknowledging Christianity, they retained in their houses various implements of Hindoo idolatry, and entered indiscriminately into all the pernicious usages of that deplorable superstition."[2] But, possibly, Mr. Marshall, who so dangerously

[1] Allen's "India," p. 320.

[2] "Life of Bishop Middleton," Vol. I., p. 227. Hough's "Christianity." Vol. V., p. 226.

avoids quotations of the above character, may object to Protestant opinions of the character of his so-called converts. We will, therefore, make one or two brief extracts from Roman Catholic writers, and the first shall be the Jesuit Father Martin: "On Saturday evening I got ready a small triumphal chariot, which we adorned with pieces of silk, flowers, and fruits. On it was placed an image representing our Saviour risen from the dead; and the chariot was drawn in triumph round the church, several instruments playing at the same time. The festival was greatly heightened by illuminations, lustres, sky-rockets, and several other fireworks, in which the Indians excel; then verses were spoken or chanted by the Christians, in honour of our Saviour's triumphing over death and hell. The chief personage of the settlement, his whole family, and the rest of the heathens who assisted in the procession, fell prostrate thrice before the image of our Saviour risen from the dead, and worshipped him in such a manner as very happily blended them indiscriminately with the most fervent Christians."[1] The Abbé Du Bois, after a life spent in India, writes thus: "For my part, I cannot boast of my successes in this holy career during a period of twenty-five years, and that I have laboured to promote the interests of the Christian religion. The restraints and privations under which I

[1] "Lettres Edifiantes et Curieuses," quoted in Trevor's ".India," p. 290. Tom. x., pp. 168-182.

have lived, by conforming myself to the usages of the country; embracing, in many respects, the prejudices of the natives; living like them, and becoming almost a Hindoo myself; in short, by 'being made all things to all men, that I might by all means save some,'—all this has proved of no avail to me to make proselytes."[1] The abbé, a Romish missioner, be it remembered, gives a most deplorable account of the concessions made to Hindoo superstitions of every form, asserts that he does not believe he made a single convert during his lengthened ministry, and abandons the whole population of India to perdition.

The reader can now judge, even from the limited amount of evidence which we have been able to submit, how far good and evil are mingled in the missionary operations of the Romish Church. Truth, no doubt, lies as it generally does, between the extreme statements on either side. Roman converts are, unquestionably, in many instances, as well conducted as those of other denominations; and it would be hard to prove on the part of the Protestants that all their proselytes were paragons of virtue. Ignorance, superstition, self-interest, desire of imitation, and other unworthy motives, may prompt Asiatics, as well as Europeans, to profess the outward form of religion in which they have no real belief. But it by no means follows, as infidels have argued, that all converts are

[1] Letters of Abbé Dubois. Passim.

hypocrites, for there is abundant evidence to prove that many have not only suffered in their worldly fortunes on account of their faith, but have sealed their testimony with their blood.

Our general conclusion is, that the *impression made by the Portuguese in the* XVIth Century, notwithstanding numerous fluctuations, *still continues to operate in Southern India*, not only on the Syrian Christians, whether Jacobite or Romanist, but also on the modern missionary efforts in that quarter. We must express a hope that, amid many tares, much true wheat has been scattered in the soil of the Deccan, and that should a reformation take place amongst the million of Roman Catholics in India, similar to what occurred in Germany, great indeed would be the effect throughout the whole of this vast region, As a writer well acquainted with India has said, "How soon in this way might hundreds of native missionaries be raised up to preach, each in his own language, the wonderful works, and the yet more wonderful love, of God."[1]

[1] Allen's "India."

AUTHORITIES.

Albuquerque, Alfonso de. Commentarios. Lisboa, 1576-40.

Andrade, I. F. Vida de D'Joãode Castro. Lisboa, 1651.

Annales de la Foi. Paris and Lyons, 1865.

Annuario Pontificio for 1870. Rome.

Ansted Prof. Geog. of India. London, 1869.

Arrian, F. Historia Indica. Amstel, 1757.

Asiatic Society of Bengal for 1834. Calcutta, 1862.

Assemanus, J. A. Bibliotheca Orientalis. Romæ, 1719-28.

Assemanus, I. S. De Syris Monophysitis Dissertatio. Romæ, 1730.

Azurare, Gomes. Chronica de Discobumento, &c. Paris, 1841.

Badger, G. P. Nestorians and their Rituals. London, 1852, 8vo.

Baldœus, P. Beschryvinge van Malabar. Amsterdam, 1672, fol.

Bàrreto. Relat. Stat. Christ, Malabar. Romæ, 1645.

Barros, Ioaode. Decadas. Lisboa, 1778, 12mo.

Bartoli, D. Dell Istoriadella Compagnia di Giesu. Romæ, 1667, fol.

Bartoli and Maffei. Life of Xavier. Trans. by Dr. Faber. London, 1858.

Bateman, J. Life of Daniel Wilson, Bishop of Calcutta. London.

Bernouilli, John. Description de l'Inde. Berlin, 1797, 4to.

Bertrand. La Mission de Maduré. Paris, 1847, 8vo.

Bingham, J. Origines Ecclesiasticæ. London, 1834.

Biographie Universelle. Paris, 1811-28, 52 vols.

Browne, Bishop. On the XXXIX. Articles. London, 1858.

Bruce. Scenes and Sights in the East.

Buchanan, Claudius. Christian Researches, New York, 1811.

Calcutta Review. Vol. II. Calcutta, 1846, 8vo.
Caldecott, R. M. Life of Baber. London, 1844, 8vo.
Camõens, Luiz de. Os Lusidadas. Paris, 1858.
Canoz, R. C., Bishop. Report of Madura Missions. Trichin, 1862.
Cardoso, J. Agiologia Lusitano. Lisboa, 1652, 1744.
Caron, Raymond. Missions Apostoliques. Paris, 1649.
Castanheda, H. L. de. Conquista da India. Lisboa, 1833.
Catholic Directory for 1867-1870. London, 8vo.
Cave, W. Scriptorum Ecclesiasticorum, Hist. Lit. Oxf., 1740, fol.
Cerri, Urbano. State of Roman Catholic Religion. London, 1844, 8vo.
Chambers, James. Bishop Heber and Indian Missions. Lond. 1846, 12mo.
Christian Observer. London, 1823-35.
Christian Year Book for 1867. London.
Churchill, Messrs. Collection of Voyages, 6 vols. London, 1745.
Conference on Missions at Liverpool in 1860. London, 1860.
Cordara. Historia Societatis Jesu.
Cordeyro, Ant. Historia Insulana. Lisboa, 1717, fol.
Correa, Gaspar. Lenda da India.
Cosmas, Indopleustes. Indica Topographia Christiana. Montfaucon.
Conto, Diogo de. Decadas IV., V., VI., and VII. of Asia in De Barros. Lisboa, 1778.
Covillam, Pedro de. Relazão do Viage a India.
Crakanthorpe, R. Defensio Eccl. Angl. London, 1625.
Crétinau, Jaques. Histoire de la Compagnie de Jesus. Paris, 1844, 8vo.
Cyclopœdia of Christian Missions. Glasgow, 1859.
D'Alembert. La Destruction des Jésuites.
D'Anville.
Day, F. Land of the Permauls. Madras, 1863, 8vo.
Dellon, C. Relation de l'Inquisition de Goa. Amst., 1719, 12mo.
Denis, M. F. Portugal. Paris, 1846.
Dialogos de Varia Historia. Lisboa, 1645.
Diodorus Siculus. Basiliæ, 1559.
Dubois, J. A. Letters on Christianity in India. London, 1823.
Duff, D. India and Indian Missions.

Duncan, G. Geography of India. Madras, 1868.
D'Ussieux. Découverte des Indes.
Elphinstone, Hon. M. History of India.
Etheridge, J. W. Syrian Churches. London, 1846, 12mo.
Eusebius. Hist. Eccles. ed. Oxon, 1843.
Fabricius. Lux Evangelii.
Faria e Sousa. Os Portugueses in Asia. London, 1695, 8vo.
,, Asia Portuguesa. Lisboa, 1666, fol.
,, The Portuguese Asia, by Stephens. London, 1698.
,, Historia de Portugal. Brusselas, 1730.
Ferreria, A. P. A Vida de D. Luiz de Ataide.
Fleury, Abbé. Discourse on Ecc. Hist. London, 1721.
Fleury, Abbé. Histoire Ecclesiastique. Bruxelles, 1713.
Fontana. Monumenta Domenicana. 1540.
Ford, R. Handbook for Spain. London, 1855.
Fox, H. W. Chapters on Missions in S. India. London, 1848, 16mo.
Francisco, de S. Luiz. Vida de D. Joaõ de Castro. Lisboa, 1835, 4to.
Franco, Ant. Synopsis Annalium Soc. Jesu in Lusitania. 1726.
Fraser. History of the Mogul Emperors.
Galvão, A. Descobrimentos. Lisboa, 1555.
Gama, Vascode. Roteiro da Viagem. Lisboa, 1861.
Gibbon, E. Decline and Fall of the Roman Empire.
Glen, I. B. de. Gouvea Histoire Orientale tournée en François. Am., 1609.
Goes, Damão de. Chronica d'El Rey, D'Monoel. Lisboa, 1566.
Geddes, M. History of the Church of Malabar. London, 1694.
Gouvea, Anto. Jornada do Arcébispo de Goa. Coimbra, 1609.
Grundler, J. E. Account of the Malabarians. 1714, 4to.
Guzman, Luix de. Historia de las Missiones. Alcala, 1601.
Hallam, H. Middle Ages. London, 1855, 8vo.
Heber, Bishop. Journal.
Helyot, Pierre. Histoire des Ordres Monastiques. Guincamp, 1838.
Henrion, M. R. A. Hist. des Missions Catholiques. Paris, 1846, 4to.
Herculano, A. Historia de Portugal. Lisboa, 1846, 8vo.
Herrera, Tordesillas Ant. Historia de las Indias. Madrid, 1730.

Hoole, E. Missions in Madras, Mysore, and South India. London, 1844, 8vo.

Howard, G. B. The Christians of St. Thomas. Oxford and London, 1864.

Howitt, W. Colonization and Christianity. London, 1838, 12mo.

Hough, J. Hist. of Christianity in India. London, 1839, &c.

Jarric, Pierre du, Histoire des choses, &c. Bordeaux, 1608, 4to.

Jesuits—Relation des Missions. Paris, 1659.

Jesuit in India, by Strickland.

Indice Chronologico Navegućões dos Portugueses. Lisboa, 1841.

Juvencii, J. Historia Soc. Jesu. Paris, 1711, 8vo.

Kaye, J. W. Christianity in India. London, 1859.

Kerr, R. H. Report on Syrian Christians in 1806, Christ Res. 1812.

La Croze, M. V. Hist. du Christianisme des Indes. Haye, 1726, 8vo.

Le Bas. C. W. Life of Bishop Middleton. London, 1831, 8vo.

Lee. History of the Syrian Church in 17th Report of C. M. S London.

Lettres Edifiantes et Curieuses. 26 vols. Paris, 1780-83.

Limborck, Phil. History of the Inquisition. London, 1618, 8vo.

Litteræ Annuæ Soc. Jes. Mongunt, 1618.

Lock. Travels of the Jesuits.

Lopes, Thomé. Navegaçã as Indias Orientaes. 1550, fol.

L'Univers. Portugal par F. Denis. Paris, 1846.

Ludlow, J. M. British India. London, 1858, 8vo.

Macaulay, Lord. History of England. London, 1864.

Madras Church Missionary Record for 1835-6.

Maffei, G. P. Histoire Indica Col. Agrip. 1593, fol.

Maffei, G. P. L Histoire des Indes. Paris, 1665, 4to.

Magistris, G. de. Relation. Paris, 1663-8.

Major, R. H. India in the XV. Century. London, 1857.

Marco, Polo. Travels of, by T. Wright. London, 1853, 8vo.

Maria, V. Viaggio all'Indie Orientale. Romæ, fol.

Martin, M. History of Eastern India. London, 1831, 8vo.

Meier. Missions Geschichte.

Michelsen, E. H. Modern Jesuitism. London, 1855.

Mill, J. History of British India. London, 1848, 8vo.
Montfaucon, B. Nova Collection Patrum. 1707.
Mullens' Missions in South India. London, 1854, 8vo.
Muratori. Relazione delle Missione.
Murray, Hugh. History of British India. London, 1855.
Neale, J. Mason. Eastern Church. London.
Newcombs. Cyclopædia of Missions. New York, 1855.
Nicolini, G. B. History of the Jesuits. Edinburgh, 1853, 12mo.
Niekamp, J. L. Hist. de la Mission Danoise. London, 1745, 8vo.
Norbert. Memoires Historiques sur les Miss. des Malabares.
Osorio, Jer. Hist. Port. por F. M. do Nascimento. Lisboa, 1804.
Osorius, Hier. Operaomnia. 4 vols., Romœ, 1592, fol.
Paulinus, P. India Orientalis Christiana. Romæ, 1794, 4to.
Pearson, H. N. Memoirs of Schwartz. London, 1839, 8vo.
Peet, J. Trans. of Syrian Liturgies in Madras Church Missionary Records for 1835.
Pereira, A. P. Historia da India. Coimbra, 1616.
Philipos, E. The Syrian Christians of Malabar. London, 1869.
Ranke. History of the Popes.
Raynal, Abbé. Histoire Philosophique des Indes. Paris, 1778.
Reports of the C.M.S., S.P.G., L.M.
Resende, G. de. A Chronica d' El Rey. D. João II. Evora, fol.
Resende, G. de. De Antiquitalibus Lusitaniœ. Evora, fol.
Ribeiro, J. P. Dissertacões Chronologicas Criticas. Lisboa.
Rollin, C. Ancient History.
Robertson, W. Disquisition on Ancient India. London, 1794.
Ragnagli di Missione. Romæ, 1615.
Raulinus. Histoire Ecclesiæ Malabarensis. Romæ, 1745, 4to.
Rowe, G. The Colonial Empire—East Indian group. London.
Sarpi, P. History of the Council of Trent.
Santarem, Visconde de. Quadro Elementar de Portugal. Paris, 1842.
Saint-Cyr, Louis. Les Nouveaux Jésuites. Paris, 1865.
Saint-Cyr, Louis. La Mission de Maduré. Paris, 1859.
Simon, R. Histoire Critique. Irevoux, 1711.
South India Conference. Madras, 1858.

Storrow, E. India and Christian Missions.

Strickland, W. Catholic Missions in India. London, 1865.

Swanston. Memoir in Journal of Roy. Asiatic Soc. for 1833-4.

Thornton, E. Gazetteer of India.

Trevor, G. India—Its Natives and Missions. London.

Trevor, G. India—An Historical Sketch. London, 1858.

Turner, S. History of the Anglo-Saxons.

Valentyn, F. Veischryring van Choromandel. Amst., 1726.

Vasconcellos, Ant. Anacephalœoses. Antuerpia, 1627.

Venn, Henry. Life of Xavier. London, 1862.

Wadding, L. Annales, 1590-1600. Romæ, 1731.

Wedell, R. Von. Hist. Geog. Hand. Atlas. Berlin.

Wittman. Storia Universale delle Cattoliche Missioni.

Wordsworth, Bishop. Theophilus Anglicanut. London, 1857.

Wrede, F. "S. Thomé Christians." Asiatic Researches. Vol. VII.

Ziegenbalg. Gospel in the East.

APPENDIX.

A.—The Archbishop of Canterbury's Appeal for the Assyrian Christians.

B.—The Christians of Assyria commonly called Nestorians.

C.—The Church Missionary Society's Work in Travancore and Cochin.

D.—The Roman Catholic Missions in Hindostan and Southern India.

APPENDIX A.

THE ARCHBISHOP OF CANTERBURY'S APPEAL FOR THE ASSYRIAN CHRISTIANS.

THE following "Appeal on behalf of the Christians of Assyria, commonly called the Nestorians," has been put forth by the Primate of All England, after consultation with other members of the English Episcopate, as well as with the influential Committee which his Grace has invited to assist him in the furtherance of the contemplated measures:—

"The ancient and once flourishing community, commonly known by the name of Nestorians, and now comprised chiefly within the limits of Assyria—the modern Kurdistân, one of the frontiers of Asiatic Turkey—have recently appealed for help to the Church of England. The appeal, signed by several Assyrian bishops, priests, deacons, and notables of the laity, and ratified with the seal of their Catholicos or Patriarch, Mar Shimûn, was addressed to the Archbishop of Canterbury and the Bishop of London (Bishop Tait). It has already been published in full, but its purport may be succinctly stated in the following quotation from a speech in reference to it by the late Archbishop Longley:—

"'The Nestorians, in this touching letter, say that they feel they are in a state of great ignorance and darkness; and they apply to us to come over and help them—to send some one to instruct and enlighten them. I have reason to believe that they are not at all wedded to Nestorian principles, and that they might easily be led to abandon them. I cannot but hope, therefore, that inasmuch as this appeal has been made to us, there may be some well-disposed people who will contribute to a mission to these poor eastern Christians. It is a very modest petition that we should send out two missionaries, who might bear comfort and consolation to those who are now really in very great distress. Their position is a very painful one. They are between two hostile forces, the Mohammedan on the one hand, and the Papal on the other; and they are persecuted by both. They appeal to us.'

"The claims of these Assyrian Christians upon the liberality of English Churchmen are too obvious to require any lengthened exposition. Isolated from the great body of Christendom, they cannot look, like other eastern Christians, to powerful European protectors. With the exception of one alleged theological error upon a cardinal point—which, however, they disclaim, and are professedly ready to repudiate—they have preserved, throughout centuries of severe persecution, the primitive creed and doctrine of the Catholic and Apostolic Church. Among them the eucharistic cup has never been denied to the laity, nor the right of marriage to the priesthood; there is no superstitious use of images or pictures; purgatory and indulgences are unknown; while the reading of the Holy Scriptures by all in the vulgar tongue is, so far as their scanty supply of books enables, diligently practised.

"To our own communion, brought back, through God's blessing upon the Reformation, to the primitive standard, this ancient body is especially and most reasonably attracted; and we are anxious that their hopes of obtaining assistance from us may be realised as they ought.

"I am not unmindful of the many other claims which press on the liberality of the members of our Church. But I would strongly recommend this request from the Assyrians as constituting one of the most urgent among them all.

"In pursuance of the intentions of the late Archbishop Longley, I now invite the faithful in this favoured land of England to contribute towards a fund by means of which candidates for the native ministry may be brought over hither to receive a better education, and delegates may be sent to the east in the name of the Church of England to suggest to this venerable and interesting community such counsels of wisdom as they ask at our hands; the object being not to make proselytes to the English Church, but to aid them in reforming heir own Church, where needful, upon a primitive basis and after primitive models.

"A. C. CANTUAR."

We heartily trust that this Appeal will prove the means of eliciting a substantial and adequate response from all members of the Church of England who—to adopt the language of the resolution on the subject passed at the recent meeting of the Anglo-Continental Society—"reverence the Christendom of antiquity, yearn for re-union on a primitive basis, and are anxious to extend the blessings of the Gospel among unbelievers." It is announced at the foot of this Appeal that subscriptions may be paid to the account of the "Assyrian Christians' Fund," at the London offices of the Society for the Propagation of the Gospel.

An appreciative notice of Mr. Badger's paper on the so-called Nestorians—as reprinted from our pages—which appeared in the last number of the S.P.G. official organ, the *Mission Field*, concludes in terms which aptly expound and reinforce the pleading of the Lambeth Appeal:—

"Why, it may be asked, is this ancient Church, which has kept the light of Christianity alive amidst Mohammedan darkness, in outward separation from the whole of Christendom? The reason is its refusal to accept the decrees of the Council of Ephesus: the Assyrian Christians refuse to call the Blessed Virgin *Theotokos* (her who gave birth to God), and they commemorate Nestorius among the saints. Their isolaled position, and their peculiar language, may account for this. The word into which *Theotokos* is translated implies in their language more than it does in Greek; and if, in refusing to accept that word, they only mean to refuse to say that our Blessed Lord is God of the substance of His Mother, it would be hard to blame them. Mr. Badger believes that they might be induced, by proper explanations, to accept the statements made at Ephesus, and to erase the name of Nestorius.

"To the reiterated appeals of this ancient Church for help to educate her people, the English Church has hitherto turned a deaf ear. Rome is active there, but cannot win their confidence: they abhor images, and the few invocations of saints in their rituals come immeasurably short of the language sanctioned by the Roman Church. Russia might aid them, but the veneration of pictures is not in accordance with their ancient customs. American Independent missionaries are at work there, but their doctrine (as well as their discipline) is utterly at variance with that of this ancient Church. They still look to us for help, which is at present limited to the education in England of two Assyrians and one Chaldæan. But we trust that an answer more suited to their needs, and to our opportunities, may now speedily be given."

The Society for Promoting Christian Knowledge will not, we believe, be behind her younger sister in contributing assistance to this movement. That corporation possesses, besides a most valuable collection of Nestorian, Jacobite, and other ecclesiastical Syriac and Arabic MSS., several accurate translations of works pertaining to our own Church and theology, which ought, with as little delay as possible, to be printed and put in circulation among the Christians of the East. One such is a version of our Prayer-book in that Syrian dialect in which the rituals of the so-called Nestorians are written. This work would obviously be of great service to the clergy and the few educated laymen of that body; it would also be of some use to the Papal Chaldæans, though these for the most part are as familiar with Arabic; and it would probably find currency, moreover, among the priesthood of the Jacobites throughout Asiatic Turkey, and of even the Christians of St. Thomas in India. The Society possesses also an Arabic translation of Jewell's "Apology," which by its arguments against Romanism, and by its vindication of the English Reformation, would be of two-fold Catholic advantage to all Christians from Egypt to Mesopotamia, and, in short, in every country where the "French of the East" is spoken. We would recommend the publication, in the first instance, of these versions of the Prayer-book and Jewell's "Apology;" but it should not be long before they are followed by the Books of Homilies and by Nelson's "Fasts and Festivals," which also the same Society has nearly in readiness for its Arabic press.

Among several indications which we have noticed of the new interest which is everywhere awaking respecting the Christians of the Far East, we may specify the following announcement of the subject proposed by the Paris *Académie des Inscriptions* for the *Prix Bordin* (of which the value is 3,000 francs):—"Faire l'histoire de l'Église et des populations Nestoriennes depuis le Concile Général d'Éphése (431) jusqu'à nos jours."

APPENDIX B.

THE CHRISTIANS OF ASSYRIA, COMMONLY CALLED "NESTORIANS."

SUCH are the lamentable divergences of opinion in our own Church, and such the pressing claims of our own people upon her zeal and devotion, that were we not persuaded that concurrence in one benevolent object is likely to promote unity amongst ourselves and the expansion of our sympathies, I should not be here to plead in behalf of a foreign Christian community.

The so-called "Nestorians" of the present day, of whom I am to speak, inhabit the mountains of Kurdistân in Turkey, and the plains around Urumîah in Persia. In the early ages of the Christian era they were spread over a much larger portion of the East, including Central Asia, Tartary, and even China; and until within the last three centuries the forefathers of those people who inhabit the plains bordering on the Tigris in and around Mosul, now called "Chaldæans"—a title given them on their submission to the see of Rome—all belonged to the same community.

They trace their conversion to Christianity to Mar Addai[1] and Mar Mari, of the Seventy, and reckon the latter as their first patriarch, from whom and his fellow-apostle they derive the validity of their orders in an unbroken line of spiritual descent. Seleucia-and-Ctesiphon was the title of the patriarchal seat until Ctesiphon was destroyed by the Saracens, A.D. 637. Under the Khalifs it was re-

---

[1] The title of "Mar" is equivalent to our "saint" and "lord" and is applied to all bishops indiscriminately. "Addai" is the Syriac for Thaddæus.

moved, first to Baghdad; then to Mosul, near ancient Nineveh; and eventually to Kochânes, in Kurdistân, the usual residence of Mar Shimûn, the ruling patriarch.

The alleged source of their evangelisation, their geographical position, and their retention of the Syriac language, are presumptive evidences in favour of their Aramæic origin, and tend to corroborate the traditional account preserved among them that their three patriarchs in succession to Mar Mari were consecrated, the first two at Jerusalem, and the third at Antioch.

Whilst there is internal evidence against the authenticity of a further tradition, still extant in the shape of a joint epistle from the four "western patriarchs"—that is, west of Mesopotamia—ascribed to the beginning of the third century, raising the see of Seleucia-and-Ctesiphon into a separate patriarchate, on account of the mutual jealousies of the Persians and Romans, and the dangers which the Assyrian patriarchs-elect incurred in going beyond the Persian boundary for consecration, there can be no doubt that the frequent wars between those two empires were a serious hindrance to free intercourse between the Church at Ctesiphon and the Churches within Roman tereitory.

Apart from these considerations, however, it is unquestionable that the metropolitan of Seleucia-and-Ctesiphon was ἀκέφαλος, or independent; and, further, that considering the manner in which the patriarchal office originated in the Church—several sees having adopted it some time between the Councils of Nice and Chalcedon, before it was formally recognised—the Churches under the jurisdiction of the aforesaid metropolitan were fully warranted in establishing the institution. The right to a patriarchate, or the property of the ecclesiastical government which it involves, is indirectly admitted and confirmed by Pope Julian III., who in 1533 consecrated Sulâka, an Assyrian convert, "Patriarch of the Chaldæans"—the designation then given for the first time to the so-called Nestorians who had seceded to Rome, which patriarchate has been continued up to the present day.

There is good ground for believing that friendly intercourse and intercommunion, as far as the political animosities between the Romans and Persians permitted, were maintained between the patriarchs of the east and the patriarchs of Constantinople and Antioch up to the Œcumenical Council of Nice. The Syriac chronicles bear witness to the fact, and the commemoration of many of the Roman or Greek fathers in the Syrian diptychs corroborate it. Their records state that Papa, who filled the see of Seleucia-and-Ctesiphon at the time, was invited to attend that council, but being incapacitated through age he deputed Shimûn-ibn-Sâbary and Shahdost to represent him. Then came the persecutions under Sapor, who rivalled Nero or Diocletian in his efforts to uproot Christianity from his dominions. The Syriac narrative of his cruelties, especially towards the clergy, is truly appalling. An instance of kindly fellowship between the Eastern Church and that of Antioch is recorded during this period. Sapor having ravaged the district around Antioch, carried away many of the inhabitants to Ahwâz, and among them Demetrianus, their patriarch, and several bishops. Papa, the eastern patriarch, visited his captive brother there and requested him to occupy his see, but Demetrianus declined the fraternal compliment.

The next recorded instance took place about A.D. 410, during the reign of Izdijerd, who applied to the Roman Emperor to send him a physician to heal him of a malady, as most of the native Christian doctors had fled or had been put to death during the persecutions under his Sassanian predecessors. The Emperor accordingly despatched Marutha, Bishop of Mayapharkat, in Mesopotamia, who, having succeeded in curing the Persian sovereign, obtained much greater liberty for his Christian subjects. Is-hâk, who was patriarch at the time, showed Marutha all the canons which had been drawn up for the Assyrian Church, and Marutha presented Is-hâk with a copy of the western canons—an interchange of courtesy such as might occur between the representatives of two sister Churches at the present day. The same Marutha, accompanied by the famous Acacius, Bishop of Amid, the modern Diarbekir, was sent by Theodosius the Younger some years later to heal the son of Izdijerd. On that occasion also the most friendly relations appear to have existed between these delegates and Yau-Alâha, who then filled the see of Seleucia-and-Ctesiphon. Socrates Scholasticus calls him "Ablatus, the Persian Bishop," and records that he, in conjunction with Marutha, "published unto the world another proof of the Christian faith, for they both, being continually given to watch and pray, cast a devil out of the king's son."[1]

Having thus given a rapid glance at the "Eastern Patriarchate"—that, I beg to remark, is the designation of the see among the so-called Nestorians—and shown that it was in communion with the other Churches of the East up to the beginning of the fifth century, I come now to the Council of Ephesus, assembled by order of Theodosius II.,

[1] Lib. vii. chap. 8.

and at the instigation of the turbulent Cyril, Patriarch of Alexandria, to try—no, to condemn—the alleged teaching of the equally factious Nestorius, Patriarch of Constantinople. (Most gladly, I conceive, would the Christian Church in general draw a veil over the scandalous proceedings of that famous Synod.) In an assembly like the present, I need not enlarge on the heresy ascribed to Nestorius, but we should bear in mind when approaching the subject that Cyril had, as Hooker says, "avouched," in his writings against the Arians, that "the Word, or Wisdom of God, hath but one nature, which is eternal, and whereunto He assumed flesh;" which delcaration, although not so meant, was "in process of time so taken as though it had been his drift to teach that, even as in the body and soul, so in Christ, God and man make but *one nature*"[1]—an error which was subsequently condemned by the Council of Chalcedon. Bearing these things in mind, I say, and also the different uses which conflicting theologians had made of the almost cognate terms οὐσία and ὑποστάσις, there is *à priori* ground for believing that Nestorius' formula of "two natures and two ὑποστάσεις in Christ" was designed to combat the fearful error, which obtained so extensively afterwards, of the confusion of the divine and human natures in our blessed Lord. Nestorius denied to the last that he held two *distinct* persons in Christ; and Basnage La Croze, Thomas à Jesu, and Mosheim have defended him against the charge of heresy.

But the question which more immediately concerns us is, whether the so-called Nestorians of the present day hold the heresy attributed to Nestorius? My own solemn conviction, after a careful study of their standard theology, is that they do not. Fortunately, some of the most eminent divines have come to the same conclusion, since even Assemanni, as Gibbon justly remarks, "can *hardly* discern the guilt and error of the Nestorians;"[2] and our own learned Richard Field, writing two centuries and a half ago, says: "But they that are now named Nestorians acknowledge that Christ was perfect God and perfect man from the first moment of his conception, and that Mary may rightly be said to be the mother of the Son of God, or of the Eternal Word, but think it not fit to call her the mother of God, lest they might be thought to imagine that she conceived and bare the divine nature of the three Persons—the name of God containing Father, Son, and Holy Ghost."[3] (That, I beg to remark by the way, is the main

[1] Book v. chap. 52.

[2] "Decline and Fall," chap. 47, note.

[3] "Of the Church," book iii., chap. 1.

argument of the so-called Nestorians against the use of the word θεοτόκος, which, rendered in Syriac into "Mother of God," is much stronger than the Greek title or its Latin equivalent *Deipara*, implying that the Blessed Virgin was as much the parent of the Divinity as of the humanity of Christ.) Field then goes on to say: "Neither do these Christians so say there are two persons in Christ, as if the human nature did actually exist in itself, but only to imply that there is a potential aptness in it so to exist if it were left unto itself. Yet the form of words which they use is not to be allowed, for it savoureth of heresy, and took beginning from heresy."[1] Therein also I fully concur with the profound divine, and I have every reason to believe that, in the event of any response on our part to their overtures for intercommunion with us, the so-called Nestorians would forego their present formula, and adopt that of the Council of Ephesus.

If we inquire how the title of "Nestorians" came to be applied to them, it cannot be denied that their adoption of a modified form of Nestorius' questionable phraseology, saying as they do at present that there are in Christ two natures, two ὑποστάσεις, and one *parsopa*,[2] laid them open to the implied stigma; but it is equally certain that it was the inveterate malice of the Monophysite party—whose signal success at the second Council of Ephesus, the "Synod of Thieves" as it was called, gave them an overwhelming influence in Egypt and the East—which branded them with the epithet. Such is the opinion of their own divines, and the ecclesiastical history of those times corroborates it.

The Greeks, however—for distinction's sake I shall so style those who depended on the Constantinopolitan patriarchate—do not appear to have shared in the unchristian rancour of the followers of Eutyches and Dioscorus towards the Easterns. The chronicles of the latter contain a circumstantial account of two embassies sent to the Emperor Zeno, between A.D. 481-485, by Firûz, King of Persia, entrusted respectively to the famous Barsoma, metropolitan of Nisibis, and Acac, who then filled the see of Seleucia-and-Ctesiphon. Both were most cordially received by Zeno, at whose request Barsoma drew up a statement of the doctrines respecting the divinity and humanity of our blessed Lord, which was highly lauded by the Greeks. Nearly a

---

[1] "Of the Church," book iii., chap. 1.

[2] For the Assyrian definition of these terms, see "The Nestorians and their Rituals," vol. ii., pp. 62-65.

century later—about A.D. 581—Hormuzd, son of Chosroes Anushirwân, despatched the patriarch, Mar Yeshua-yau, to the Emperor Maurice, on a similar errand; and about A.D. 628 another Mar Yeshua-yau, accompanied by several metropolitans and bishops, was sent to the Emperor Heraclius. In these two last-named cases, also, the visitors were requested to draw up a formal declaration of their creed, which being regarded as orthodox, they were invited to celebrate the holy eucharist, the Greeks communicating with them, and they subsequently communicated at the celebration by the Greeks. I sincerely wish that time permitted me to read over a translation of those remarkable creeds of the Eastern bishops which were submitted to the Church at Constantinople in the sixth and seventh centuries.

The names, dates, and other coincidences in these narratives leave no doubt on my mind of their authenticity, and I adduce them to show that, far from sympathising with the Jacobites—as the Monophysites then began to be styled, after their famous leader James, or Jacob Baraddæus—in their enmity to the so-called Nestorians, the Greeks actually held intercommunion with them up to A.D. 628. The subsequent cessation of brotherly intercourse between them appears to have been mainly due to the political state of the East, which ensued very shortly after, on the irruption of the Saracens.

As to the continued commemoration of Nestorius by the Assyrians, they allege that it was usual for other Churches to request them to insert the names of their saints, martyrs, and patriarchs in the "Book of Life"—that is, the diptychs. Especially was this done by the Constantinopolitan see on the occasion of a new patriarch; and to this custom they attribute their commemoration, up to this day, of Ignatius, Polycarp, Ambrose, Athanasius, Gregory, Nazianzen, John Chrysostom, and many other Fathers of the East and West. The request was generally acceded to, after the names were approved by a provincial synod; but they point out several instances, including Gregory Nazianzen and Chrysostom, whose names the Greeks afterwards begged them to erase, which they refused. The same took place on the elevation and subsequent deposition of Nestorius; but as they saw no just reason for joining with the Greeks in their condemnation of him, more especially as John, Patriarch of Antioch, and many other bishops, had not concurred in the sentence passed upon him at the Council of Ephesus, they objected either to anathematise him or to remove his name from the diptychs, and sent an answer to the following effect: "Cursing is disallowed by us, as being contrary to the injunction of Christ, 'Love your enemies, and bless them that curse you.'" Whatever may be thought of such a reply in this particular instance, there can be no doubt that the Christian Church would have been more exemplary had it been less profuse of its anathemas. Nevertheless, I am persuaded that if that were the only bar to intercommunion with ourselves, the reputed followers of Nestorius would be ready to abandon his commemoration, on the reasonable condition of being allowed to believe that his formula respecting the divinity and humanity of Christ, though different from that of the Catholic Church, was not necessarily heterodox or repugnant to the truth.

This my persuasion is founded as well on the opinions and practice of the so-called Nestorians of the present day as on the reasoning and procedure of their old divines. The latter argue that Nestorius was neither their spiritual head nor fellow-countryman, but a native of Germanicia and Patriarch of Constantinople; and the name "Nestorian," as designating their community, like the term "Protestant" with us, is never used in any of their rituals. The existing members of their Church very seldom call themselves "Nestorians," except out of bravado, or to distinguish themselves from the members of other local Christian communities, preferring the national designation of *Surâye* (Syrians), or the more comprehensive title of *Meshihaye* (Christians). I have chosen to call them "Assyrians" in order to distinguish them from other "Syrians," such as the Jacobites. Field styles them "the Assyrians, unjustly named Nestorians."[1]

The gradual cessation of intercourse between this people and the other Churches in the east and west appears to have been contemporary with a glorious effort on their part to extend the principles of the Gospel. Alternately persecuted and protected by the Abbaside Khalîfs, and while the Greek patriarchates were content to remain inactive, as they have continued up to the present day, as Dean Stanley says, "like islands in the barren sea of Islam," evangelists from the see at Baghdad carried the glad tidings of salvation to the utmost limits of Asia and to the islands of the Indian sea. "From the conquest of Persia," writes the captious but accurate Gibbon, "they carried their spiritual arms to the north, the east, and the south. In the sixth century, according to the report of a Nestorian traveller,[2] Christianity was successfully

---

[1] "Of the Church," book iii., chap. 1.

[2] Cosmas, "Indicopleustes."

preached to the Bactrians, the Huns, the Persians, the Indians, the Pers-Armenians, the Medes, and the Elamites: the barbaric Churches, from the Gulf of Persia to the Caspian Sea, were almost infinite, and their recent faith was conspicuous in the number and sanctity of their monks and martyrs. The pepper coast of Malabar, and the isles of the ocean, Socotra and Ceylon, were peopled with an increasing number of Christians, and the bishops and clergy of these sequestered regions derived their ordination from the Catholic of Babylon (Baghdad). In a subsequent age, the zeal of the Nestorians overleaped the limits which had confined the ambition and curiosity both of the Greeks and Persians. The missionaries of Balch and Samarcand pursued without fear the footsteps of the roving Tartar, and insinuated themselves into the camps of the valleys of Imaus and the banks of the Selinga . . . and in their progress by sea and land the Nestorians entered China by the port of Canton and the northern residence of Sigan [near Pekin]. . . . Under the reign of the Caliphs, the Nestorian Church was diffused from China to Jerusalem and Cyprus; and their numbers, with those of the Jacobites, were computed to surpass the Greek and Latin communities. Twenty-five metropolitans or archbishops composed their hierarchy."[1] These remote branches, like the once flourishing sees of Africa, are long since withered, and the community at present consists of a patriarch, seven metropolitans, ten bishops, 250 presbyters, and about 15,000 families, of which one-third occupy the district around Urumîah, and the remainder the mountains of Kurdistân.

Apart from the moot point of the Two *Hypostases*, the doctrines of the Assyrians are in general accord with those of the Greeks; wherein they differ from the latter, their teaching and practice approach more nearly to our own. Like the Greeks, they retain the Nicene Creed without the *Filioque* clause, and baptise by immersion—confirmation with the "oil of unction," as a subsidiary part of that ordinance, being administered at the same time. With regard to the Eucharist, they believe in the Real Presence, and deny transubstantiation; administer in both kinds to the laity; never reserve any of the consecrated elements; forbid more than a single celebration at one altar on the same day; and, like the Greeks, use leavened bread, and allow infants to communicate.

Besides baptism and the Lord's Supper, some of their divines reckon orders, the oil of unction, absolution, the holy leaven, and the sign

[1] "Decline and Fall," chap. 47.

of the cross, as sacraments, thus making up the mystical number of seven; nevertheless, the term "sacrament" is only applied to the latter five in the sense in which marriage is so denominated in our own Homilies. No special "outward signs" of "ordained by Christ Himself" accompany their transmission of holy orders, and the grace conferred by the imposition of hands is regarded as one of ministration and spiritual authority, not a gift of conveying personal sanctification upon those who are called to any sacred office in the Church.

The "oil of unction," which is used in holy baptism, is styled "an apostolical tradition;" "*the matter*," says Mar Abd-Yeshua, one of their most eminent theologians, "is pure oil; *the form*, the apostolical benediction." They know nothing, happily, of the Romish doctrine of extreme unction. They also annoint a new altar—a service equivalent to our consecration of churches; but it is specially prescribed that a different oil—not that of baptism—shall be used on such occasions.

Absolution, with them, has nothing in common with the Popish sacrament of penance. Their doctrine regarding confession and absolution seems to be in perfect accord with our own. Auricular confession as an obligatory duty is unknown among them. Such as wish to communicate of the holy Eucharist assemble together, or individuals consult the priest privately, and then meet in the porch of the church, and, whilst kneeling or sitting in a humble posture, the priest reads over one or more absolutions, in the form of petitions, from the "Book of Pardons," consisting chiefly of prayers that God would mercifully pardon his penitent children. In the case of a penitent who had denied the faith, he is also signed with oil in the name of the Trinity.

In the belief that Mar Mari and Mar Addai committed to the Easterns a "holy leaven," to be kept for the perfecting of the administration of the Eucharist until our Lord's second coming, the Assyrians observe the traditions very strictly, and the renewal of the leaven—for which there is an appropriate office, attributed to the twelfth century—takes place every year with great solemnity. The superstition is comparatively harmless, for, although it tends to enhance their estimation of the sacramental bread used by themselves, it does not lead them to question the potentiality of the ordinary leavened cakes or bread used by other Churches to receive consecration.

The sign of the cross, as a sacrament, amounts with them to no more than this: that the use of signing with the sign of the cross—with which the invocation of the Holy Trinity is always associated among them—is an apostolical tradition most fit to be retained in the Church;

for "by it," says Mar Abd-Yeshua, "Christians are ever kept, and by it all the other sacraments are sealed and perfected."

Passing on to the subject of our Thirty-first Article, the "Marriage of Priests," it it unquestionable that in the early ages of the Eastern Church under notice marriage was not forbidden to any ordained person. Two canons of the so-called Apostolical Constitutions preserved by them attest the fact; and accordingly, we find that the Patriarch Babai, about A.D. 498, and his successor Shîla, were both married and had children. A synod convened by the former expressly decreed that "all the ministers of the Church should marry, each having one pious and well-conducted wife, agreeably to the law, in order that they may be kept from falling into sin." That decree was reversed by a subsequent synod under Mar Awa, A.D. 536, which positively forbade any married priest being raised to the episcopate, which decree has been rigidly observed ever since, so that Dean Stanley is at fault when he says, as he does in his brilliant "Lectures on the Eastern Church," that the Nestorian or Chaldæan patriarch is allowed to marry. Equally mistaken is the late learned Dr. Neale, who in his notes to my work on the Nestorians, which he kindly edited, attempts to throw discredit on Babai and Shîla, calling them both "men of infamous character." The slander is borrowed from Romanist authorities, and is utterly without foundation; for the Syriac "Lives of the Patriarchs," which is remarkably impartial, speaks most highly of the piety of those two prelates. But the ambitious aim of retaining the highest office in the hierarchy in the same family—an aim which was kept in abeyance for several succeeding centuries—eventually prevailed, and in A.D. 1450 the then patriarch, Mar Shimûn, ordained that the succession should descend from uncle to nephew. That ordinance still obtains, and is, moreover, not unfrequently carried out in appointments to the episcopate also—an arrangement which virtually deprives the Church, clergy and laity included, of their ancient right to elect their bishops, and reduces to a dead letter the subsisting canons to that effect. Vicious as such a system is, it has a counterpart in various modified forms in the West as well as in other Eastern Churches, and I trust that the disestablished and emancipated Church of Ireland will insist on its right to elect its own bishops.

On the other hand, however, it is lawful for all Assyrian priests and deacons to marry, after ordination as well as before. They may also marry a second or a third time, being widowers, "as they shall judge the same conducive to godliness." In former times they possessed many convents, and some of the clergy and laity who elected to live a more devotional life took upon them certain vows, of which celibacy was one. At the present day they have no such convents, and, as far as I could learn, no such conventual establishments ever existed among the mountain community, although a church is occasionally met with, at some distance from a town or village, called *Daira* (convent), occupied by a solitary priest who has taken the vow of celibacy and acts as pastor to the adjoining parish. But the celibacy of the clergy is not necessarily perpetual; for on just cause being shown, the bishop is empowered to release them from the vow and permit them to marry, with this simple restriction, that the marriage shall be celebrated in private. Further, there are no nunneries among them: those styled nuns do indeed take a vow of celibacy, but they reside in their own homes, and are expected, until loosed from their vow, to devote themselves to works of Christian benevolence, in the same way as some of our Sisters of Mercy.

Regarding the state after death, the Assyrians are in accord with the Greeks; and whilst repudiating the doctrine of Purgatory, maintain the efficacy of prayers for the righteous dead. Pardons and indulgences, such as are fabricated and sold by the Church of Rome, are utterly repugnant to their theology and practice; and with respect to pictures and carved images, they vie with the old Iconoclasts in their abhorrence for them as objects of religious worship. I have known them to wrench off and destroy brazen crucifixes—always, however, preserving the cross, which they hold in high veneration as the emblem of the Crucified One. It is carved at the entrance of all their churches, and is devoutly kissed by the in-coming worshippers; it is placed upon the altar, with two candles symbolizing the Gospel and Epistles, and Christ in His divinity and humanity the Light of the world; their simple Church vestments are ornamented with it; and, in fact, its use is universal among them, being regarded, as I have already remarked, as "the sign by which Christians are ever kept, and by which all the sacraments are sealed and perfected." They have no relics, but clay and dust taken from the tombs of reputed saints are frequently carried away by the more ignorant, and preserved as antidotes against evil; and some passages of one of their service books, which by the learned are looked upon as interpolations of a recent date, attribute supernatural virtues to the remains of saints and martyrs. Indirect invocation of saints, calling upon Christ to accept their intercessions in behalf of His earthly worshippers, are of frequent occurrence throughout their rituals; but direct invocation of the saints is comparatively rare, and the addresses come immeasurably short of the language sanctioned by the Church of Rome. The strongest which I have met with is the following:—"O thou holy Virgin, through whom our race, corrupted by the deceitfulness of sin, was sanctified, pray with us to thy Sanctifier to sanctify us, and that through the shadow of thy prayers He may preserve our life, spread the wings of His pity over our frailty, and deliver us from evil. O mother of Him who causes us to live, thou handmaid of our Creator, be to us a wall of refuge at all times."

If to the foregoing sketch of the tenets of the Assyrians I subjoin that their copious rituals are sublime in diction and teem with scriptural thought and language; that their services, like their churches, though simple in the extreme, exhibit all the features of primitive order and ancient ecclesiastical usage; that their reverence for the Word of God is supreme; that although the old Syriac of their rituals is barely intelligible to them, nevertheless in theory they recognise the principle that all the services should be conducted in a language "understanded of the people;" and, further, that the clergy and laity generally are decidedly predisposed to religion—I judge that enough will have been said to convey a tolerably comprehensive account of the existing Assyrian Church.

Our first intercourse with that community took place in 1842, when I was delegated by the then Archbishop of Canterbury and the Bishop of London,[1] under the joint auspices of the Gospel Propagation and Christian Knowledge Societies, to visit their Patriarch, Mar Shimûn, and to co-operate with him for the general welfare of his people. My interview with him in the Tyâri country was eminently satisfactory. He was surprised and gratified to find that the Anglican was an episcopal Church; that we had ritual services, and held higher views of the sacraments than he had heard ascribed to us; for I beg to observe that even in that secluded region, as elsewhere throughout the East, our Church had been identified, as it still is to a great extent, with Nonconformists, under the general designations of "English" and "Protestant." The scheme then initiated for establishing schools throughout the mountains was abruptly thwarted through the invasion of the Christian villages by the ferocious Kûrds under Bedr Khan Beg, which resulted in the flight of Mar Shimûn, several priests, and some hundreds of his

[1] Archbishop Howley and Bishop Blomfield.

people to Mosul, where I was temporarily located, and had fitted up a room for daily service and weekly communion in English. Deprived as the refugees were of a church, I readily granted them the use of my chapel, in which the patriarch and his clergy regularly officiated, and the odour of the incense burnt in their earlier services still pervaded the air when ours commenced. The refugees, as well as a sprinkling of Jacobites and Chaldæans, were generally present at our offices, so that the room was literally crammed with worshippers; and in the course of a few weeks the Assyrians became so well acquainted with the order of our English ritual that they always uncovered their heads at the reading of the Gospel, as they do in their own churches. In daily intercourse with the patriarch and his learned archdeacon for upwards of a year, I had abundant opportunity of explaining to them the doctrines and discipline of the Anglican Church, and so desirous was Mar Shimûn of establishing intercommunion with us, that he eventually requested me, one day during the service, to receive him as a communicant. If I hesitated to do so, it was simply from prudential motives, and lest the action might be misconstrued by gainsayers, and I further pointed out to him the propriety of deferring the step until some definite terms of intercommunion had been agreed upon by our respective Churches. The patriarch fully appreciated the wisdom of these suggestions, but from that time forward, notwithstanding the offer held out to him of supremacy over all the Chaldæans if he would submit to Rome, his mind was fully bent on effecting a union with us. Unfortunately, the Church at home was not prepared to entertain the overture: our Convocation was little better than an ecclesiastical myth; no mere Church society could dispose of such a question, nor any number of individual bishops; consequently, the proposal fell to the ground, and the mission was abandoned, notwithstanding the repeated and urgent appeals of the patriarch that it might be continued.[1]

Still, I have reason to hope that our transient effort was not wholly in vain. The public celebration of our worship, which had been witnessed by large numbers of different native communities, convinced them of our ritual order, and on their return home the refugees carried away with them the knowledge which they had acquired of our doctrines and discipline, and scattered it far and wide throughout the mountain villages, from whence it was conveyed to their brethren in Persia. Efforts were subsequently made to induce Mar Shimûn to

[1] See "The Nestorians and their Rituals," vol. i., pp. 289-296.

accept the proffered co-operation of the Americans at Urumiah to instruct his flock; but his reply to Mr. Layard, six years after my departure from Mosul, was, that "he wished to be helped in that labour by priests of the Episcopal Church of England, whose doctrine and discipline were more in conformity with the Nestorian than those of the American missionaries."[1] I visited the patriarch again in 1850, while on leave of absence from my appointment in India, and was received by him and the Christian mountaineers generally with the warmest demonstrations of affection. He dilated on the temporal and spiritual destitution of his people, and complained bitterly that our Church had turned a deaf ear to his prayers. Alas! I could not hold out any hope that we were then better prepared than formerly to come to his relief. Since then the good old man has been gathered to his fathers, and his nephew has succeeded to the patriarchate, under the same title, Mar Shimûn.

One almost wonders that, after such treatment at our hands, the Assyrians should still recur to us for aid. Nevertheless, as recently as November, 1867, Mr. Rassam, the British Vice-Consul at Mosul, was charged to deliver a letter, signed by two bishops, several presbyters, deacons, and influential laymen, addressed to the Archbishop of Canterbury and the Bishop of London, begging that delegates might be sent out to aid them in promoting the spiritual welfare of the mountain community. The genuineness of that document was hastily discredited by the Urumiah missionaries, but a later epistle from the patriarch expressly confirms it, and reiterates the appeal for help.

The practical question now is, What ought to be done? This is a question which concerns not the primate alone, but the whole Church. It is a subject, moreover, of vast importance, involving as it does the necessity of an appropriate organisation on our part for the eventual restoration of this ancient community, which might be applicable in similar cases. The Church of Rome possesses such an organisation, and has largely used it, not to build up, but to disintegrate the ancient Churches of the East, and to reduce them to her obedience. Laying aside her ambition for supremacy, it is high time that we placed ourselves in an equally advantageous position—a position to which, as a true branch of the Catholic Church, we are fully entitled—to restore the lapsed Oriental communities, including those on the western coast of

[1] "Nineveh and Babylon," p. 425.

India; and whilst leaving them in full possession of their ecclesiastical status, rites, and ceremonies, to promote the unity of Christ's mystical Body by joining them to ourselves in one communion and fellowship, holding one Faith, one Lord, one Baptism.

What hinders, indeed, that, in due subservience to more urgent demands upon her devotion and charity, the Church of England should not occupy the Assyrian field thus providentially opened to her best energies? One objection urged is that we should thereby be interfering with a people canonically subject to the Greek patriarchates. Even were this so, the argument loses all its force from the simple fact that the Greek Church is utterly powerless to undertake the task. Moreover, it should be borne in mind that our object is not to subject a foreign community to our jurisdiction, but to promote Christian union, on terms which may lead, under the Divine blessing, to eventual intercommunion between all the Eastern Churches, and between them and ourselves. But I maintain that the Greek Church possesses no canonical authority over the Assyrians, and never did. "By comparing," says Bingham, "the broken fragments that remain in the acts and superscriptions of the ancient Councils with the Notitia of the Empire, and comparing both with the later Notitia of the Church, it plainly appears that the Church was divided into dioceses and provinces, much after the same manner as the Empire." The territory in which the Eastern patriarchate, with its chief see, Seleucia-and-Ctesiphon, was originally situated, appertained to Persia; and as it never formed part of the Roman Empire, so that see was never included either within the patriarchate of Constantinople or that of Antioch. A reference to the ancient dioceses comprehended within those patriarchates will fully bear out this statement.

A somewhat similar objection is raised in an opposite quarter. The American Independent or Congregationalist missionaries at Urumiah regarded our first efforts among the so-called Nestorians—although strictly confined to the mountain community—as an unjustifiable interference, and they have not hesitated to characterise my proceedings among them as intolerant, Popish, Puseyite, &c., for no other reason than because my replies to direct questions by the native Christians indicated the differences which unfortunately exist between Nonconformists and ourselves, and led the Assyrians to prefer our doctrine and Church government to theirs. No one is more ready than I am to recognize the zealous exertions of the American missionaries at Urumiah to benefit the Nestorians in and around that place; for besides translating the Holy Scriptures into vulgar Syriac, they have established schools among them, and by the diffusion of light and knowledge have undoubtedly aided them to resist the persevering efforts of Pápal missionaries to bring them into subjection to the see of Rome. Their success, up to a certain point, was mainly attributable to their conservative mode of procedure, allowing all who joined them to retain the use of their rituals, and to adhere to their own ecclesiastical discipline. But, unless I am grossly misinformed, a different policy has been adopted of late years, whereby those who become associated with them are required to renounce their ancient use, and to conform to the Presbyterian or Congregationalist standard. No step could be more impolitic on their part, or more fatal, eventually, to the permanence of their influence; for such is the tenacity with which the Eastern Churches generally adhere to episcopacy and their ancient ritual services, that any attempt to substitute the Nonconformist model in their stead is sure to fail in the long run. (The movement which is now going on among the so-called Protestant Armenians in Turkey is an example in point.) It is mainly owing to the fear of similar encroachments that Mar Shimûn refuses to sanction the labours of the American missionaries in the mountains; and, judging from a recent appeal from a bishop and several of the clergy at Urumiah—some of them in the service of the missionaries—many of the community *there* are anxious that their Church should be reformed without being destroyed. Would that the American missionaries could join heart and hand with us in so noble a work!

APPENDIX C.

THE CHURCH MISSIONARY SOCIETY'S WORK IN TRAVANCORE AND COCHIN.

THE Society's work in this field is, we think, very interesting and very hopeful. Whether we look at the picturesque region in the south-west corner of all India, in which it is carried on; or at the peculiarity of the elements of which the small population of nearly two millions is composed; or at the character for enlightenment of its native rulers, it has many features of interest; and the progress of the mission hitherto gives us every reason for hope for the future.

We know not where else in all India we should look for the same number of persons, in proportion to its size, who call themselves by the name of Christians, as in the territory of Travancore and Cochin. There are the Christians who hold communion with the Jacobite Patriarch of Antioch, in number some 120,000 persons. They have been there since the sixth century of our era, unmolested by the native rulers, and even allowed by them a certain social status in the country. There are the Romanists, who date, of course, since the arrival in India of the Portuguese, somewhere about 140,000 in number. They consist partly of those who, through the violence of the emissaries of Rome, have been proselytized from Syrianism to Romanism; and partly of those who have become Romanists from heathenism. Then there are the Protestant Christians in connexion with the London Missionary Society in the extreme south of Travancore, somewhere about 30,000 in number. They are principally Shanars, of the same race as those amongst whom our Tinnevelly Mission has been so successful. They speak the Tamil language, and their affinity, of course, would be much more with the native Protestant Christians in Tinnevelly than with the Malayalim-speaking Protestant Christians of their own kingdom of Travancore. Finally, there are the Christians in connexion with the Church Missionary Society, numbering somewhere about 13,000. If we were to count together all who bear the Christian name in Travancore and Cochin, we should find the number to amount to not far short of one-fifth of the entire population; and to these we might add, as another peculiar element of the population, somewhere about 1,500 Jews, who reside in the important town of Cochin.

The most influential, though not the most numerous class of the heathen population is the Brahmin class. They have great influence at the courts, and great influence everywhere throughout the kingdom. They are, of course, the class who are deeply interested in maintaining caste and retarding the progress of Christianity. In fact, we may look upon caste as a *priestly* idea from the beginning, cleverly devised for the purpose of keeping the priestly Brahmins at the top of the social tree. It is a matter of wonder that, with princes so enlightened as the Travancore princes have been for several generations, and with the Syrian church existing so long amongst them, the Travancore Brahmins should be, of all Brahmins in India, almost the most privileged race of them. One cannot but fear that the Syrian Christians, in the centuries of the past, can have but little witnessed for Christ, and but little declaimed against the monstrosities of Brahminism. If they had, it is very probable that they would have received less quarter and less toleration from the native princes. At present, the indigenous Brahmins of Travancore and Cochin (Numboory Brahmins, as they are called,) number about 14,000. Foreign Brahmins (especially from the Tamil country), who do not rank so high, and are not at all privileged in the same way as the Numboories, number some 36,000. The Nairs, who rank next to the Brahmins, are a high-spirited and influential class of people. The reigning family of Travancore belongs to this class, and they are the principal landowners of the country. The Chogans, who are generally servants to the Nairs; the slaves, no longer legally so, but actually slaves to the other classes; the Araans, who are the aboriginal dwellers on the slopes of the western ghâts, cultivators of the soil, and worshippers of the spirits of their ancestors; these make up the rest of this varied population.

There could not have been a more interesting experiment made than the Church Missionary Society was induced by many friends to make, in the Lord's name, in Travancore. The experiment was, in short, to raise up into a living and witnessing church the fallen and lifeless church of the Syrians. Lifeless, indeed, that church might have been called. The fountain of life was closed against the people by the word of God being in a language (the Syriac) not understood by the Malayalim-speaking people. The liturgical services of the Church were mostly in the same language. No witness for Christ was borne before the heathen. The problem, therefore, which the missionaries, on arriving in Travancore in 1816, had to deal with was how they might, with God's blessing on their efforts, impart spiritual life to the Syrian church, and so raise it. It was to try this experiment they were sent forth. And what an interesting experiment it was! If God should enable them to succeed, what a mighty lever for working India they would have prepared! But all experience shows that to raise into life a dead church is not an easy task. They translated the word of life into the language of the people. They were allowed to take, and they took, a systematic part in the education of the young priests intended for ordination in the Syrian Church. They preached wherever they had an opportunity, but they asked no Syrian to abandon the communion of his Church. They laboured in the education of the young. Twenty years were allowed for the testing of this experiment. At the end of that time it was perceived on all hands that the gravitation downwards of a fallen Church was greater than had been at first thought of. A new method of proceeding was adopted. From 1838 to the present time the Gospel has been preached to all alike, Syrians and heathens, and all have been exhorted to come out, and separate themselves from false communions, and join themselves with a pure scriptural communion.

The blessing of God seems to have followed the new plan. Since 1838, twelve thousand persons of all classes have come out and joined the Protestant Church of England. Ten young men, who belonged to the Syrian communion, have abandoned it, and have been educated, trained, and admitted to the ministry of the Church of England. One young man, a member of a Brahmin family, all of whom became Christians a few years ago, is now also a promising native clergyman. The converts are from all classes, those from the Syrians and the Chogans being the most numerous, the mountain-men and the slaves helping considerably to swell the number. Thus, out of these various elements there is being one Protestant Bible Church formed in the land. The same thing that missionary work is doing everywhere throughout the world is going on here. It is drawing together into one brotherhood in Christ races and tribes once altogether separated, the uniting power being the cross of the Lord Jesus Christ. The Brahmin party have been greatly incensed, and at one time it is certain that the missionaries could not have held their ground in the country had it not been for the influence of the British name. The work has steadily held on its way. May the Lord cause it to grow more and more, until it covers the land!

What is to be expected from this native Protestant Church in Travancore and Cochin? What is their distinct Christian influence? Does the word of the Lord sound out from them to their Syrian and heathen neighbours? Could their pastors thank God for them, "remembering their work of faith, and labour of love, and patience of hope in the Lord Jesus Christ?" Is there amongst them an anxiety to win souls to Christ? Are the distinctions of caste abolished, and are they of one mind in the Lord? We will only say that we know that there are native clergymen in Travancore who, by the grace of God, are behind none in their longing desire to save souls. We could enumerate many instances where the Gospel has spread simply through the faith and love of the converts themselves. We think, on the whole, that the questions above asked can be answered in the affirmative with regard to the Travancore mission as much as with regard to any mission with which we are acquainted. This native Church has, we think, a strong claim on the prayers of the friends of missions, that the Holy Spirit might be poured upon it, that so its witness for Christ might become more and more decided, and that the converts to the faith might be more and more multiplied.

We have to ask now an important question about this native Church. When may we expect that it will take its stand as an independent Church, *i.e.*, a Church independent of pecuniary aid from a foreign Society? When may we expect that it will become, under a bishop or bishops of its own, an independent branch of the Protestant Church of England? We think that this is a question which ought to be asked, and which all who are interested in missions are asking now. Most dangerous would it be to deprive a native Church of our aid in men and means before it is ripe for standing by itself. But we ought not to postpone the time of its standing alone unnecessarily by a day. The vigour of a native Church is not improved by an excess of fostering. If there is spiritual life in it, that life will expand itself more purely and more vigorously when human aid is withdrawn, and it is led to cast itself on the heavenly comfort and strength of the Holy Spirit. And, besides this, the claims of *all* India are too great, the field is too wide, to admit of our spending more time than is necessary on any one point of it. The Church Missionary Society thoroughly realises this idea to itself, and its present action in reference to the Travancore native Church is that of gradually leading it on to realise it too. The Society does not forget the difficulties of the native Church, composed as it is so largely of new converts from so many classes, and it does not expect too much. But not less steadily and urgently is it setting the idea before the native Church in a practical way. For several years past the native Church has been accustomed to look upon the support of their spiritual and other teachers as coming out of a Sustentation Fund raised by themselves, and *supplemented* by the Society; and they are taught that their own contributions must increase year by year, and the Society's supplementary grant decrease year by year, until it altogether ceases to be granted.

It is pleasant to know that the sum raised by the native Church is increasing year by year. It is to be hoped that the present native pastors, and those who may hereafter be ordained, will see the importance of endeavouring to maintain themselves on as small a sum as possible, in order that their own Christian people may be able the sooner and the more easily to maintain them without foreign aid. The neighbour Syrian Church sets an example in this respect to our native Protestant Church. The bishops, catanars and deacons, receive no pecuniary aid whatever. Their support comes entirely from their own people. We think that this is an example which the native Protestant Church in Travancore would do well to consider.

APPENDIX D.

HINDOSTAN.

The Catholic Missions in Hindostan do not offer, as those in China, the grand spectacle of entire provinces praying to be baptized, or the still more exciting interest attached to the persecuted Christians, as those of the Annamite kingdom at present. In Hindostan, which is the most important district of all Asia, next to the Chinese empire, from the extent of its territory and the number of its inhabitants, there are thousands of Christian settlements requiring to have their faith strengthened and enlivened; also, a quiet but steady movement among the pagans, the Mussulmans, and the heretics towards Catholicity, which claims development; in fine, there are 150 millions of souls to be enlightened and saved. Eight hundred missioners, under the direction of seventeen bishops, are combating there night and day, sometimes struggling against the inertness of whole populations retained in error by their habits of sensuality, sometimes fighting against the secular prejudices of the different races, and again, often pitted against the proselytism of heresy, having for its aid political supremacy and the power of gold; all these struggles carried on in obscurity, without either the courage inspired by the prospect of martyrdom or the hope of a near and general victory. And yet this continual struggle requires an untiring devotedness which nothing can discourage, not even its fruitlessness, for it is the duty of a missioner to give himself to the cause with all his heart, and without any calculation as to his chances of success. He must work as if the entire victory depended on his individual exertion. This is a noble and inspiring position, which carries with it a certain consolation, since it is evident that God alone can be the inspirer of all the ardour and perseverance felt by the missioner, and that He bestows these gifts in order to further and hasten His own merciful designs.

In Hindostan, as in most missionary countries, the zeal of the missioner has a double object to attain: 1st. To maintain the Christians in the holiness of their vocation while surrounded by an infidel population; 2nd. To try and convert the pagans, and also to preserve the Catholics from the effect of Protestantism, which, having been introduced into the country by the English influence, is dangerous to them, as it is also an obstacle to the conversion of the infidels to Christianity, even though the natives have little esteem for the religion of the English.

I.

The extent of each of the vicariates, and the insufficient number of evangelical workers, necessitates a special organisation in order to ensure the regular service of the missioners.

M. P. M., Superior of the Foreign Missions, has made known, in a letter addressed to the Central Councils of the Propagation of the Faith, the mode employed for the visitation of the Christian settlements in the Vicariate-Apostolic of Pondicherry, where there is a population of 108,000 Catholics dispersed over all points of the territory:

"In order to watch over the faith of so many Christians, and to bring from the darkness of paganism the great number of souls, the mission has been divided into several districts, according to the number of Catholics, and also to the number of missioners. Each district is composed of several villages, whose inhabitants are either all, or at least, the greater number Catholics. The missioner resides in the centre of the district, but the administration of sacraments, which obliges him to visit continually from one end of his parish to the other, and, above all, the immense distances of certain villages, prevent him having sufficient time to instruct all the Catholics, or to appease the quarrels which often arise amongst the families. It was in order to remedy, as much as possible, these inconveniences, and to encourage the Catholics in fidelity to their faith and the practice of virtue, that Monsignor Godelle resolved, some few years since, to consecrate two missioners to the office of continually travelling from one district to another, preaching retreats, in imitation of those which are given in Europe." (Letter of the 15th October, 1864.)

The hopes entertained by Monsignor the Vicar-Apostolic of Pondicherry have been realised; for, notwithstanding their natural apathy of character, the populations have been roused, and abundant fruits have followed the holy exercises. The Superior charged with this laborious ministry gives the following edifying details in his letter:

"We have," he writes, "begun our apostolic journey by Selam, a populous and pretty considerable commercial town, situated at the foot of the chain of eastern Ghauts, forty-six leagues south-west of Pondicherry. There are only a few Christians in this town, but there are many more in the neighbouring villages. The mission lasted for twenty days, in order to give sufficient time for every one to take advantage of it, and they certainly did avail themselves of the opportunity. Almost everywhere I passed, several Christians, moved by the instructions they had heard, came and threw themselves at my feet, saying, 'Father, I have never before understood all that you have just told us. I have for ten, fifteen, twenty years led a wicked life, having formerly made bad confessions, but the good God has sent you now to bring me salvation. Pardon me.' Then they commenced their general confessions, shedding tears of sorrow, and I could scarcely contain the emotion I felt in witnessing the deep contrition of these poor strayed sheep thus restored to the fold.

"From Selam we went to Yedapadhy, a village in which, from time immemorial, discord has reigned supreme, notwithstanding the efforts of the missioners to make peace, the people resisting all such attempts. God was pleased to bestow this much-desired blessing as a fruit of the holy exercise of the mission. The retreat had only commenced two days when the inhabitants, of their own accord, made peace, and came to throw themselves at our feet, promising to submit humbly to whatever we should command. A banquet was given as a pledge of the reconciliation. The two men who were heads of each faction, and had made themselves most remarkable by their animosity, were designated to be organisers of the feast. Men, women, and children, all desired to take part in the entertainment, and, as there was no house large enough to hold such a number of guests, the court of the church was made to serve for the banquet-hall. The next morning all began to attend the confessional; even the pagans seemed inclined to become Christians. Each time that I walked out they crowded round me. 'Father,' they would say, 'where are you going? We will accompany you, and will sit at your feet to hear your good advice.' One of the old men of the village one day accosted me in a friendly manner, and when I passed on after speaking a few words, I heard him say to his neighbours, 'Ah! if we followed the good advice the father gives us, we would be much better than we are.'"

In Madura, where only the great centres possess missioners, the Christians are only visited from time to time, generally about once a year. The greater number, therefore, of missioners (they number about fifty native and European) pass their lives travelling through the vast districts allotted to them, trying to visit all the Christians dispersed in the middle of the pagan population.

The Rev. Father Ant. Batut, of the Society of Jesus, writes to his brother the following description of these apostolic excursions:

"The missioner's suite consists of three persons—a catechist to instruct the Christians, a disciple for the material service, and a man for guiding the ox or the horse that carries our conveyance. When the missioner reaches the first Christian settlement he is going to visit, he at once installs himself and his suite in the church. They give this name of church to four mud walls thatched with straw. This building is made to serve all purposes. It is the church, the presbytery, the refectory, and the dormitory; a plank of timber, supported by four legs, is made to answer alternately table and bed. Each day the charity of the Christians supplies a ration of rice for the support of the Father and his suite, the preparation for confession and communion is made, baptism is given to the children, extreme-unction administered to the dying, abuses are corrected, and all exhorted to a more fervent life. This labour continues for eight, ten, and fifteen days, according to the importance of the locality; then the missioner prepares to depart: he bids farewell to his Christians, after having advised them to assemble every day for prayers, but, above all, to come to say prayers for mass together every Sunday. If the village is not too far from his own residence, the missioner can make a few rare visits to administer the sacraments to the sick, but, generally speaking, he is only able to visit once in each year." (Letter of February, 1865.) These journeys occupy the missioner for two or three months, after which he returns to his home to rest for a few days, and sets out for some other point in the district.

The Rev. Father Serasset, of the Society of Jesus, having been sent from Dharwar (vicariate-apostolic of Bombay) to Moudgal, a considerable town, situated in an independent territory, has enjoyed the consolation of discovering the last vestiges of Christianity, which had been formerly flourishing, but is now reduced to a few hundred Christians. We shall make extracts of the accounts of his mission, written by him to his brother, the parish priest of Develier, near Delémont (diocese of Bale).

"Moudgal is about 140 miles distant from Dhawar. Our Fathers had founded there a Catholic flock, that had long after been remarkable for the wisdom of their laws. This mission belongs to the vicariate-apostolic of Madras, but as it is without a pastor, I was invited to visit it. I felt inward pleasure at the idea of visiting those spots that had been the territory where the zealous devotedness of the children of our Society had converted so many pagans; but on arriving there, my anticipations were changed into sorrow instead of consolation. The dwelling of our former missioners is now a heap of ruins; the church, to the infinite regret of the Christians, has been destroyed lately, in order to give place to a new one, and the traditions and memories of the old building have all disappeared. All that now remains is the tomb of the most celebrated of the missioners of this country, Father John Paradisi, whose memory is still held in great veneration by all our Christians. They never quit the church without blessing the tomb of him whom they call their father in the faith. The epitaph of Father Paradisi describes, in a few words, his life and his eulogy. Here is the translation of it:

"*Here lies the body of John Paradisi, aged* 88 *years.*
He had the care of this Mission for 41 *years,*
and converted a number of souls to the true faith.
After giving us an example of every virtue
He departed this life on the 13*th of January*, 1793.

"I arrived at Moudgal a few days before the festival of Christmas-day. The Christians were all assembled there, and numbered about 400. They are generally dispersed about the district, being employed in weaving and manufacturing stuffs; but they are faithful to their old traditions, and return to Moudgal to celebrate together the feast of Christmas and that of the Epiphany; they number about 600 when all together. Those poor Christians were sadly in want of a mission, for they were living without approaching the sacraments, and were afflicted with discord and division amongst each other. After hesitating for a few days, there was at length a general movement in favour of the mission. From Christmas to the Epiphany a continual festival was kept up." (Letter of the 3rd September, 1864.)

II

The conversion of the idolaters and the Mussulmans is impeded by almost insurmountable obstacles, notwithstanding the great zeal of the missioners.

"To preserve the faith in the hearts of our Christian flock," writes the secretary of Monsignor Hartemann, Vicar-Apostolic of Patna, "seems to be the only thing we can hope to realise at present, until it pleases Almighty God to render this arid and immense country fruitful." (Letter of the 20th November, 1864.)

Monsignor Dufal, Vicar-Apostolic of Eastern Bengal, expresses the same sad regrets. His lordship writes as follows from Noucolly to the Central Councils on the 21st February, 1865:

"Notwithstanding our constant efforts, the number of conversions is very small, almost insignificant when we compare them with the population of this vast country. Seventy-six during the year 1864! Alas! it is indeed so difficult to make any amongst the Hindoos, that the catechists are very few. I do not speak of the Mussulmans, who come next in number after the Hindoo population, and who are nearly all steeped in profound ignorance, and without any desire to improve themselves. They are plunged in earthly pleasures, and brutally attached to a religion that encourages their sensuality. If by chance you happen to meet some who appear less brutalised, and you make an effort to enlighten them, they answer you by a smile of pity, as much as to say that you are losing your time in attempting to argue on such subjects with them. One of them said to me a few days since, 'If I were to join the Christians, what would become of me? I should inevitably be banished as a vile miscreant from the society of my acquaintances, friends, and relations. No, I shall die a Mussulman; and I hope Allah will have mercy upon me.'

"The Hindoos are not so entirely debased as the Mussulmans. Their character is generally more noble, and they seem more desirous of instruction, particularly such of them as are above the lower ranks. From a mere desire of knowledge, they consent at first to listen to you; and, after a little argument, they finish by esteeming you, as they recognise you to surpass them in intelligence. They will even be convinced, possibly, of the holiness and truth of the Christian religion;

they will admire the heroic devotedness and virtues that the Christians are continually displaying, and which contrast so strongly with the superstitions and trickery of the Brahmins, all which they acknowledge while witnessing the folly and abominations practised by these Brahmins, as well as their ceremonies, stained with cruelty, and which constitute their exterior worship. They understand all this, but there they come to a stand-still, and they are yet far from conversion. I believe their hour of grace has not come; but still, I don't despair, but, on the contrary, I rely hopefully, and even rejoice at the happy symptoms of progress I witness; for, a few years since, the Hindoos were inaccessible to Europeans, and particularly to missioners. It is, therefore, a great step in advance to be able to speak to them of religion. As an additional cause for hopefulness, I will relate a significant fact. In one district the Hindoos of rank have decided on sending their daughters to a Christian school. This progress has been brought about by one of themselves, who has persuaded his companions in religion that it would be very advantageous to secure a good education, even for their women. Now, if those in the higher ranks, who pass for the most enlightened, give this example, many will assuredly follow it."

The position of the Hindoo females is well known. The Christian religion, in raising woman from her state of degradation and inferiority, can alone bestow on her the honour and dignity that Providence has assigned as her position in the family. The Hindoo women are well disposed to become Christians.

"At the termination of an instruction at which a number of pagans had assisted," writes M. Prieur, in the letter already alluded to, "seeing that they seemed much struck with what they had heard, for they acknowledged themselves that their gods are no more than demons, 'Well,' said I, 'will you not join our holy religion, and, receiving baptism, become one of us, and adore the only God who has power to make you happy?' The women looked at their husbands and answered, 'If they wish, we consent readily;' but the husbands did not evince equal alacrity. 'We will think about it before we decide,' they replied.

"Father Bruni, of the Society of Jesus, missioner at Negapatam (Madura), gives us the following details: A Mahratta widow had become the slave of a rich pagan, who had formerly lent her husband fifteen rupees; she was, according to the laws of her country, obliged to work for the creditor until the debt should be liquidated. Her four children were obliged to suffer with their mother. I had sent my catechist to purchase their ransom. He worked for two days without taking almost any nourishment. After long discussions on the subject, the pagan demanded seventeen rupees, and the catechist had but fifteen; fortunately, the widow was still possessed of a sheep and a small quantity of rice. These were both sold for two rupees, and the entire sum required was forthcoming. The whole family have just been received into an establishment for catechumens." (Letter of the 31st of May, 1864, addressed to Rev. Father Tassis).

One of our chief obstacles in establishing the Christian religion amongst the Hindoos is their social system of castes. The missioners are endeavouring to put an end to this exclusiveness by means of orphanages and schools. Besides the advantage of a Christian education obtained in all these establishments, there is a special benefit gained in Hindostan—it is, that these schools are productive of Christian marriages.

In most vicariates the number of schools is considerable.

Mangalore possesses 11; Coimbatour, 12; and these two represent 400 pupils. Mysore, 17; Madura and Vizagapatam, 19 each; Bombay, 26; Quilon, 35; Pondicherry, 80; attended by 2,000 scholars.

To these elementary schools we are to add the ecclesiastical seminaries, destined for the education of native priests, and also for the children of the influential classes. Several of those establishments are in full activity. For example, the college of Negapatam (Madura) contains 150 pupils. The college of St. Francis Xavier at Calcutta has more than 200. "The high reputation of this latter college, and its influence in spreading the Catholic religion in India, must be evident to you. In a city where the Protestant sects possess so many and such well-organised schools, as far as material advantages are in question, added to their scientific and literary institutions, it is of the highest importance that the Catholic religion should be represented by a college capable of sustaining an honourable emulation." (Report to the Central Councils on the Missions of the Society of Jesus, 6th May, 1865.)

The orphanages are destined to render still more important services to the country. We read very interesting details about them in a letter addressed to the Central Councils by the Abbé Pierron, of the Foreign Missions, and Pro-Vicar Apostolic of Coimbatour:

"In the orphanage for boys, established at Carmattampatty, and in the other for girls at Coimbatour, 128 children have been educated and instructed during the year 1864. Several of those pupils have been married or placed in Christian families. These are children of pagans, the greater number of whom belong to castes that have never allowed the Christian religion to penetrate amongst them. When they leave the orphanage, they become, by their marriages, little centres of Christianity, and the newly-converted group round them by degrees, and many are thus encouraged to enter the Catholic religion who would otherwise never have dreamed of quitting paganism. You are aware that India is partitioned into divisions and sub-divisions of an infinite number of castes, who never intermarry, and of their entire number there are many in which there is not a single Christian. When, therefore, we speak of conversion to the pagans belonging to the latter castes, the objection is always presented to us, 'If I become a Christian, who will marry my children? If all my caste and all my village are willing to become Christians, I shall be converted also.' How can we answer these objections when put forward by people who have but a faint idea of Christianity, and who esteem earthly pleasures their only happiness? But when we can point out some of their compatriots already married, and living happily in the Christian religion, all these objections about marriage disappear, and they yield easily to our representations of the necessity of their being Christians." (Letter of 25th November, 1864).

The history of these children gathered into the orphanages reveals sometimes, in remarkably striking instances, the paternal solicitude of the Almighty for these poor abandoned souls. The following are the details of a letter, written on the 10th of last June, to the Abbé Massardier, Vicar of St. Didier-le-Sceauve (diocese of Puy), by the Rev. Father P. L. Verdier, of the Society of Jesus, missioner at Palamcottah (Madura):

"A little girl, about nine years of age, was suddenly deprived of her father and mother, both having been carried off by cholera. Being far from her native country, and without protection, she fell into the hands of a bayadere (Indian women that dance before the pagodas, and are called *bayaderes*). This wretched woman, incited by a desire worthy of her profession, stamped, with a hot iron, the diabolical mark of the trident on the poor child's arms. The unfortunate little orphan, in whose soul divine grace had already commenced to shine, felt herself seized with horror of this strange woman who had so quickly become her mistress and her executioner, and she escaped from her. The fury, having discovered where the child was hiding, thought to carry her away by force; but the orphan resisted, and the affair was carried before the tribunal. In reply to the exclamations of the bayadere, the little victim exhibited her arms, burnt as they were, and cried out indignantly, 'Are you my mother, cruel woman? By what right have you been guilty of such extreme cruelty to a child? No! no! I shall never consent to live under the control of your wicked power.' The English magistrate took the orphan under his protection, and placed her in an hospital. For a year, she got her ration of rice daily there, and attended at the Protestant school; however, as no one took care of her after school hours, the magistrate began to fear she might fall into evil ways. He had heard of our orphanage at Adeikalabouram, and he asked me to receive into it his young protegée; I accepted the charge readily. After a little time, he visited the establishment, in order to see the orphan, who came to him looking as merry as possible. 'Well, are you happy here?' he said, when she presented herself. 'O yes,' she replied, 'I am happy, thanks to your goodness in having sent me here.' 'Repeat your prayers for me,' said the magistrate (who is a Protestant); the child recited the Lord's prayer. After his visit, he never met me without inquiring for the orphan, and expressing his admiration of the devotedness of the Abbé Bossan, who has consecrated his life to this work, so pleasing in the sight of God, though he is little known or appreciated by men. The magistrate is aware that this missioner has given up all his personal property for the support of those children, and that for their sake he leads a life of privation and penury.

"This orphanage of Adeikalabouram contains eighty-five little girls and forty little boys, all born in idolatry. It serves also as an asylum for twenty-one widows, converted from paganism, and eleven old men, converts also. Since the foundation of the establishment, it has already sent to heaven six hundred abandoned infants. All this good work is under the charge of nuns of the order of Marie Reparatrice (Our Blessed Lady of Reparation).

"The four principal orphanages of Madura educate four hundred and seventy orphans, and those of Bombay, of Poona, and of Bandora, in the vicariate of Bombay, contain nearly five hundred. They are not all equally considerable; for these kinds of institutions are very expensive, and many of the vicariates are too poor to be able to extend these institutions as much as they are needed. Agra and Calcutta possess each two orphanages; Mangalore has three; Mysore and Patna, four each; Vizagapatam, five; and Central Bengal, six.

"At Coimbatour, the girls' orphanage is directed by native nuns; and *àpropos* of these religious, the Abbé Pierron remarks that the increasing number of vocations to the religious life is a striking proof of the progress of Catholicity in Hindostan.

"Amongst the pagans (he says), the general question, the principal affair which occupies their thoughts, is marriage. They often marry their children before they are well out of infancy. For us Christians, who live in the midst of such opinions, how much virtue and grace it continually requires to surmount these prejudices! Nevertheless, amongst our nuns, we have young girls belonging to the richest Christian families. During the past year, five nuns were professed into the Third Order of St. Francis of Assisium, two young ladies have entered the novitiate, and three have become postulants. On the 8th of last September, the chapel of the convent was literally crowded with Christians, amongst whom were many Protestants, all eager to assist at the profession, this being a ceremony so unusual in these infidel countries. The nuns are twenty in number, fourteen of whom are professed." (Letter of 25th November, 1864.)

Though the Indian soil seems still arid after all the dew of the missionary labours and fatigues, yet it is evident that sterility is not over the whole land, nor by any means is it hopelessly unfruitful, and God sustains the missioners' zeal with some consolation. The work of the orphanages and the schools prepares a future generation of Christians.

The apostolate of the pagan adults presents so many obstacles, already explained, that we must not be surprised at the slight results. The following is a list of the conversions brought about in some of the vicariates during the year 1864:—

Coimbatour, one hundred; Mangalore, one hundred and seventy-four; Mysore, two hundred; Vizagapatam, three hundred; Madura, one thousand four hundred; and more than three thousand children baptized who were at the point of death.

It seems, nevertheless, that in the vicariate of Pondicherry, the apostolate is more hopeful and more fruitful than in most of the other parts of Hindostan. We read the following details in a letter from the Abbé Ligeon, of the Foreign Missions, addressed to the Abbé Maury, director of the seminary of the same Society, in Paris:—

"I have just been visiting the two villages of Pandjalam and Vailamour, the inhabitants of which were baptized about four years since; those are all my children in Christ Jesus. I begot them in the midst of privations and trials, and I love them with a love of predilection. Amongst the pagans who came to see me, I remarked a woman whose child I had baptized when it was so ill as to be in danger of death. I asked news of it. 'He is dead,' she replied.

"'Say rather he is living,' I answered; 'for though his little body has been laid in the earth, his soul is now gone to heaven, in consequence of the blessing I gave him.' The poor woman appeared consoled and happy.

"Two families of Vailamour came to visit me, and asked to be baptized. They were rich in children of all ages, from a baby of one to twelve years old. They immediately set about learning their prayers, and followed me to Nangattour. Here a number of pagans joined the Christians in learning their prayers. On the day of my departure, I blessed ten marriages and sent home seventeen neophytes. Scarcely had I baptized the latter, when ten others presented themselves, entreating I would baptize them. I gave a catechist the care of instructing them for two months, and desired him to conduct them to me at the end of that time. Since this visit, I have had a continual arrival of catechumens. At Attipakam, I baptized three fathers of families, one of whom belonged to the pariah caste, and has since been called to the kingdom of our Lord Jesus Christ, after having received the white robe of innocence. All his relations are being instructed, preparatory to their receiving the same grace of regeneration.

"Deviavaram, where I gave a mission with the Abbé Prieur, has given also its share of converts to the Faith. I baptized there seven idolaters, and a few days afterwards I had the consolation of regenerating thirteen more.

"Those details give clear evidence that God always alleviates the pains and trials he sends us by adding some unlooked-for blessing, in order to excite and animate our courage in His service. If the vicariate of Pondicherry contains still five millions of idolaters, it is at least consoling to the labourers in this mission to know that eight hundred have been baptized during the last year. The pagans are in general well-disposed towards Catholicity, notwithstanding the prejudices of the castes which we have to combat; and we have every reason to hope that the harvest of souls would be still more abundant amongst them if we had a greater number of apostolic labourers." (Letter of the 6th March, 1865.)

The vicariate of Quilon is more than hopeful; for the religious movement there seems to meet with neither obstacle nor opposition.

The Rev. Father Victor, of the Sacred Heart of Jesus, barefooted Carmelite, writes, on the 13th of last September, to the Abbé Bize, Professor at the Seminary of Palignon (diocese of Toulouse):—

"I have very consoling news to give you of my district. They continue to evince the same eagerness to embrace the true faith, and testify the same affection for the missioner. My arrival in a village is looked on as a general festival, and my departure causes an equal sorrow. My first blessing on arrival is received with joy, and my parting one with tears. My life passes in crossing mountains, where I have no shelter except the shade of the trees; but everywhere I meet penitents that quite surprise me, and conversions that make me forget all my fatigue and labour. In one of the small pagan towns, where a Catholic priest had never before entered, I have had the happiness of erecting a church dedicated to Our Lady of Mount Carmel."

Under the influence of divine grace, those pagans often give extraordinary edification, and make the most heroic sacrifices that they may remain faithful to their vocation.

"In the month of August, 1864 (writes the Abbé Pierron), a young man belonging to the caste of the Vellalers suddenly quitted the village, accompanied by his wife and two children, and went to visit the missioner at Carmattampatty, saying to him that he wished to become a Christian, no matter what the consequences might be to him. As this young man belonged to a very influential family, and was possessed of a certain competency, the priest received him at first with great reserve, fearing that he had only yielded to some sudden and rash impulse in coming to him; but he soon gave evident proofs of the sincerity of his conversion. The parents of the young man, on hearing that he had joined the Christians, and that he was learning their prayers, were very much excited, and made great efforts to bring him back to the village. They went so far as even to threaten the missioner; and, finding that ineffective, they tried to coax him. But, in spite of all the threats of the pagans and the supplications of his wife, he came to him, accompanied by her children: the young man remained firm in his resolution. We knew he would be expelled from his caste, disowned by his family, despised by all; but yet he was ready to pay this price, and Christian he would be." (Letter of the 25th of November, 1864.)

Sometimes God turns even their most bitter sufferings into occasions of drawing souls to His service who had been until then in a state of utter ignorance.

"You are aware (writes the Secretary of Mgr. Hartemann), that the Hindoos are cruel in character, and that they throw into the Ganges, under pretext of making them drink of the sacred river, all their sick and infirm, or aged relatives, in order to get rid of them. Some years since, a water-carrier brought to the convent a Brahmin woman he had found half-dead in the streets. The poor creature had escaped from her relatives, who were about to drown her, in consequence of her being so infirm. The nuns welcomed her with tender charity, and took such care of her that she recovered her health. They then asked her what she intended to do with herself. 'Ah!' replied she, 'I intend to become a Christian; I desire to love that God who has taken pity on me, and even died to save me.' In the absence of the Rev. Father Vincent, director of the convent, I had the consolation of baptizing her, as well as a young Hindoo girl, of eighteen years of age, and three young female children.

"Recently, an old Hindoo woman was found at the gate of the convent in a deplorable state. The good sisters brought her inside, and lavished kindness on her. This poor woman had been the mother of eighteen children, and the last remaining one had cast her into the street. The sisters spoke to her of God, of Jesus Christ, and of the sacrament of baptism. Sufferings had prepared the unfortunate woman to receive the grace of God; she prayed that they might baptize her, desiring to die in the religion of Him who died on the cross for her. They thought she was approaching her last hour, I was sent for hastily, and I baptized her: but she is recovered." (Letter of the 24th November, 1865.)

III.

In some parts of Hindostan, the Protestants make the greatest efforts to place obstacles in the way of the Catholic missioners; but we thank God that the result of the enormous expense lavished by our enemies has been a total failure in accomplishing their object.

"The number of conversions this year amongst the Protestants of Madura is most consoling, above all, when we remember the power brought against us by the Protestants, both in money spent, the threats held out against those who become Catholics, and also the many who had been made Protestants at the beginning of this century. The Mission of Madura at present numbers fifty-three Protestant European ministers and twenty-three native ones. But they have failed in seducing away any of our Christians, whilst we have gained from them all those of the district of Surinam who had been enticed into error when this district was under the jurisdiction of the priests of Goa. Their partisans are very few in the north and middle districts, notwithstanding the number of their schools and their efforts to proselytise. It is in the southern province of Tinnelly that Protestantism has most life, because it has been for a long time established there, with the assistance of the English Government." (Annual Report of the Missions of the Society of Jesus, 5th April, 1864.)

During the year 1864, there were one hundred heretics converted in Madura. "All the missioners agree in saying that the twenty-five thousand Hindoos who still remain of the fifty thousand that had embraced the Protestant religion towards the end of the last century and the commencement of this, would all become Catholics if we could protect them, and provide means for their being established elsewhere." (Annual Report of the Missions under the care of the Society of Jesus, 6th May, 1865.)

"In the vicariate of Hyderabad (writes Mgr. Murphy), the colleges, schools, orphanages, and other institutions, are in full vigour and prosperity. They have become the sources of immense benefit to our people by saving them from Protestantism and instructing them in the Catholic faith." (Letter of the 16th June, 1865.)

There were sixty conversions of Protestants in Hyderabad during the year 1864.

Those in the vicariate of Mysore numbered twelve; and Pondicherry, eighty-six.

The secretary of Monsignor Hartemann writes from Patna, on the 20th of November, 1864:—

"The mission is making progress, notwithstanding the obstacles. Our establishments of education, though of such recent creation, have already caused a panic in the camps of Protestantism. The Anglican Bishop of Calcutta is journeying through India at the present moment, and preaching a crusade against the Catholic institutions destined for the youth of the country. His want of success at Darjeeling has not caused his zeal to slacken. Darjeeling is situated at the foot of the Himalayan mountains. We have a convent of Loretto nuns there, with a boarding-school. At great expense, a Protestant school was established to destroy, if possible, our establishment. The Anglican Bishop preached in Patna with the same object in view, and ordered a college to be founded to counterbalance the influence of our institution of English ladies of St. Marie de Baviere. A convent of the same order is about to be established at Allahabad, the seat of the government of the north-western provinces, and one of the four principal cities of India."

Another letter, written from Patna by the same missioner, on the 24th November last, from which we have already given extracts, gives ull details of the immense services rendered to the mission by the nuns of Saint Marie de Baviere. "It is through their influence (says the secretary of Mgr. Hartemann) that we hope for some conversions here. Their devotedness excites the admiration of the Protestants and of the thousands of pagans surrounding them. How much sorrow alleviated! How many souls saved by their exertions! Holy sisters, who have left all to consecrate themselves (under the burning sun, and for ever in presence of an incessant enemy, the cholera) to the education of the daughters of English soldiers and of pagans!"

We find the same devotedness of the nuns of Patna amongst all the religious sisters who consecrate their lives to the care of children and the sick. It is everywhere the same abnegation, the same zeal, because it is the same spirit which animates all those souls. They have also their share in the sufferings of the apostolate, and this is sometimes even to the sacrifice of life. They fall victims to this great labour, and to the insalubrity of the climate. During the last twenty years, in the single orphanage of Calcutta, forty-two Irish sisters have died.

IV.

The letters that we have just laid before the notice of our associates give us a pretty good idea in general of the state of the Catholic missions in Hindostan. They inform us of the nature of the obstacles which oppose the more extended diffusion of the Gospel—the inertness of the native Hindoos, the prejudices of caste, Brahminism and Mahometanism, the doctrines of which encourage sensual habits, and, in fine, though of course in an inferior degree, the Protestant influence They show us how, instead of being discouraged and hopeless in the face of so many obstacles, the missioners redouble their zeal for the propagation of the faith in the mountains of Himalaya and on the coast of Malabar.

The bishops are as laborious as the simple missioners. Here it is Mgr. Godelle, of Pondicherry, who has no other bed to lie on but the bare ground, with a bag for his pillow; there it is Monsignor Hartemann, of Patna, who sets out for a three months' visitation, with an inflamed and ulcerated leg, traverses, at the point of his life, dangerous torrents, and enters immense forests infested with tigers, and, on his return, is seized with an attack of cholera.

We have rapidly indicated some of the trials to which the missioner is exposed. We must add to the account how much aggravated all those sufferings are in a country ravaged by plagues of all kinds. Not to speak of cholera, which is, we may say, a permanent plague on the banks of the Ganges, the storms, and the continued aridity and famine, have devastated latterly, and completed the misery of a population already very poor. The vicariates of Bengal, both central and eastern, and that of Hyderabad, suffer at present from two terrible cyclones that ravaged parts of India during the months of April and November, 1864. At Mazulipatam, for example, "neither the church, the missioner's house, nor the schools (all destroyed by the inundation), have as yet been rebuilt, for want of means." (Letter from Mgr. Murphy, of the 16th June, 1865.)

An exorbitant increase in the price of provisions was caused by the American war, in consequence of the grain crops having been given up for the cultivation of cotton. At present, famine has succeeded to the unusual want of rain, which dried up the earth in 1865. "Since the month of November, 1864, there has been a complete cessation of rain (writes the Abbé Gouyon, of the Foreign Missions, from Pondicherry —letter of the 5th of August, 1865). The vicariate is entirely destroyed: large trees are dried up to the very roots, the people are perishing from hunger, in the fullest strength of the term; and everywhere we see nothing but misery and nakedness, for the price of cotton is not lowered."

A letter, written from Patna, on the 24th of November last, to the Central Councils, confirms these sad details. "The famine is causing us universal desolation, and yet we have so many children to support in our orphanages! Our Hindoos are dying of hunger; a woman in the neighbourhood has devoured her own child."

The total number of Catholics in Hindostan rises to about 800,000; but this, when divided into the several vicariates, presents very considerable variations. For instance, in Quilon, there are 52,000 Catholics; in Pondicherry, 108,000; Madura, 160,000; Verapoly, 200,000; while Agra contains only 12,000; Patna, 8,000; and Eastern Bengal, 600. How is this inequality of results to be accounted for, notwithstanding the equally-devoted zeal of the missioners in each of those districts? We must remark, in the first place, that the impediments to the progress of the true faith are not everywhere existing with the same force. For example, the northern provinces have been always remarkable for their obstinate attachment to pagan superstition and the doctrines of the Koran. "We must also remember that some of the Hindostan missions are of recent foundation, and others date from the sixteenth century. Through many vicissitudes, these last have preserved Christian traditions, which rendered the apostleship of our missioners more easy." In fine, without seeking to penetrate the secrets of Divine Providence in the distribution of its graces, "May we not be permitted to believe that the protection of St. Francis Xavier, the great Apostle of India, has been especially bestowed upon those countries which were formerly the great battle-field of his conquests and are to-day the guardians of his glorious relics?"

EXTRACTS.

THE PRESENT STATE OF THE MISSIONS.

"Taking first the Syrians, they are located entirely in the native States of Travancore and Cochin, and number about 200,000. They have their own Metropolitan Bishops and Clergy, and now own allegiance to the Jacobite Patriarch of Jerusalem. They possess churches, and "lands and funds" to a limited extent; but how far the latter may be free from State assessment does not appear. The native government does not interfere in any way with their affairs."

"The Roman Catholics, among whom may be reckoned at least 100,000 Syrians, whose submission to Rome dates back to days of Portuguese supremacy, number a million and a quarter, of whom 550,000 are in the Madras British Provinces, and nearly half a million in the Madras Native States, chiefly Travancore and Cochin. The bulk of the remainder are in Bombay and Bengal."—From "Church and State in India," by Sir Theodore C. Hope, K.C.S.I., C.I.E., pp. 8, 10.

BISHOPRICS OF ASIA.

Calcutta, 1876; Madras, 1861; China, 1873; Colombo, 1875; Bombay, 1875; Lahore, 1888; Travancore and Cochin, 1890; Singapore, 1881; Rangoon, 1882; Chota Nagpore, 1890; Lucknow, 1892.—"Churchman's Almanack," 1893, pp. 29, 30.

Goa: Archiepiscopal See in Portuguese territory (Patriarchate of the East Indies). Suffragan Sees: Cochin (in British India), Damaun, Macao, and Meliapur (in Portuguese territory).—From the "Catholic Directory, Ecclesiastical Register and Almanack," for 1893, pp. 65, 66.

It is well-known that the Baptists, Wesleyans, and others have established numerous and successful missionary stations.

An excellent paper on the Eastern Churches, including the Syrians, was read at the Liverpool Church Congress by the Rev. F. S. May, D.D.

PORTUGAL.

The most westerly Kingdom of Europe, and a part of the great Iberian Peninsula, lies in 37°—42° 8′ N. lat. and 6° 15′—9° 30′ W. long., being 360 miles in length from N. to .S, and averaging about 100 in breadth from E. to W. Continental Portugal contains an area of 34,606 square miles, with a population in 1881 of 4,306,554, exclusive of the colonies. The Azores and Madeira (1,237 square miles, pop. 401,624) form part of the kingdom, which thus has a population of 4,708,178. The chief products are wheat, barley, oats, maize, flax hemp, and the vine in elevated tracts; in the lowlands, rice, olives, oranges, lemons, citrons, figs, and almonds. There are extensive forests of oak, chestnuts, sea-pine, and cork, the cultivation of the vine and the olive being among the chief branches of industry; the rich red wine known to us as "port" is shipped from Oporto. Its mineral products are important, copper, lead, tin, antimony, coal, manganese, iron, slate, and bay-salt, which last, from its hardness, and purity, is in demand. Its manufactures consist of gloves, silk, woollen, linen, and cotton fabrics, metal and earthenware goods, tobacco, cigars, &c. The exports consist to the extent of 50 per cent. of wine, which is the chief industrial product of the country, cork, cattle, copper-ore, fruits, oil, sardines, and salt. The imports are manufactured goods—hardware, cotton and woollen stuffs, machinery, wheat, sugar, dried fish, coal, &c. There is a commercial marine of 36 steamers and 433 sailing vessels, about 110,000 tonnage. Railways, 1,000 miles in extent, are open for traffic. For many years the national income has been considerably less than the expenditure; this deficiency has added to the national debt, which now amounts to about £31 a head of the population.

DEPENDENCIES.—These, in proportion to the mother-country, are of very great extent. They include the Cape Verd Islands, off the West Coast of Africa (1,847 square miles, population 107,026); Zighinchor on the Casamanza, Bissao, and a few other territories to the south of the Gambia, which are officially known as "Portuguese Guinea" (350 sq. miles, pop. 10,000); the Fort of San Joao Baptista de Ajuda, at Whidah, the principal port of the Kingdom of Dahome, where the

Portuguese are allowed to remain on sufferance, but exercise no sort of jurisdiction; the fertile islands of St. Thomas and Principe, in the Gulf of Guinea (417 sq. miles, pop. 22,000); the Kingdom of Angola, on the West Coast of South Africa, which includes the territory of Landana and Kabinda to the north of the Congo, and the whole of the coast to the south of that river as far as Cape Frio, and has Loanda for its capital (115,000 sq. miles, pop. 1,000,000); the Province of Mozambique, with the Lower Zambezi river, Sofala, and Delagoa Bay, on the East Coast of Africa (80,000 sq. miles, pop. 500,000); Goa, Daman, and Diu in India (1,295 sq. miles, pop. 481,467); part of the island of Timor, in the East Indian Archipelago (6,294 sq. miles, pop. 300,000), and Macao, in China, at the mouth of the Canton river (5 sq. miles, pop. 68,086). The possessions enumerated have an area of 204,848 square miles, with 2,548,872 inhabitants. In this estimate account is taken only of territories within which Portugal actually exercises some jurisdiction. Thus, whilst official statements give an extension of 659,000 square miles to Angola and Mozambique, the area is here reduced to 195,200 square miles.

PORTUGUESE AFRICA.

Recent treaties with France (May 12, 1886), Germany (Dec. 30, 1886), Belgium (May 25, 1891), and England (May 28, 1891), have considerably curtailed the "possessions" at one time claimed by Portugal. But even thus these possessions are twenty-six times the size of the mother country, their "government" entails an annual loss of £135,000, and the development of their resources is quite beyond the means of so small a country. Much wiser had it been had Portugal divested herself of a considerable slice of her colonies, and employed the resources thus obtained towards the development of those territories which she chose to retain.

In the meantime Portugal has not unsuccessfully striven to attract foreign capital to her colonies. In Angola, a railway from Loanda to Ambaca (188 miles) has been nearly completed by an English company. Another railway from Delagoa Bay to the border of the South African Republic (57 miles), has somewhat arbitrarily been confiscated by the Portuguese government, and the English and American shareholders now claim £2,000,000 damages, and 250,000 acres of "mineral lands" as compensation.

Among the companies among which nearly the whole of the province of Mozambique has been parcelled out, only that called after the province, but confined to the territory between the Zambesi and Sabi rivers, can be said to have fairly started upon its career. Among its directors are the Duke of Marlborough and Mr. Moreing. Colonel Machado, a very able Portuguese engineer, has been appointed its first "governor," and as friendly relations have been established with the British South Africa Company, we may look forward to the speedy commencement of more serious work than that of establishing "mining claims." The first task awaiting the company is the construction of a railway from the Pungwe and Busi rivers to Manica and Fort Salisbury.

Charters have likewise been granted to the well-known Portuguese explorers Serpa Pinto (Limpopo to the Sabi) and Carvalho (Rovuma to the Lurio), and Colonel Pavia de Andrada (Zambesi). All these charters provide for the construction of railways, and, if only a portion of what is hoped for can be realised, Mozambique, in the course of a few years, will be one of the most prosperous parts of all Africa. The Portuguese territories in Africa are as follows:—

—	Square Miles.	Population.	Inh. to 1 sq. m.
Madeira	315	134,000	425
Cape Verde Islands	1,486	111,000	74
Guinea	11,600	150,000	13
S. Thomé a Principé	456	21,000	46
Angola	517,200	3,500,000	7
Mozambique	310,000	1,500,000	5
PORTUGUESE AFRICA	841,055	5,416,000	6

—From "Whitaker's Almanack," 1893, by kind permission of the Editor.